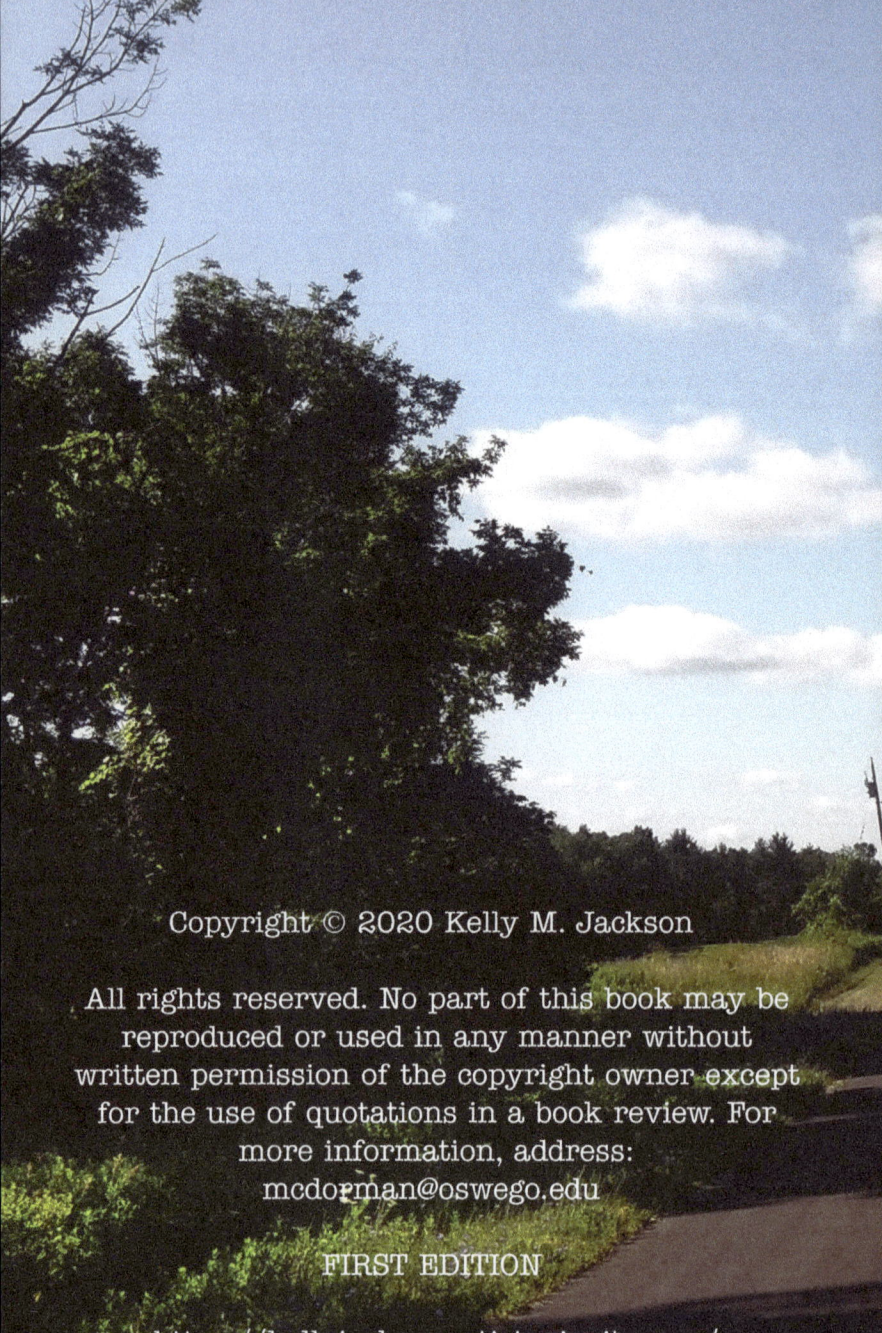

Copyright © 2020 Kelly M. Jackson

All rights reserved. No part of this book may be reproduced or used in any manner without written permission of the copyright owner except for the use of quotations in a book review. For more information, address: mcdorman@oswego.edu

FIRST EDITION

https://kellyjacksonartist.wixsite.com/wildandfree

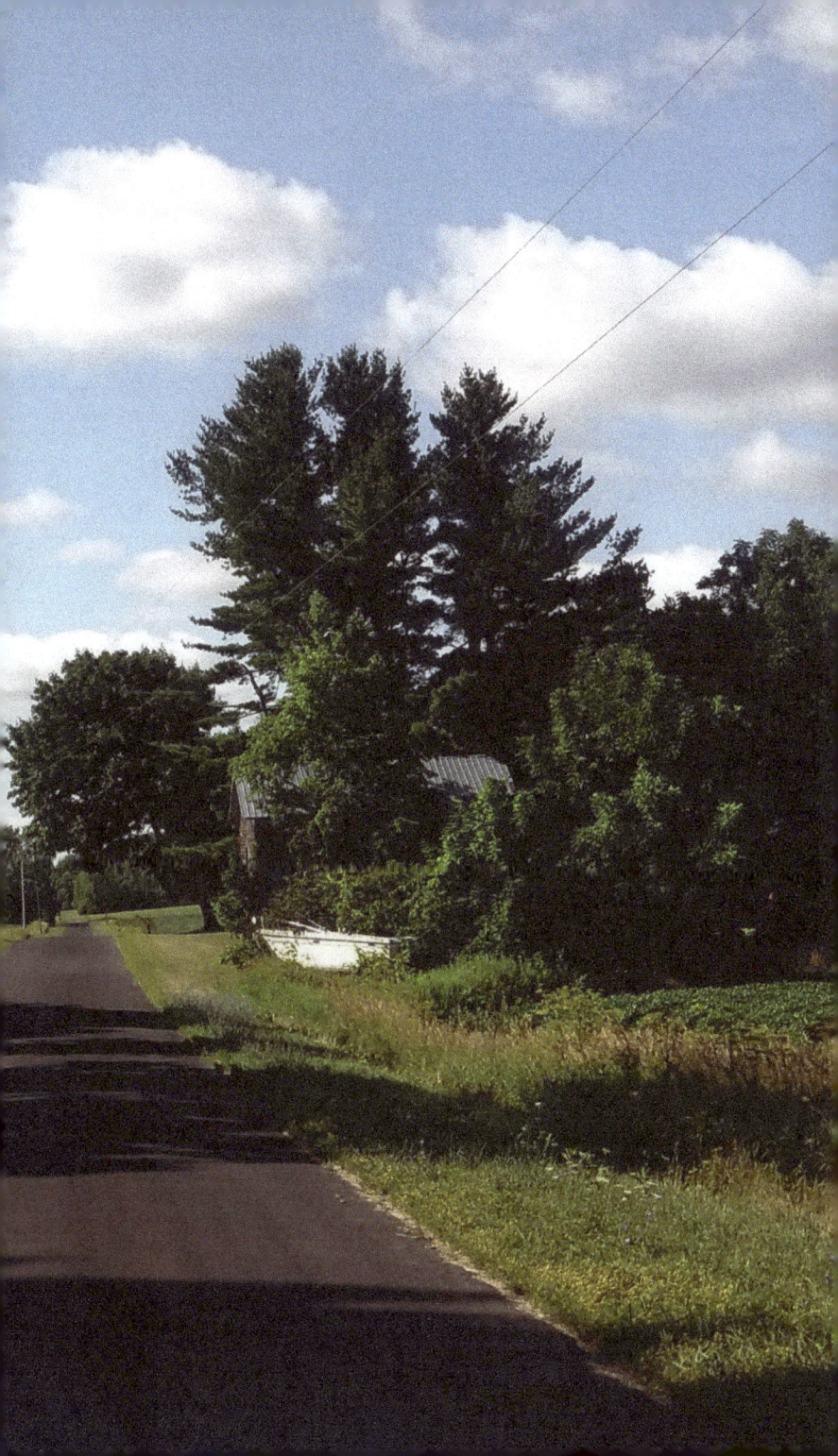

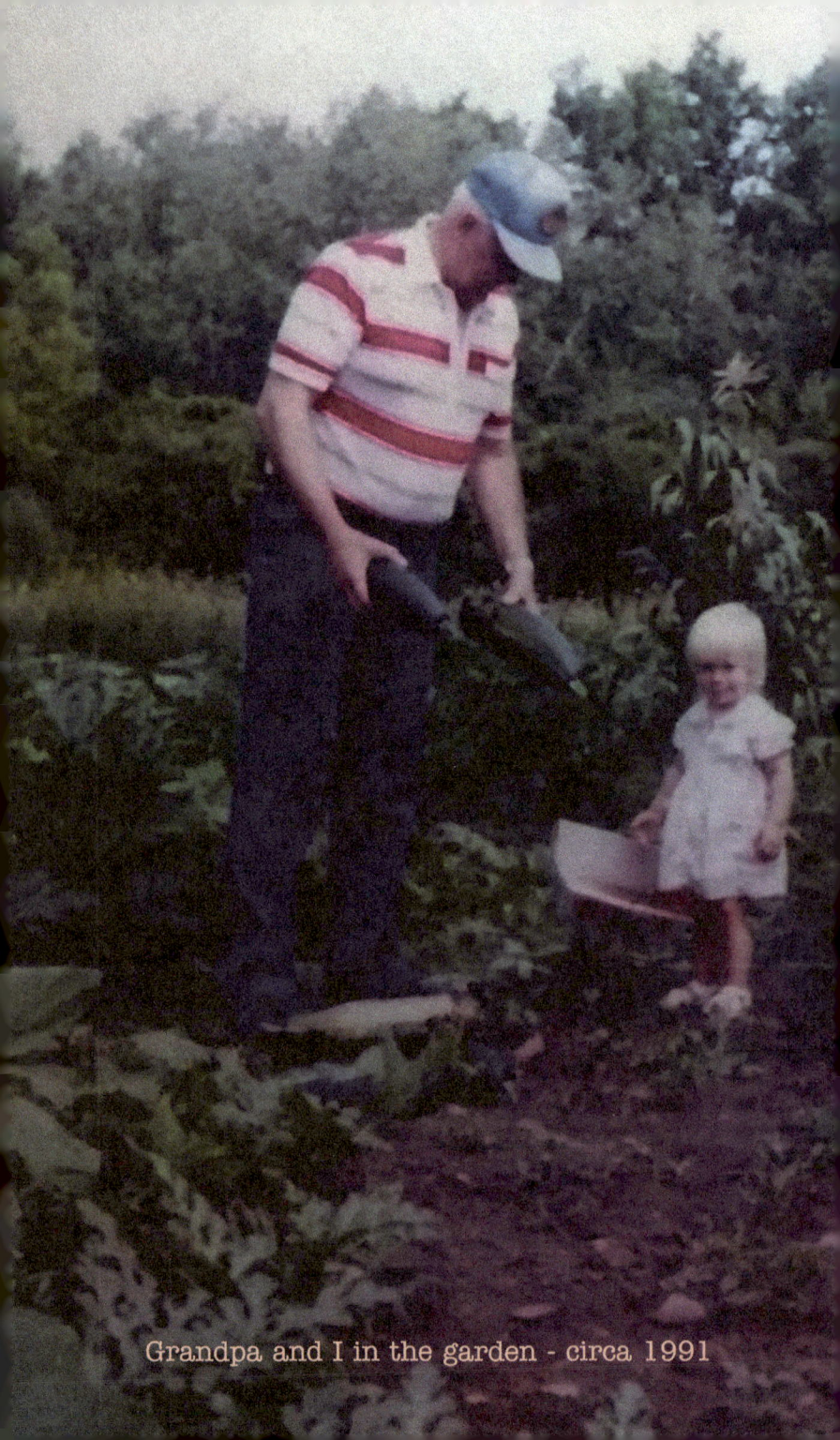
Grandpa and I in the garden - circa 1991

...

When compiling a book of your
favorite things, it's only fitting
to dedicate it to your
favorite person.

This book is for you, Grandpa.

This book is dedicated to
my grandfather,
Edward W. McDorman.

...

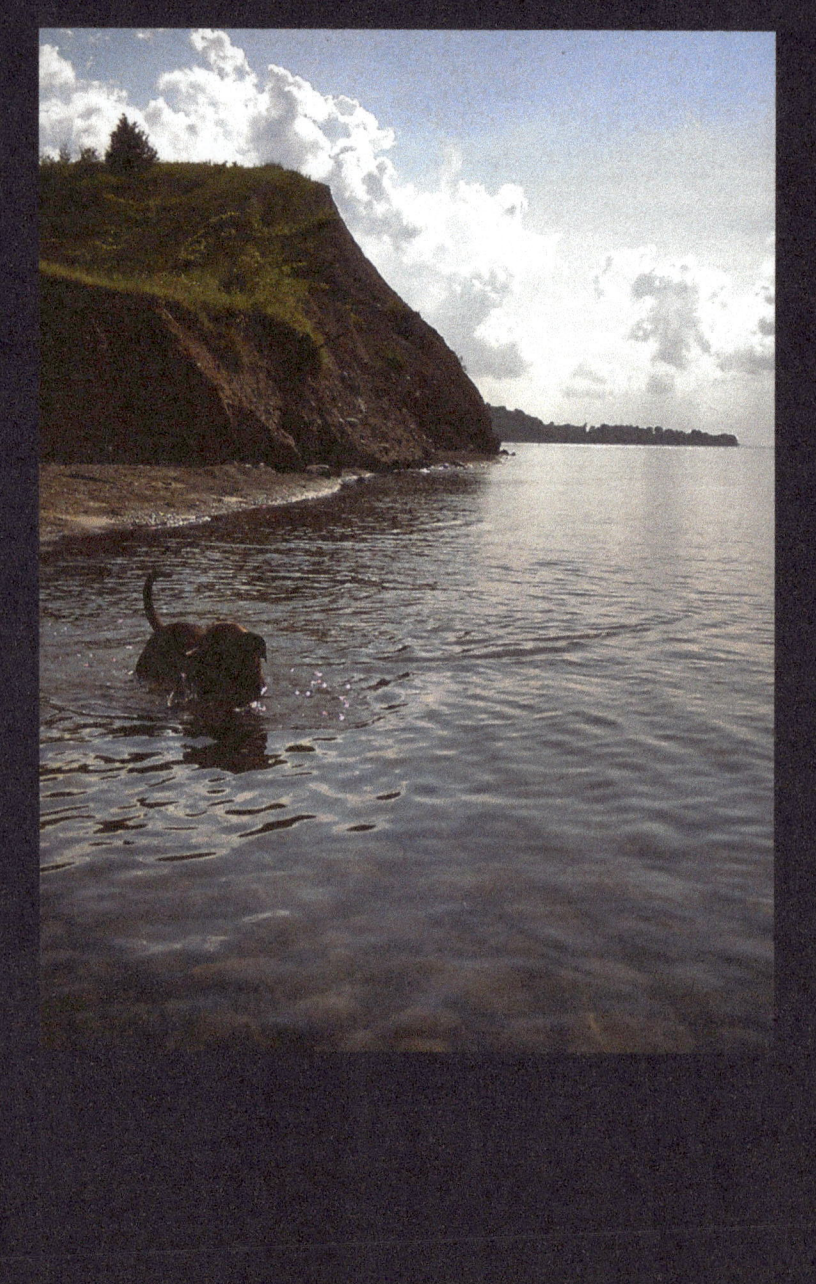

Introduction

I have been recording my favorite things
since I was 16. Even as an adult I carry my
little book, a pen and crayons in my purse.
It's a sort of therapy for me to be able to
record and reflect on life as its happening.
Quotes and photographs, ticket stubs from
concerts, song lyrics, funny conversations,
newspaper clippings and memories. In the
pages of my journals I have pressed flowers
and little words of wisdom from teachers,
stories I've recorded from my grandparents
and drawings. I enjoy pulling them out and
curling up with them when I'm feeling down,
turning to the comfort and warmth
of my memories.

Over the past 14 years I have completed over
35 little journals. My Grandpa is always
telling me that I should publish a book with
all the things I've written down.
So here it goes Grandpa.

This book is my collection (so far)
of all the magical, wonderful things
I love about life.

xx *Kelly* oo

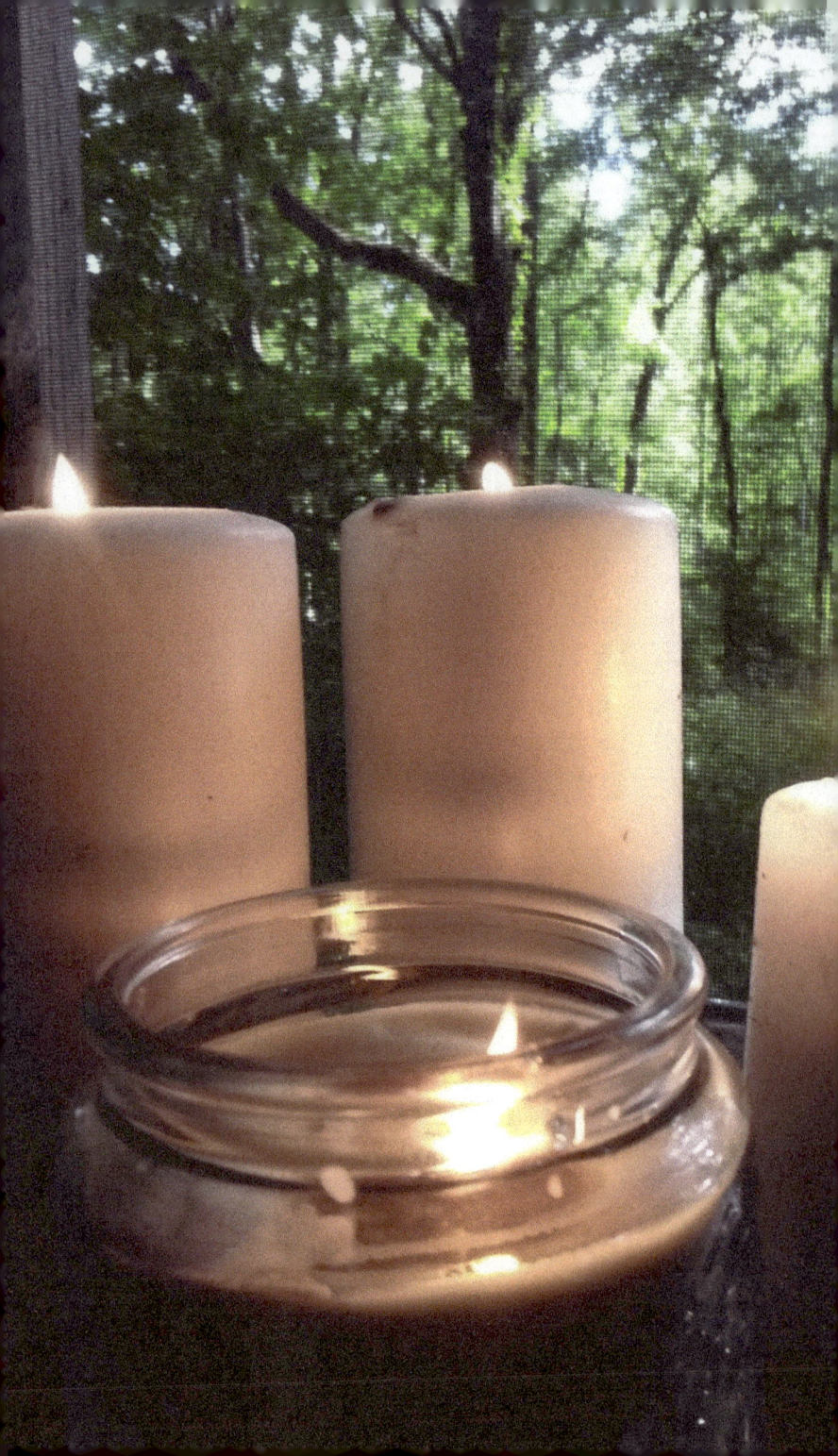

An Old Fashioned Country Girls Favorite Things

Photographs and Words
by Kelly M. Jackson

Dear Reader:

Light a candle, make a drink, forget about the dishes piled up in the sink. Cozy right up in your favorite chair, and my favorite things will take you there...

To a place in the country, where the creatures freely roam...
at the end of a dirt road, where you are safe and loved and home.

My sincere hope is that these pages will remind, rekindle or introduce you to some good old-fashioned country magic and make you feel at home - wherever you are in the world.

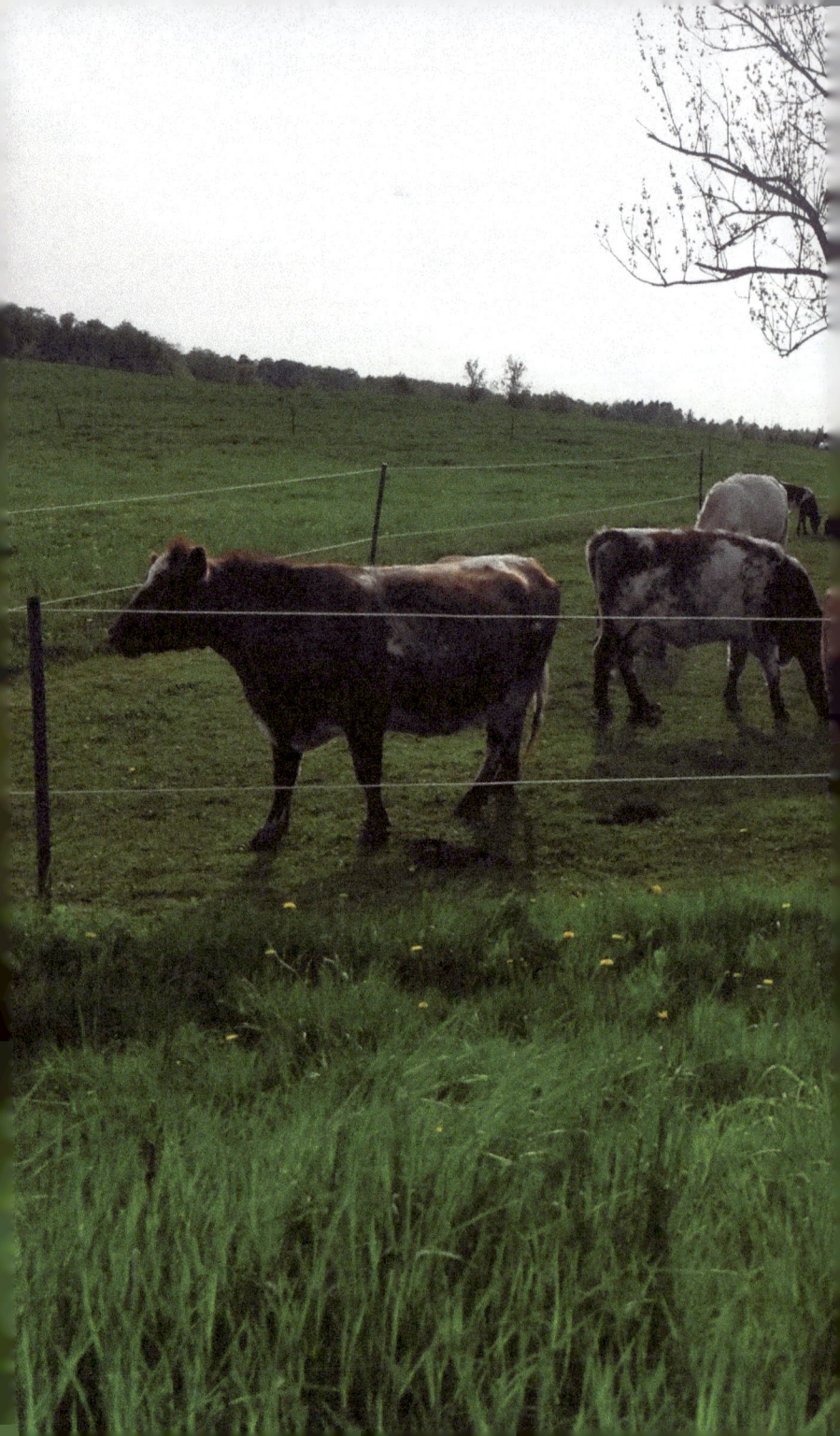

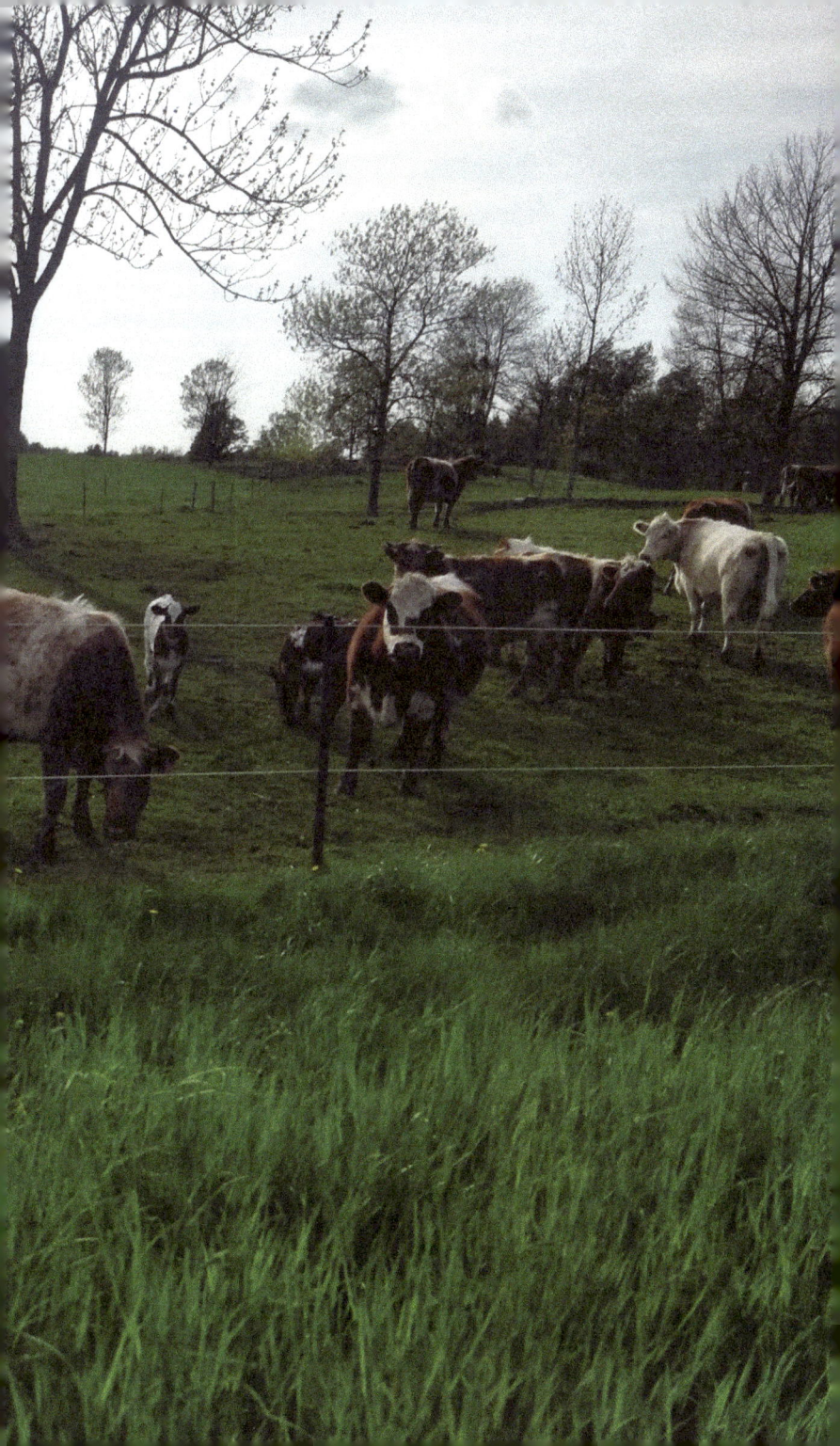

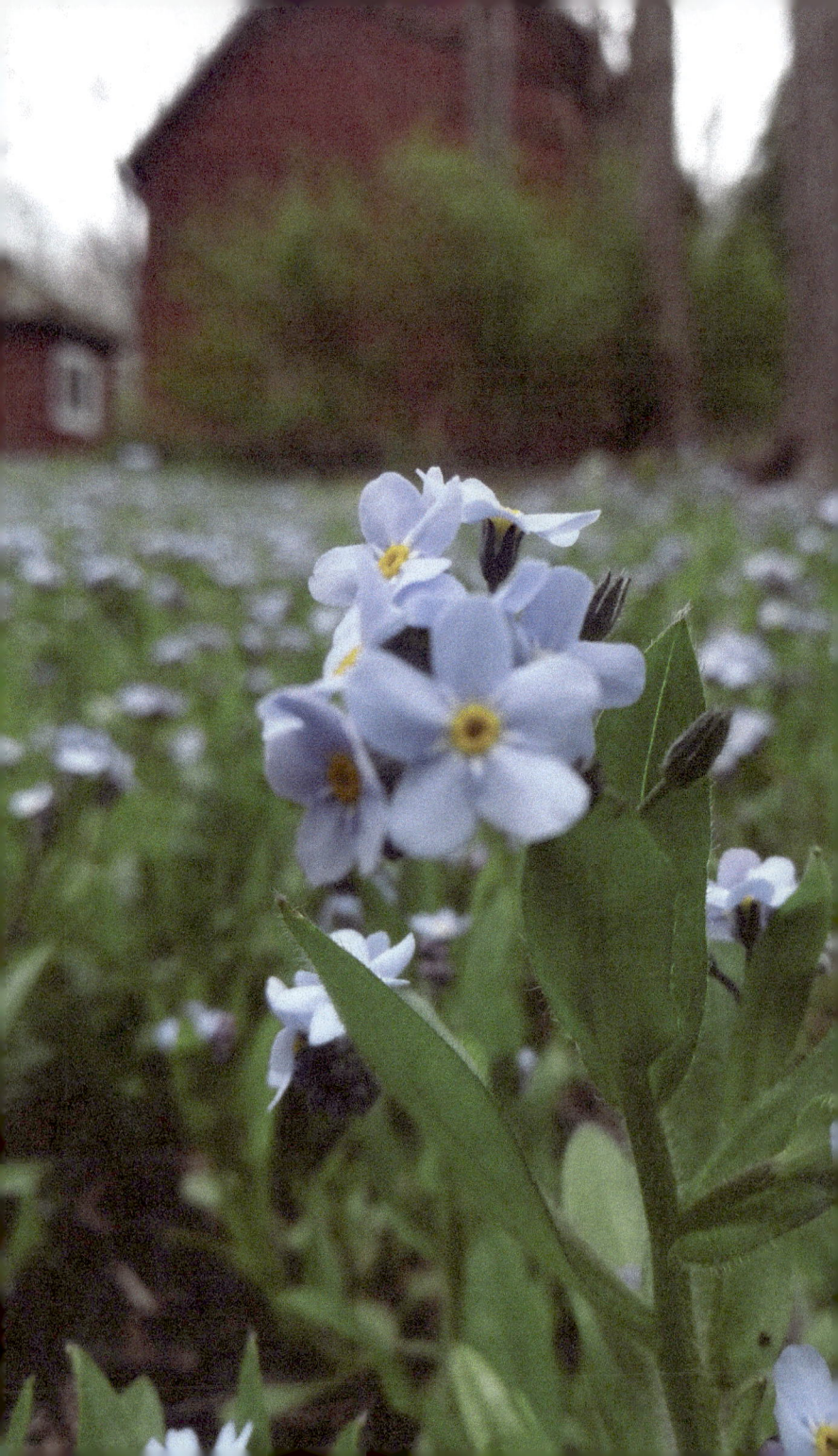

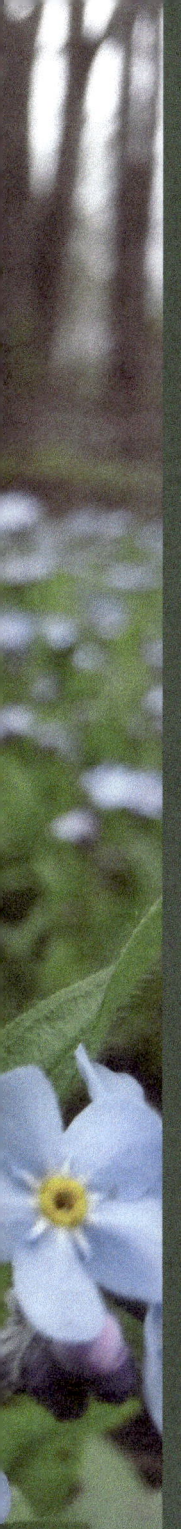

forget me nots

pick up trucks

fawns with their little
white spots

moon shadows on the
forest floor

floral fabric

sunflowers

the smell of tomato plants

springtime rain showers

honeysuckle candles

canoes leaned up against
old barns

bonfires

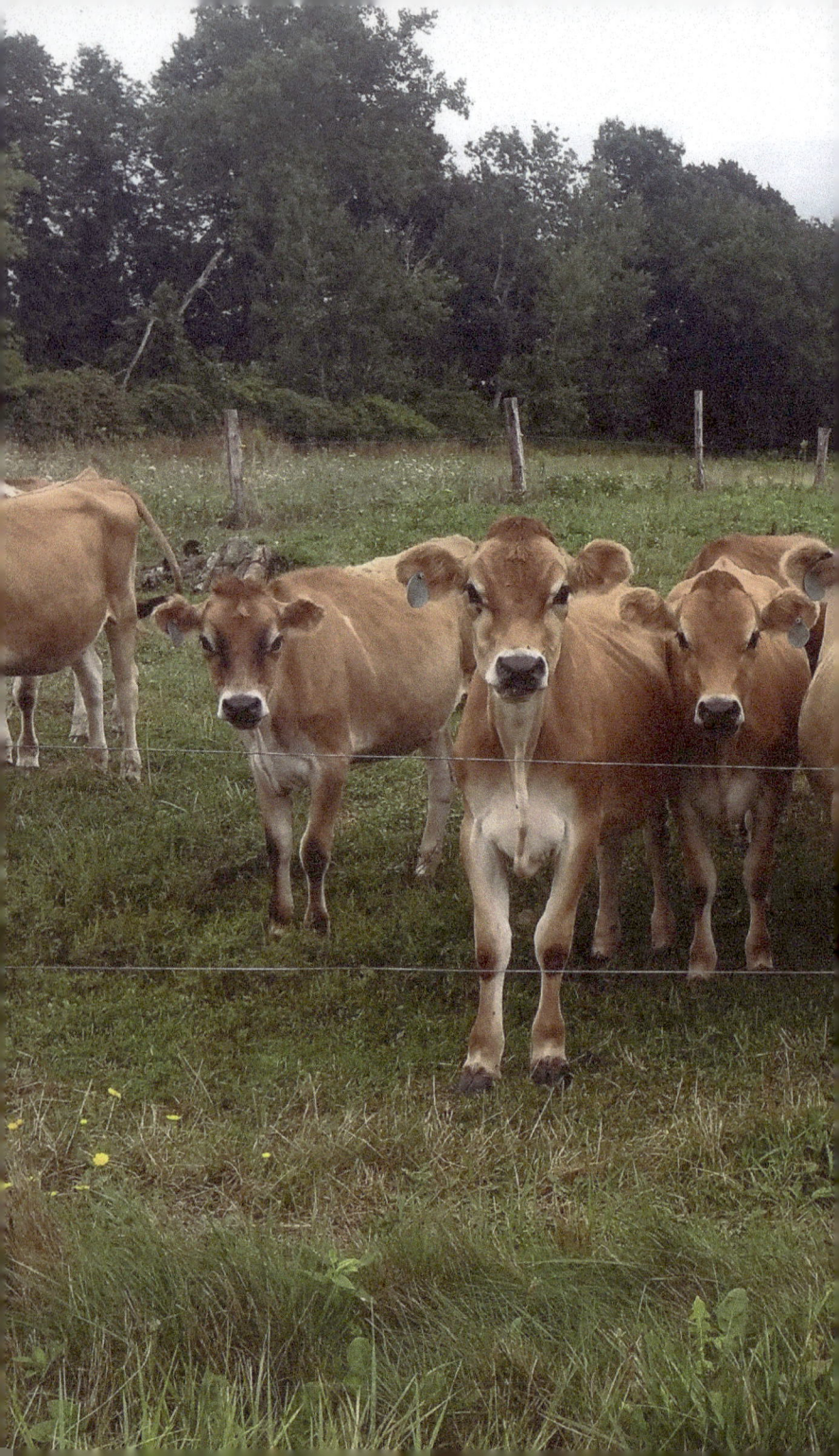

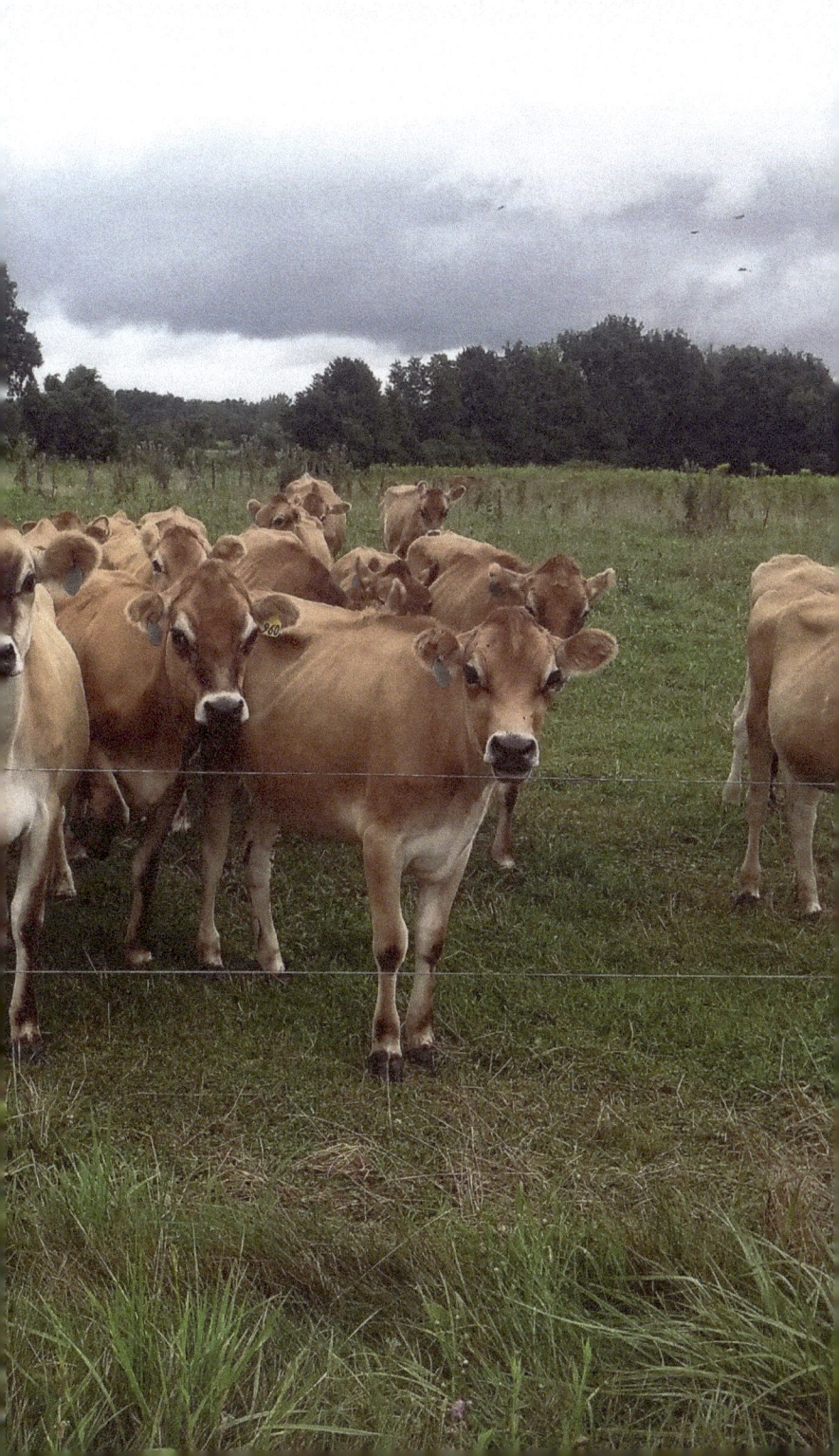

goldenrod

home movies on old projectors

monarch butterflies

wild onions

opossums

vintage seed packets

dirt driveways

snuggling in sweat shirts that are way too big

helping turtles cross the road

the patchwork of farmland from the sky

pulling carrots from the garden

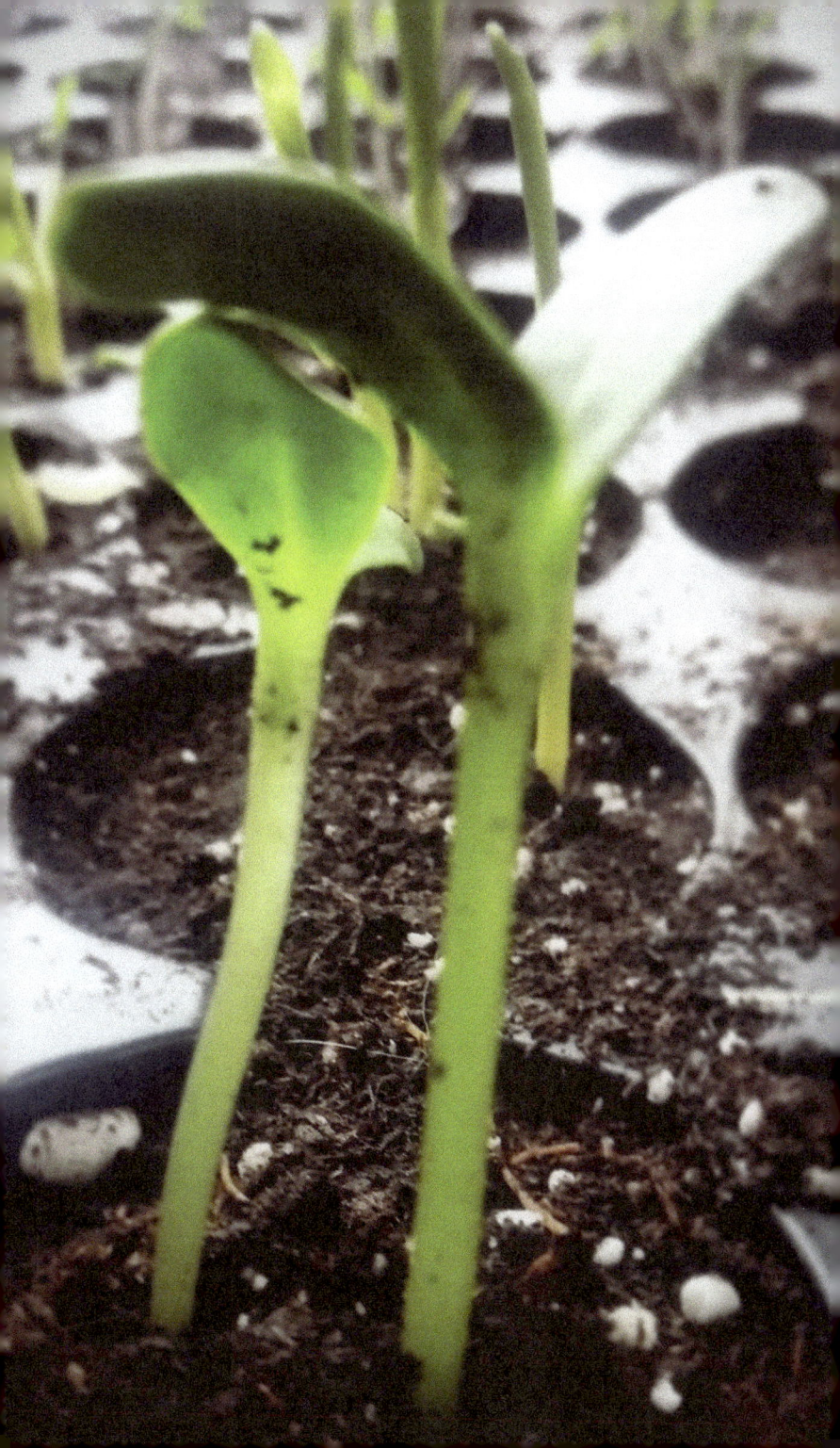

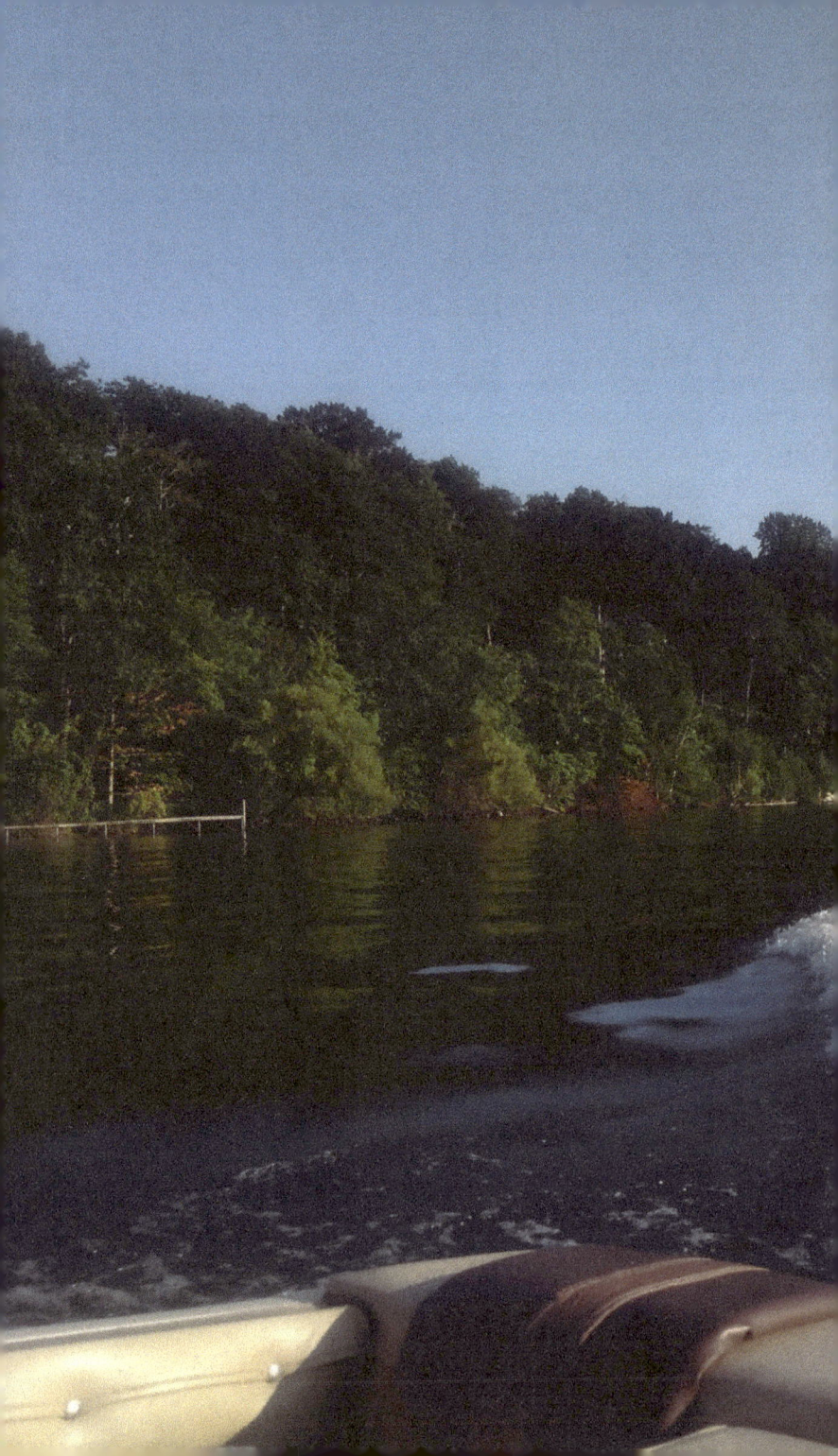

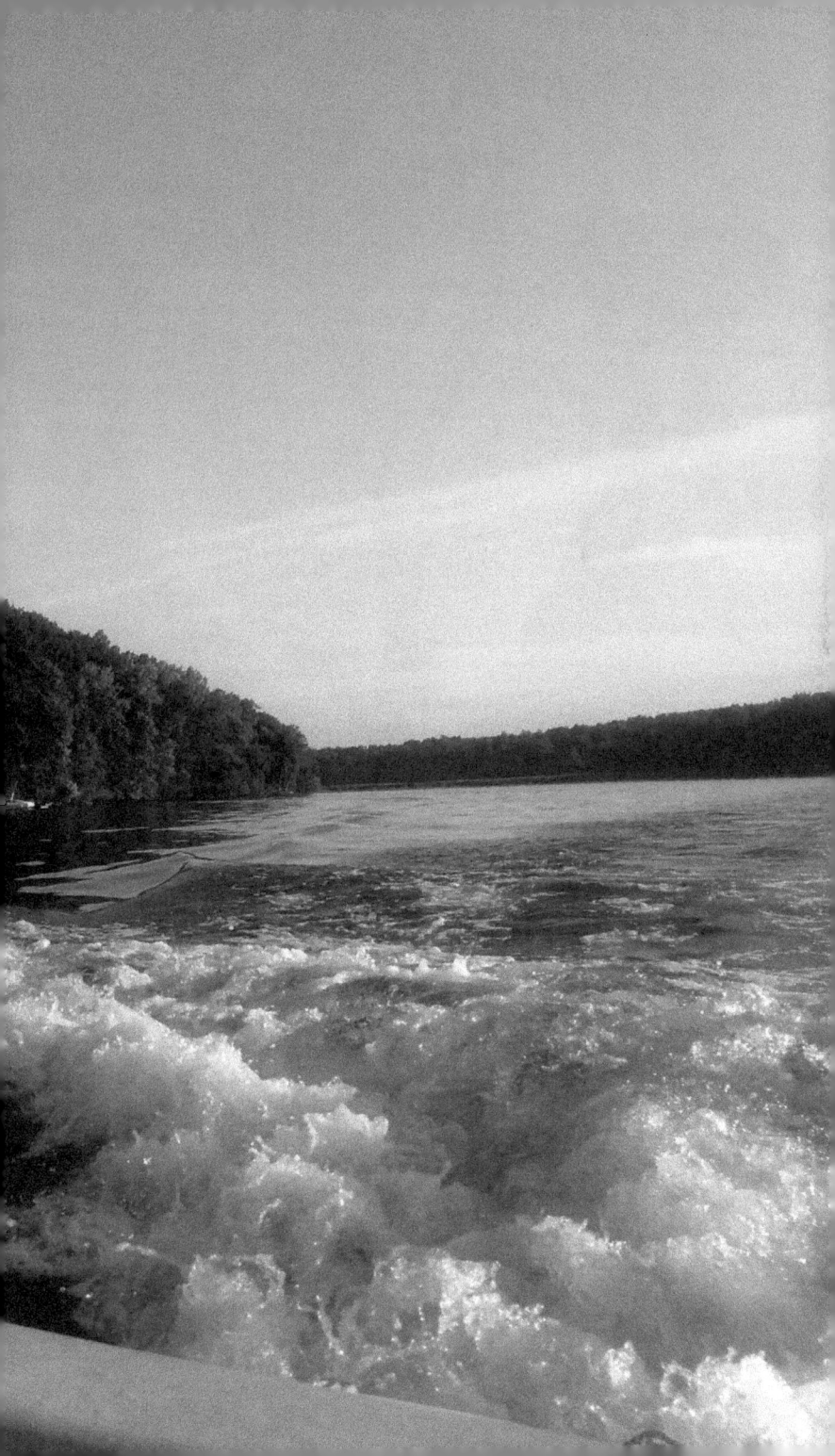

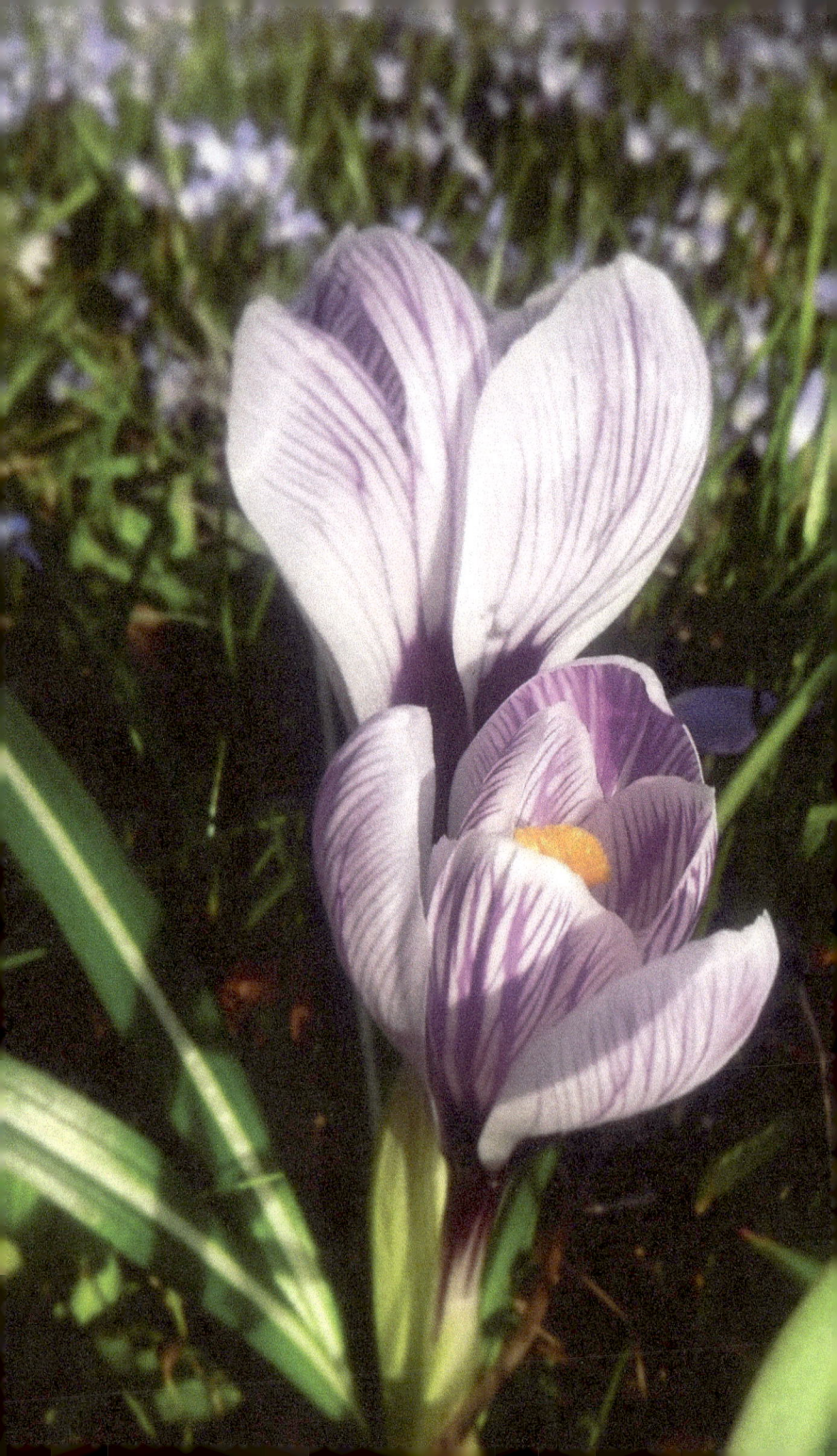

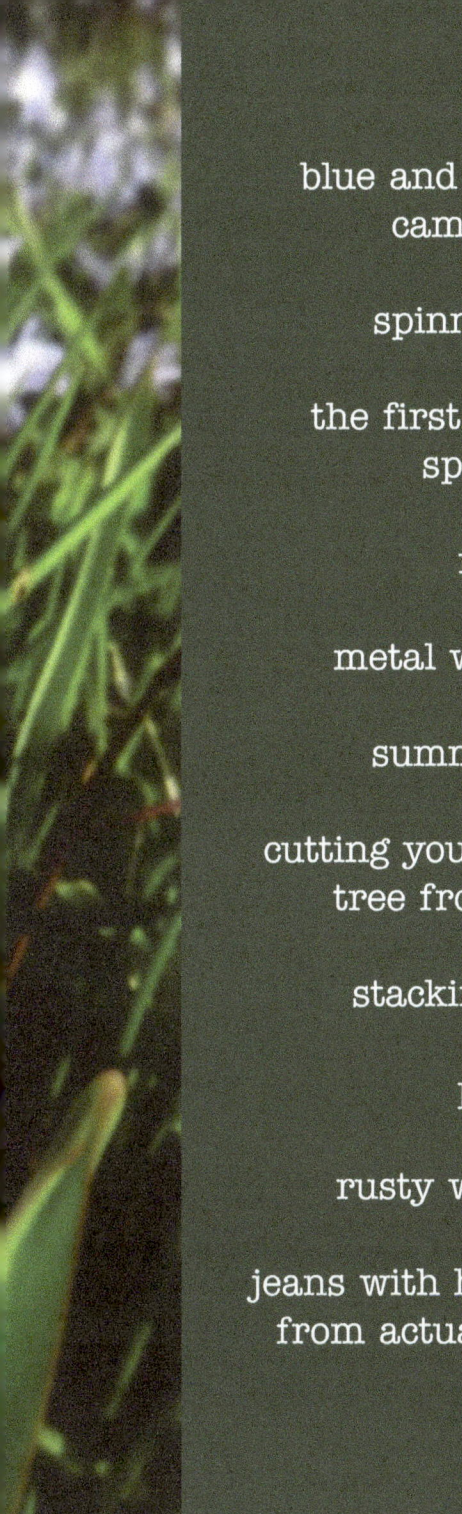

blue and white speckled camping ware

spinning wheels

the first flowers of the springtime

ravens

metal watering cans

summer solstice

cutting your own Christmas tree from the woods

stacking fire wood

picnics

rusty wheelbarrows

jeans with holes in the knees from actual wear and tear

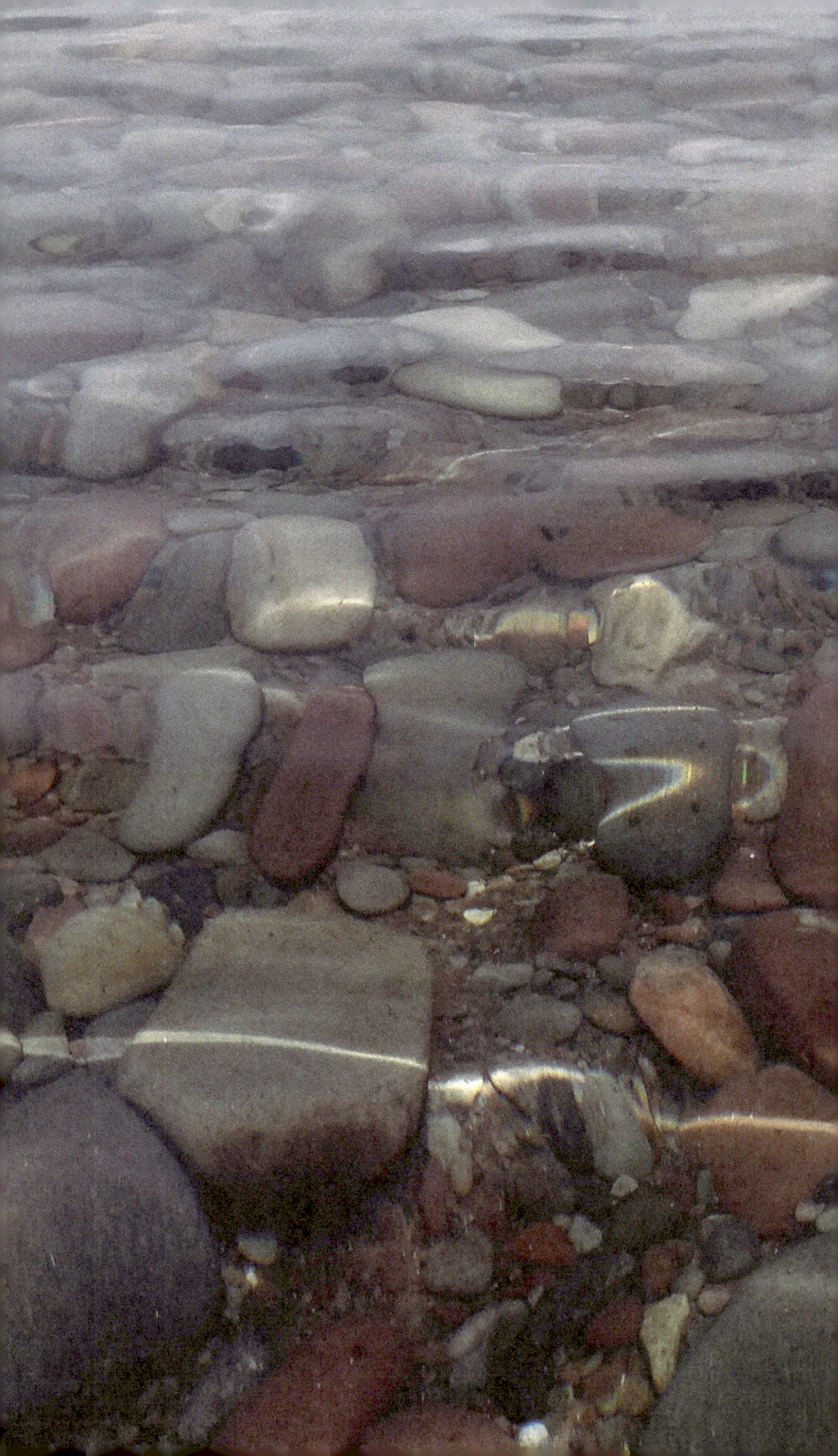

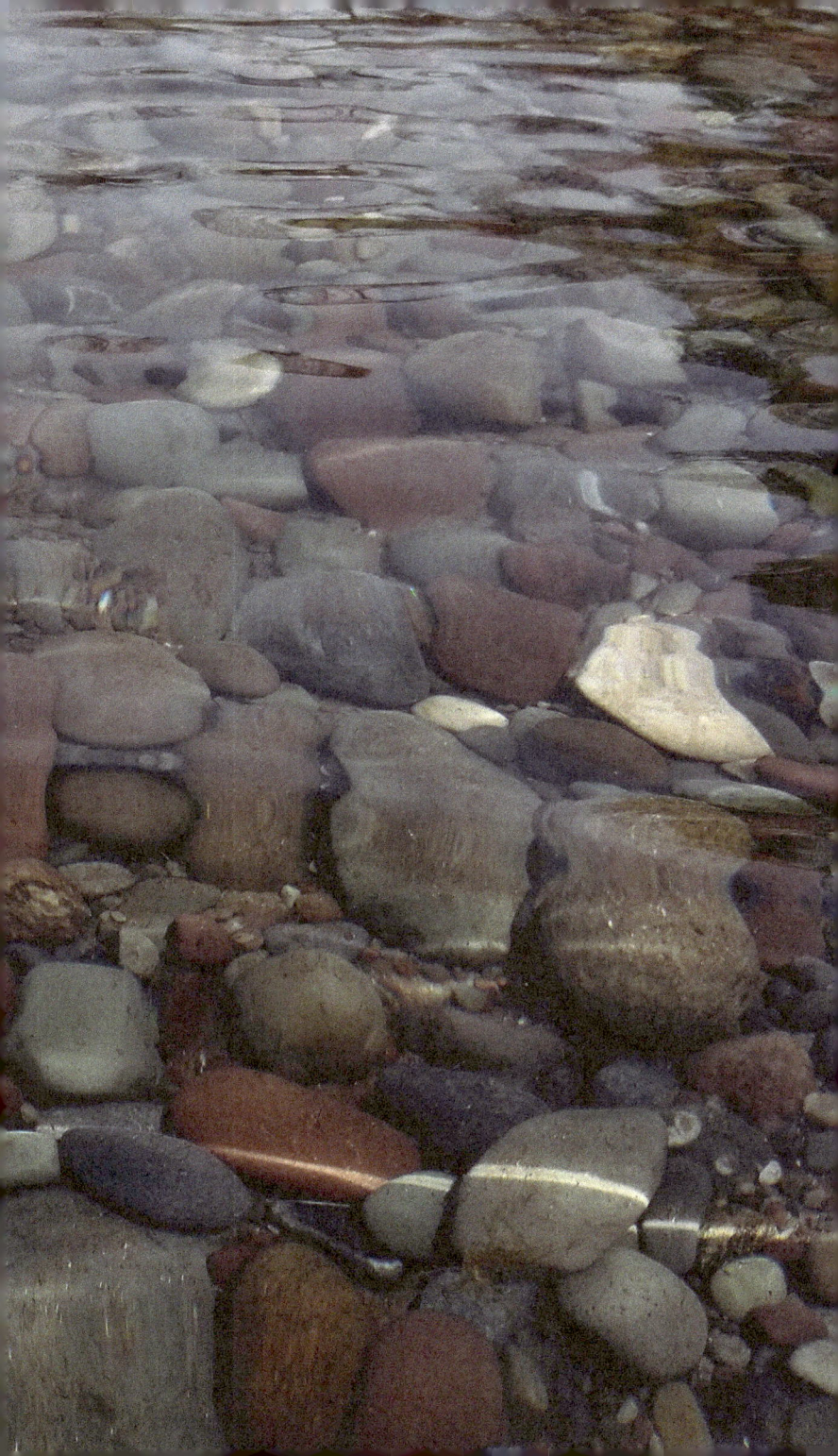

crystal clear lake water

hot tea with lemon and candied ginger

oil lamps

handmade mittens with colorful yarn

geraniums in terracotta pots

the smell of lavender

lace curtains blowing in a soft summer breeze

vegetable gardens

mud puddles

rosy cheeks coming in from the cold

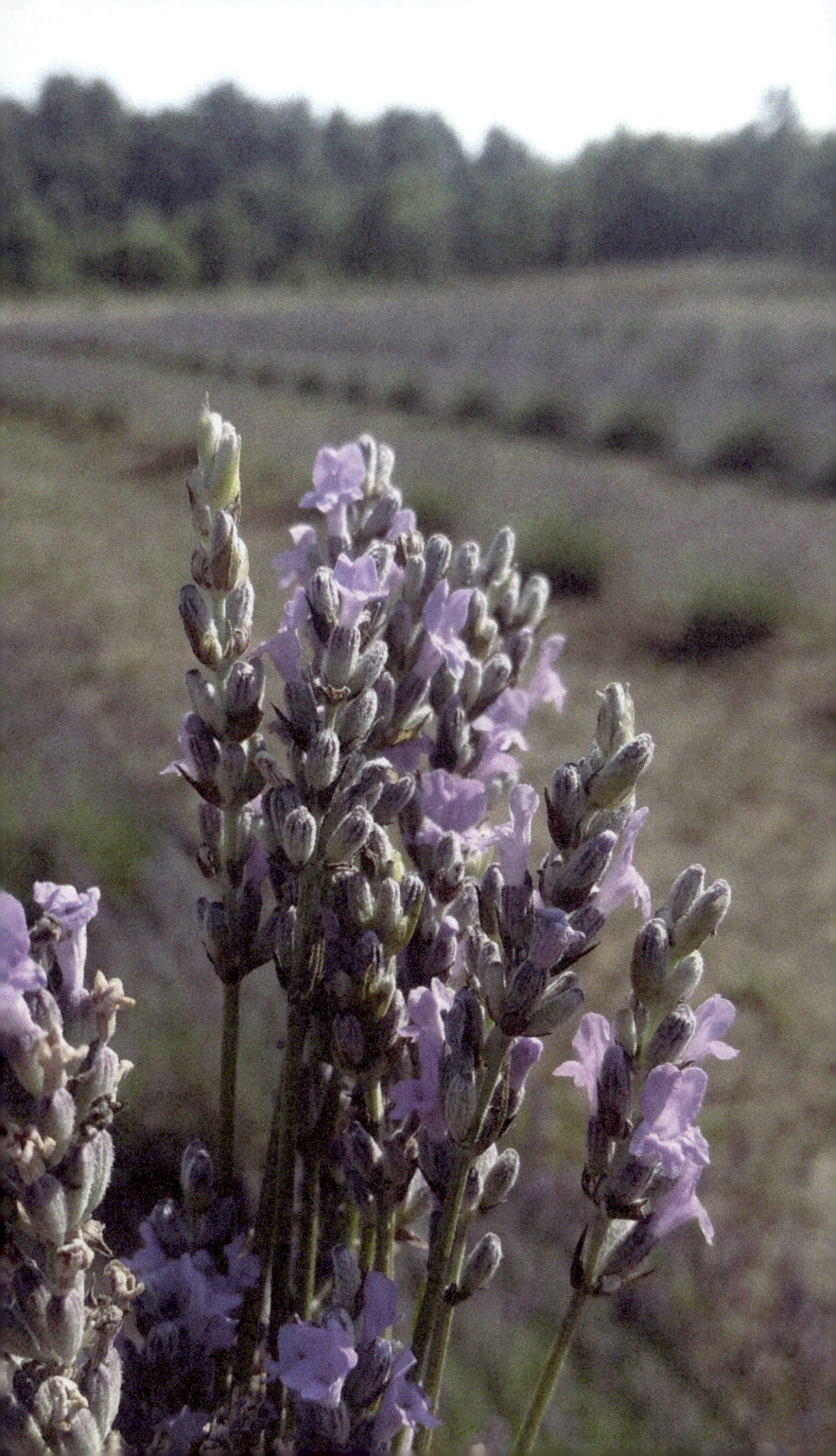

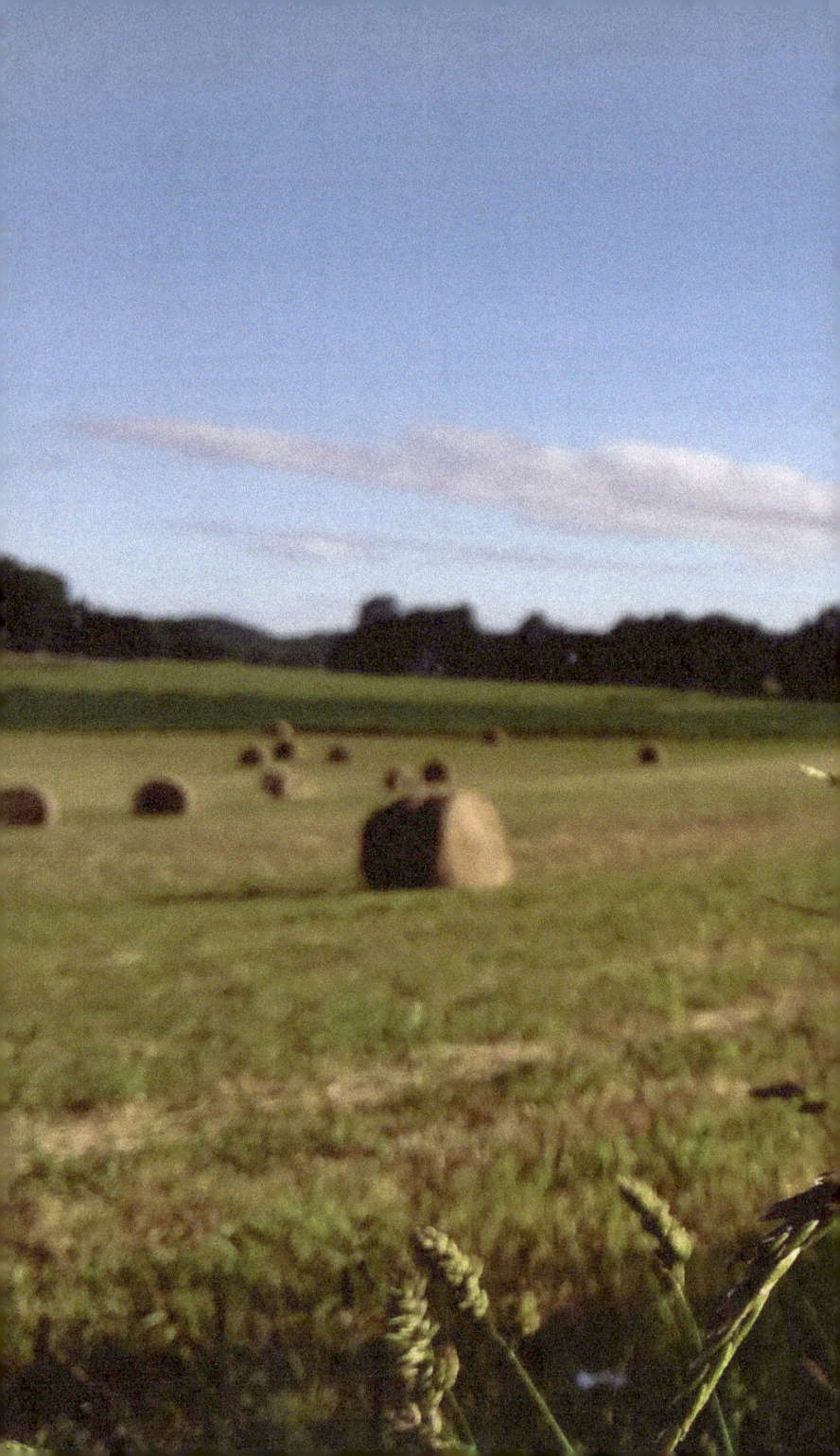

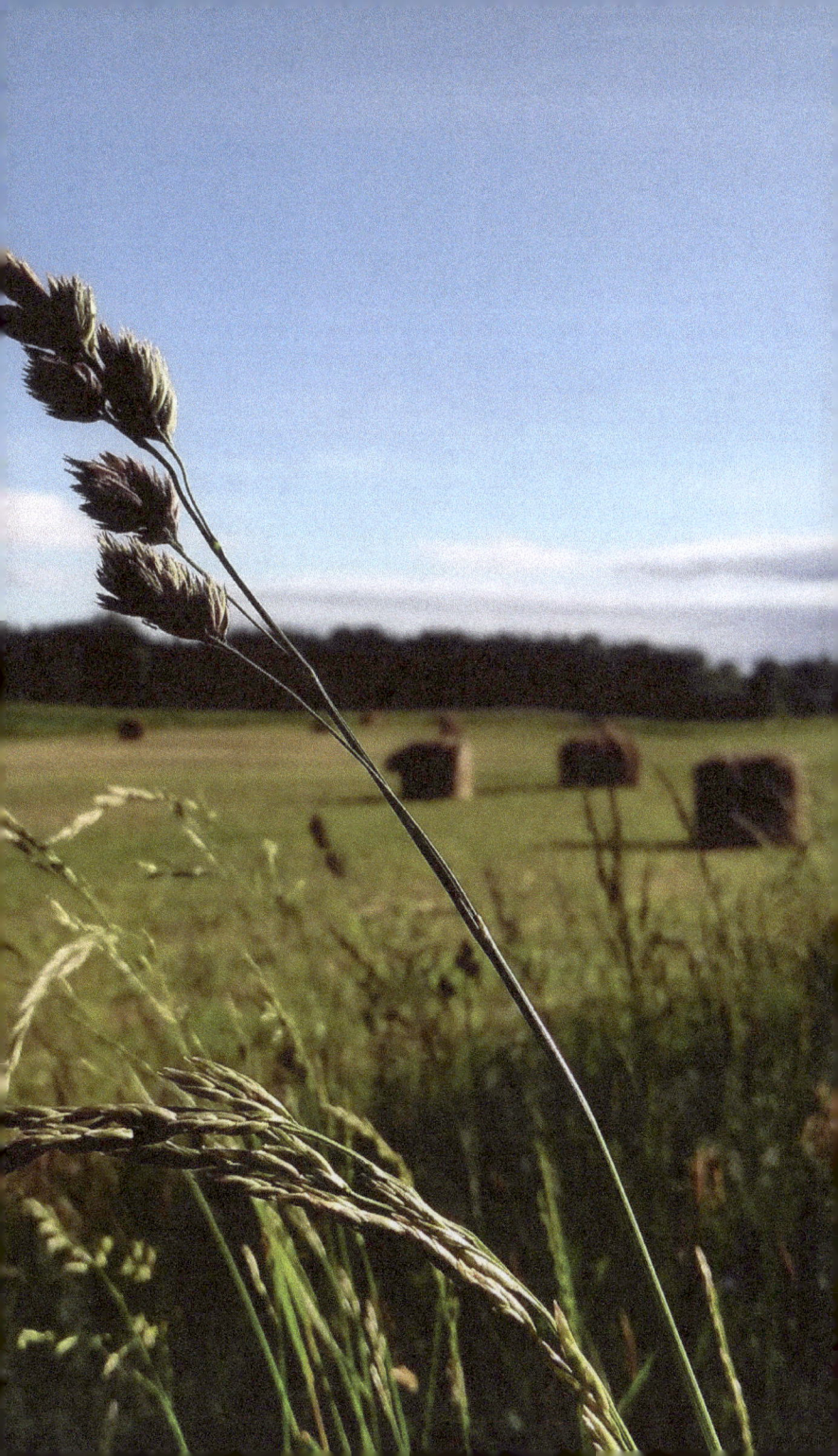

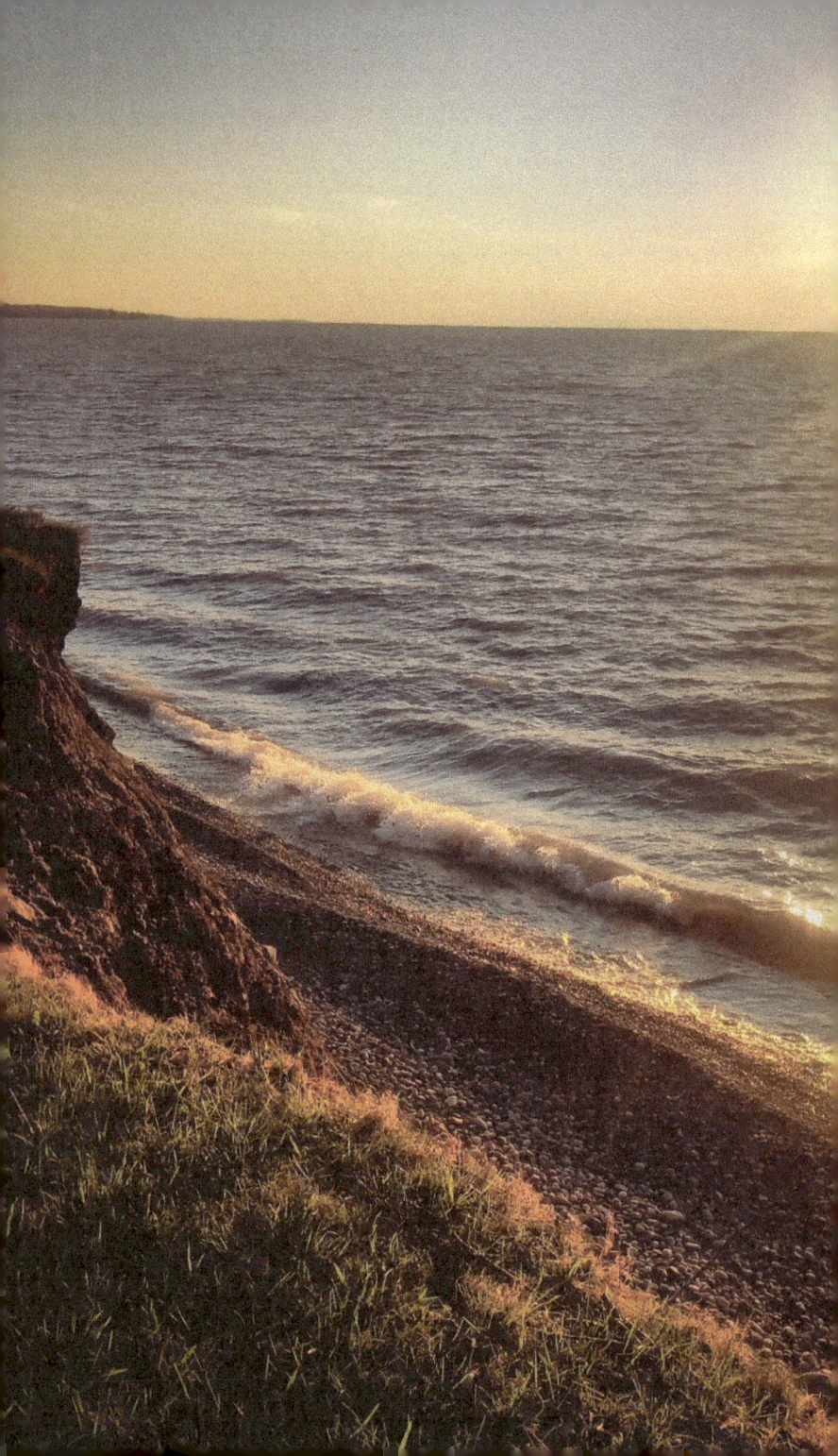

the bluffs

the smell of freshly
mowed grass

sage

colorful rag rugs on
wood floors

wood stoves

flannel shirts that are two
sizes too big

squirrels collecting nuts

hollyhocks by mailboxes

small town coffee shops

old wives tales

fiddle head ferns

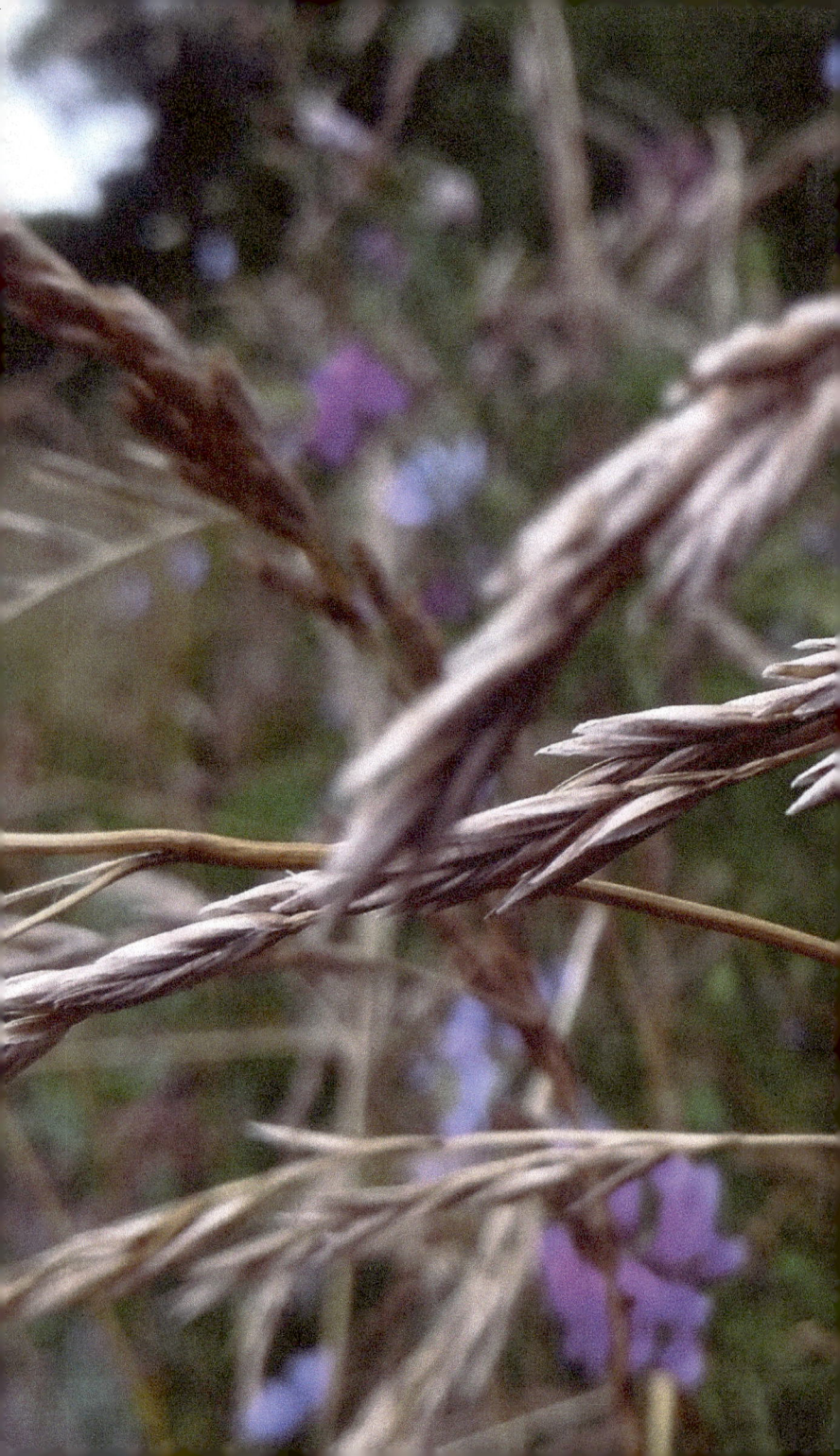

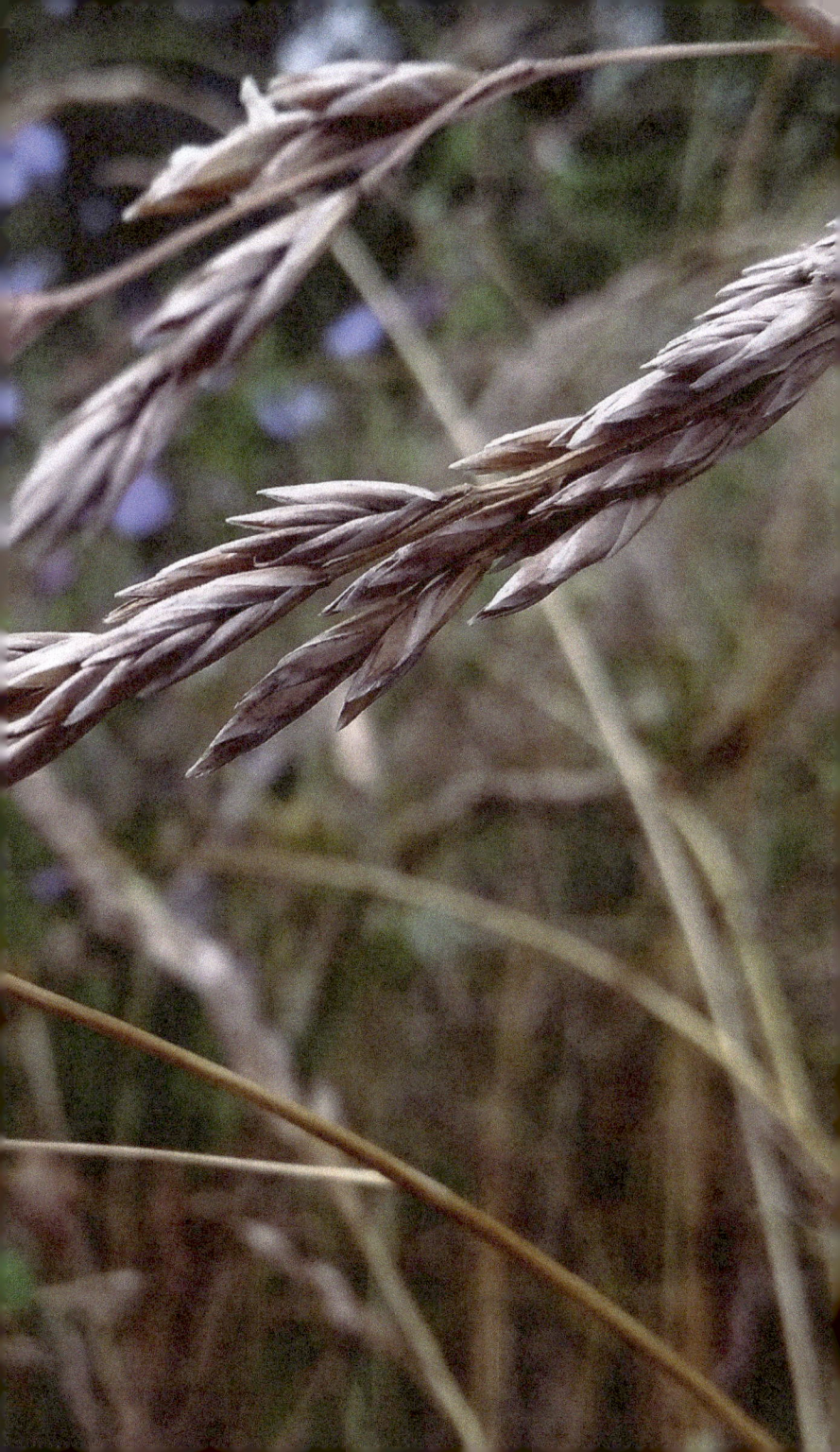

twinkle lights

the sound and smell of coffee brewing in the morning

going barefoot

the sound of a tractor echoing against the woods

dead end country roads

baby blue bird eggs

black and white photographs in little golden edged frames

jean jackets

heirlooms passed down from grandparents

strawberries

homemade jam

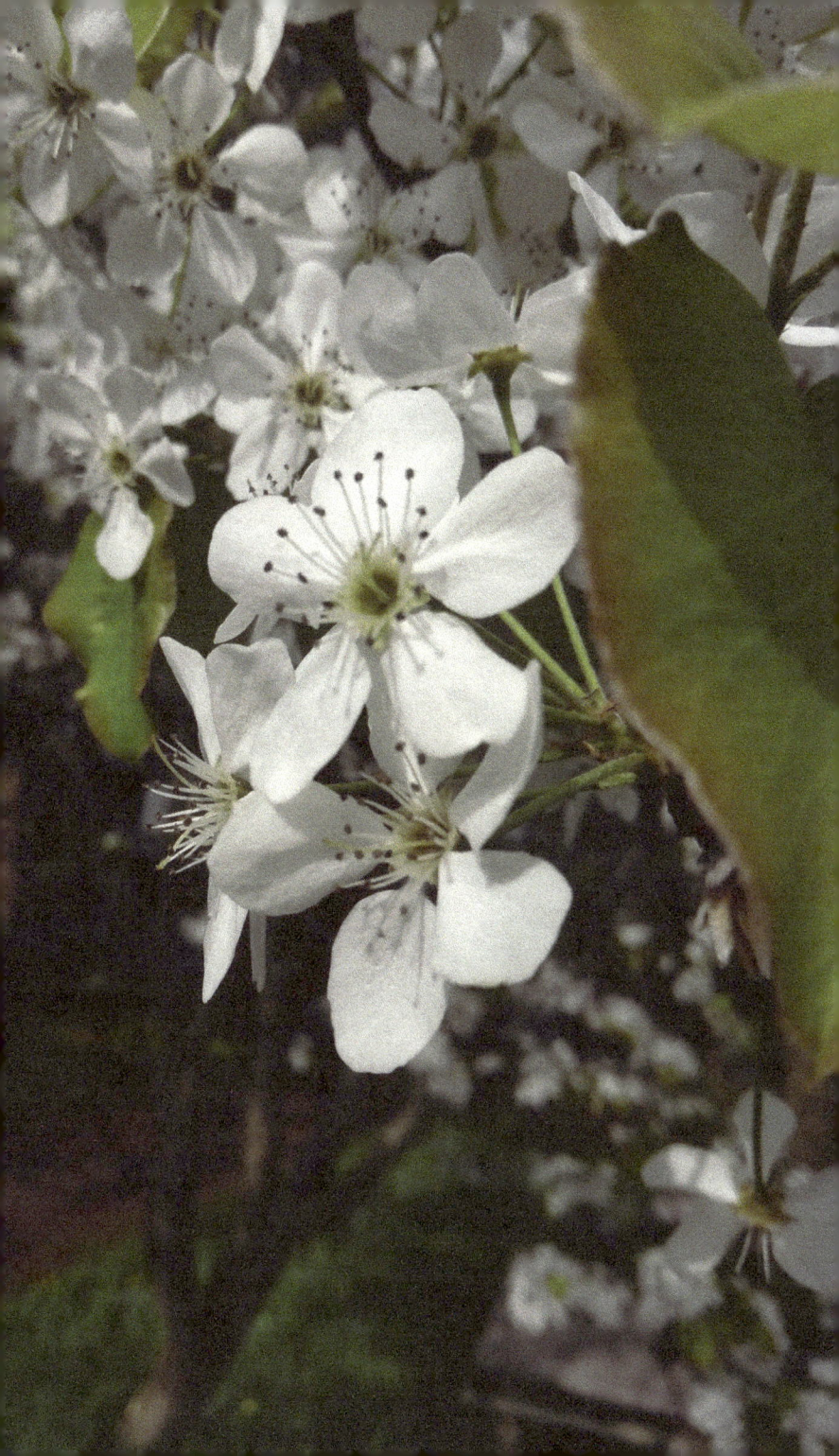

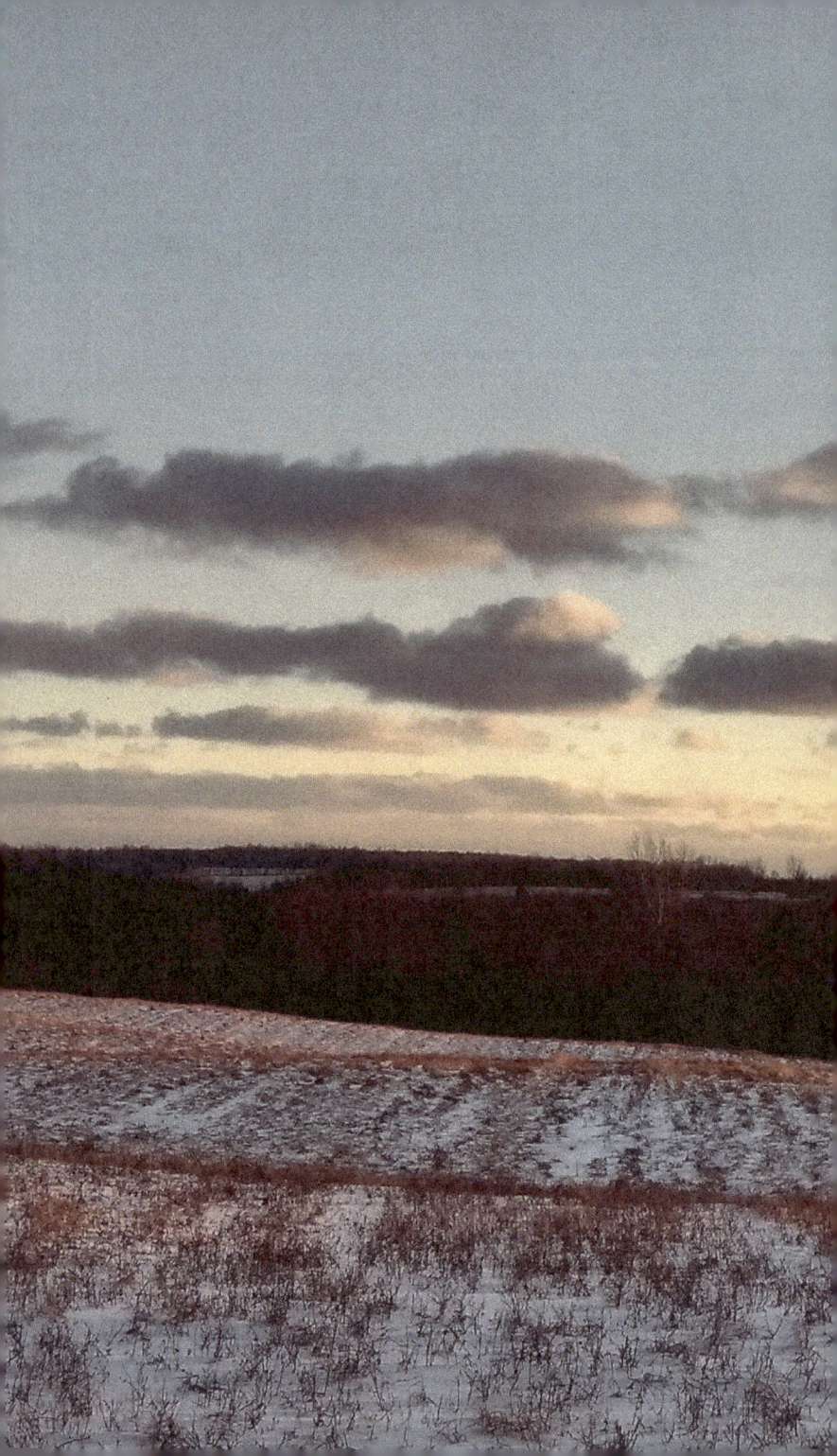

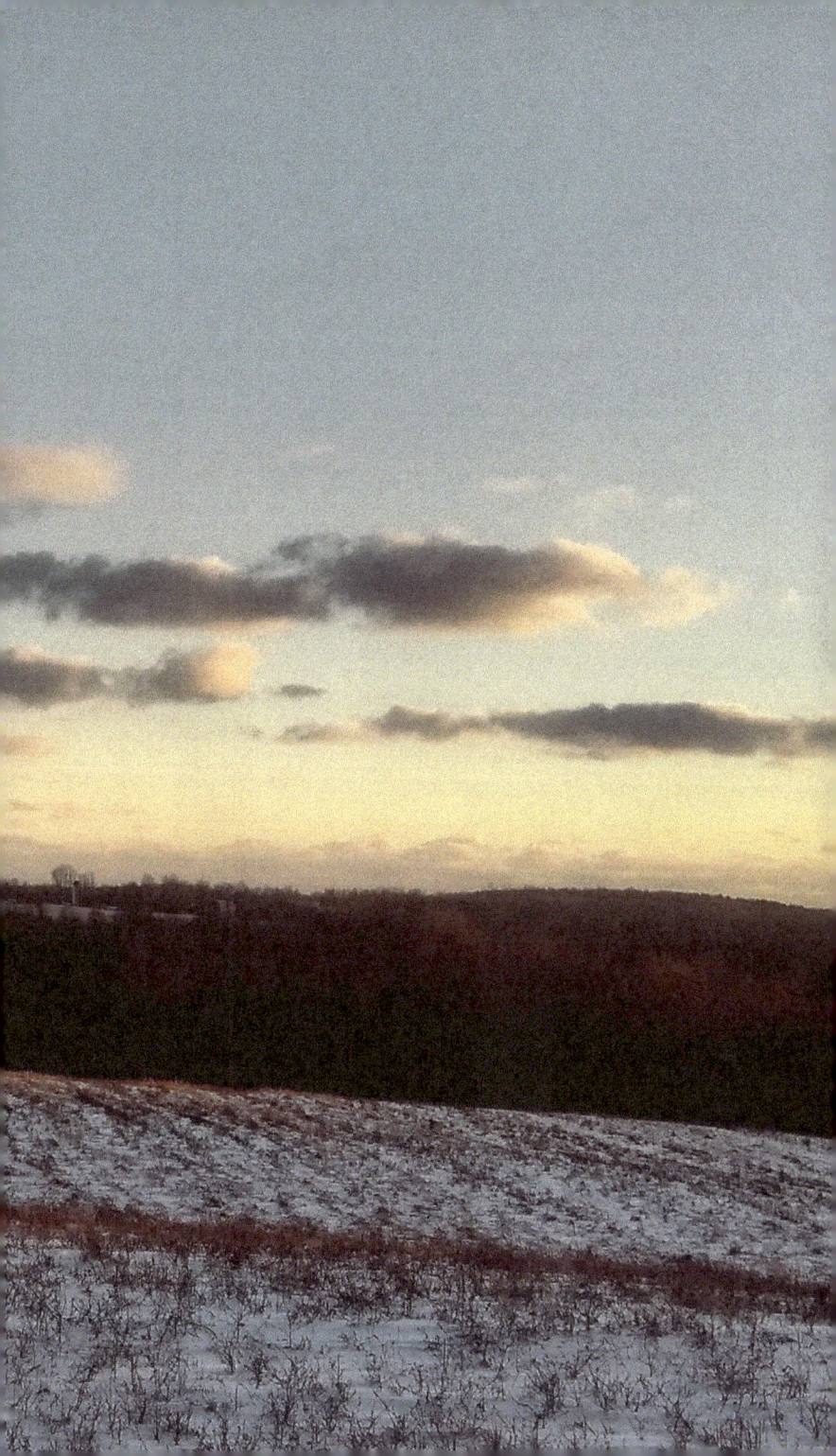

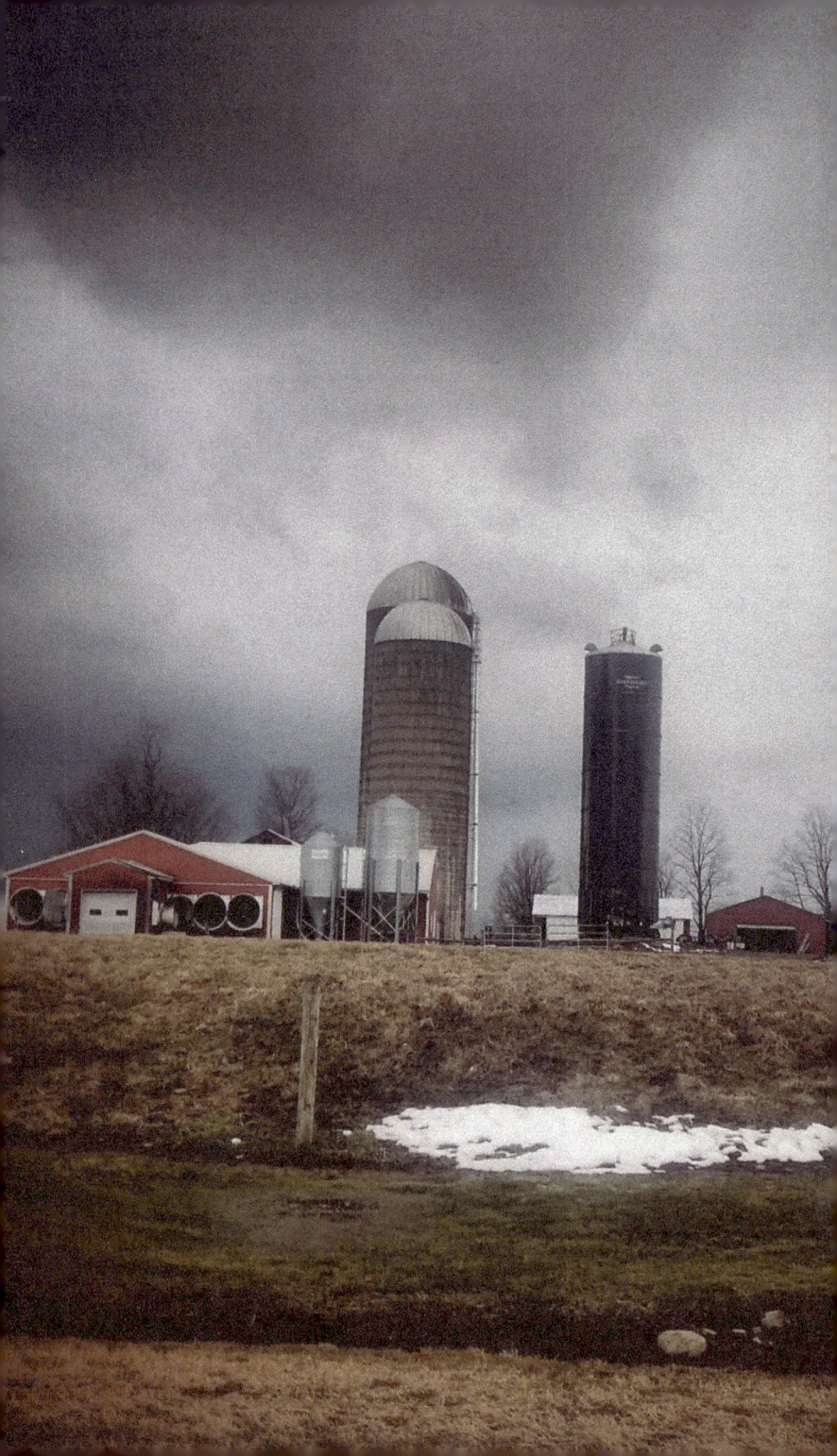

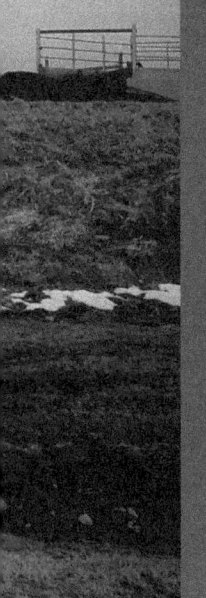

roadside vegetable stands

wicker baskets full of colorful yarn

bunny rabbits

muck boots of all different sizes lining the doorway

sweet cherries

fireworks over the water on the Fourth of July

songbirds in the springtime

barn cats

the moon rising through the trees

hummingbirds

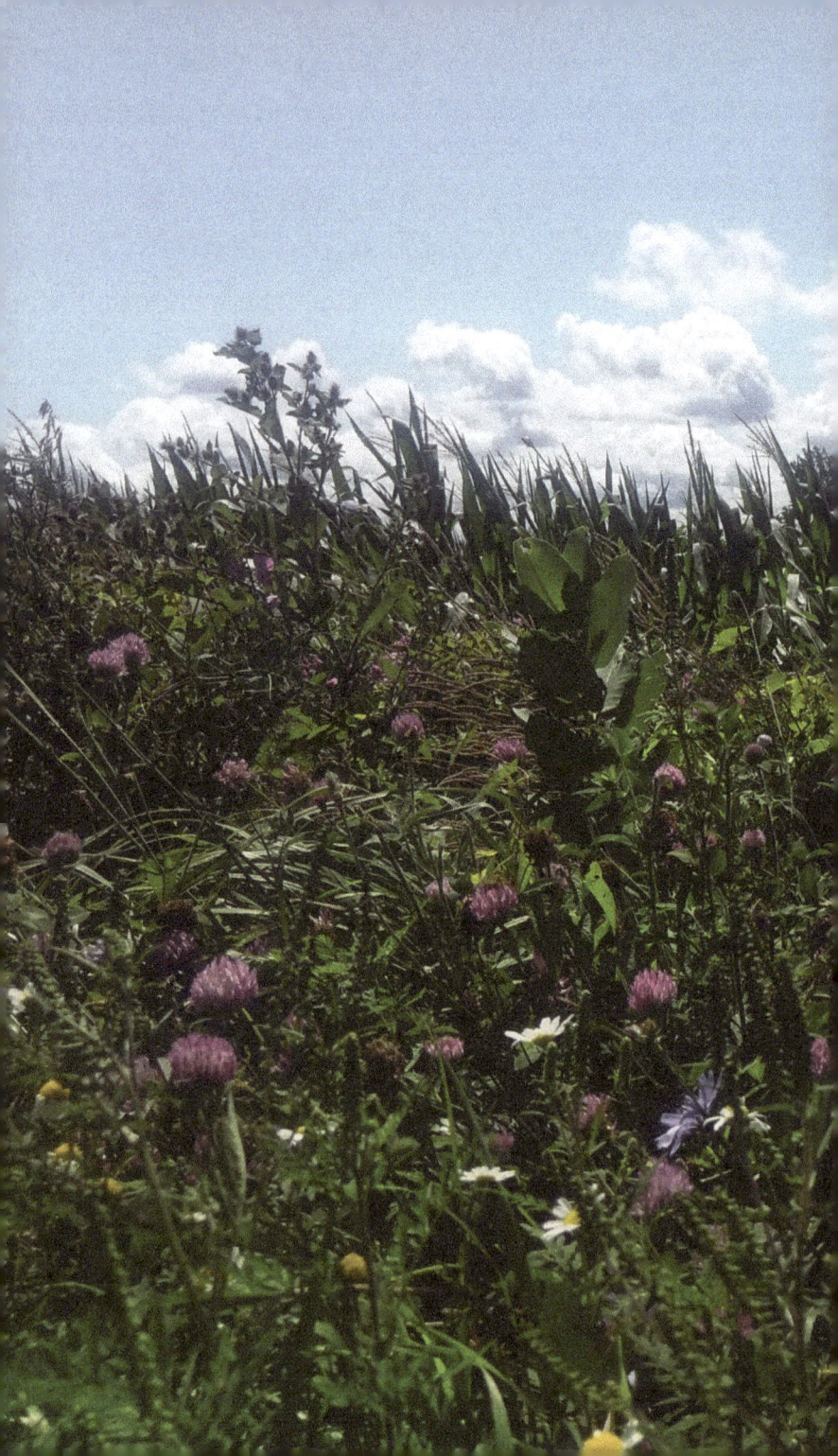

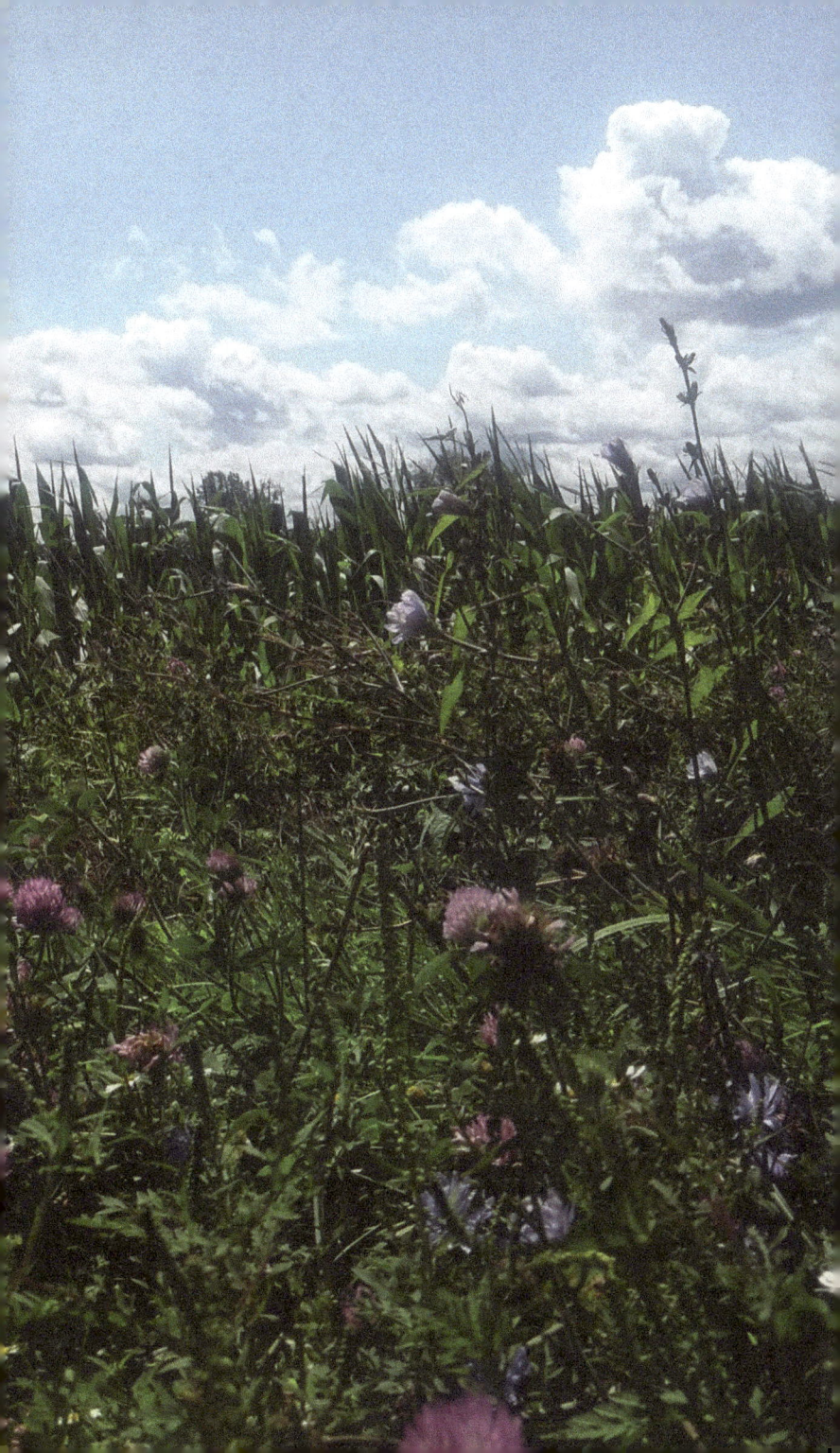

black eyed susans

the sound of screen doors
slamming shut

collecting driftwood

the smell of the soil after the
earth has been turned up
by a plow

rainbows over the countryside

the smell of fresh basil

flower bouquets from farmers
markets

red and black plaid

patchwork quilts made from
pieces of memories

cows in the field

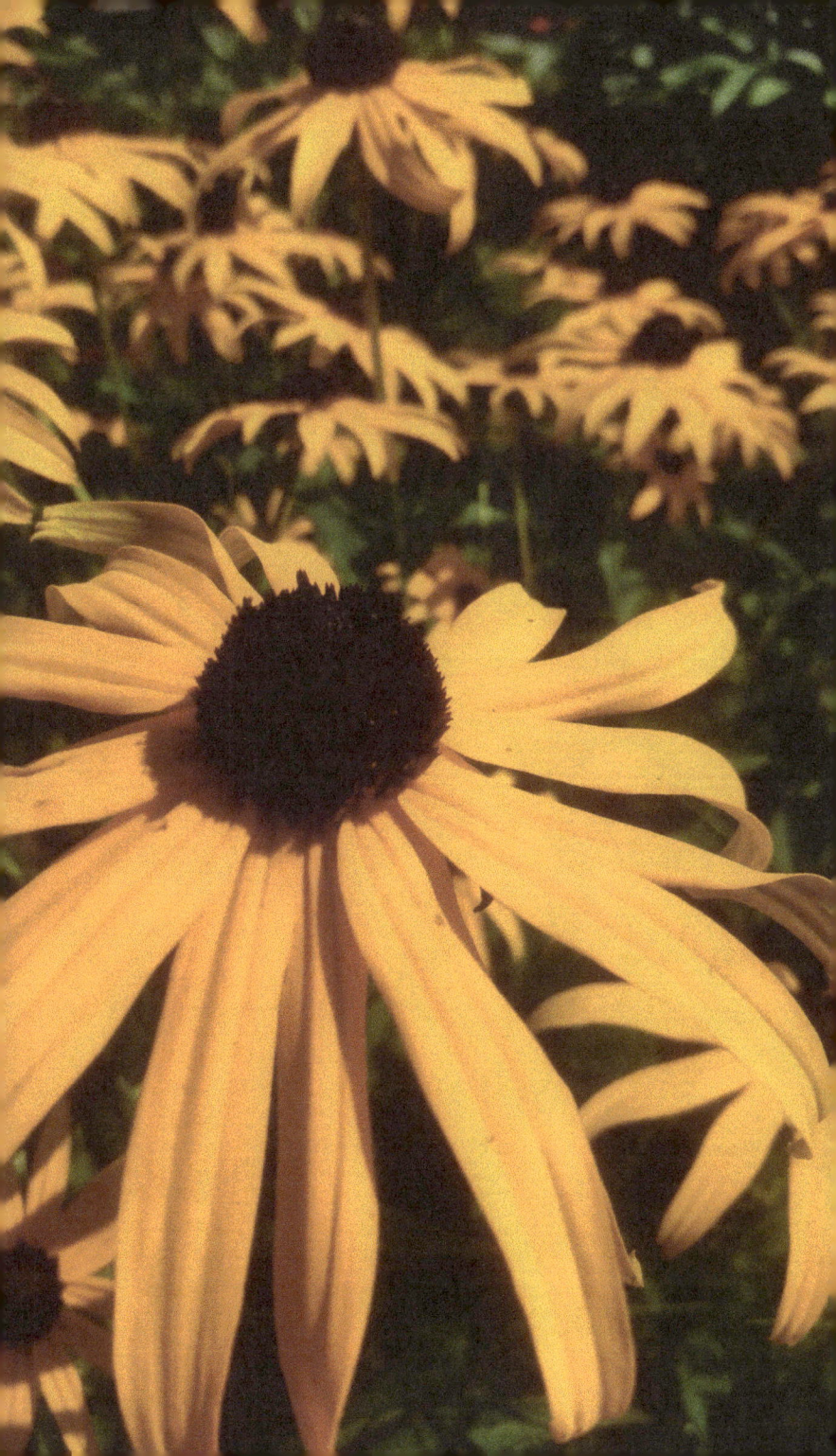

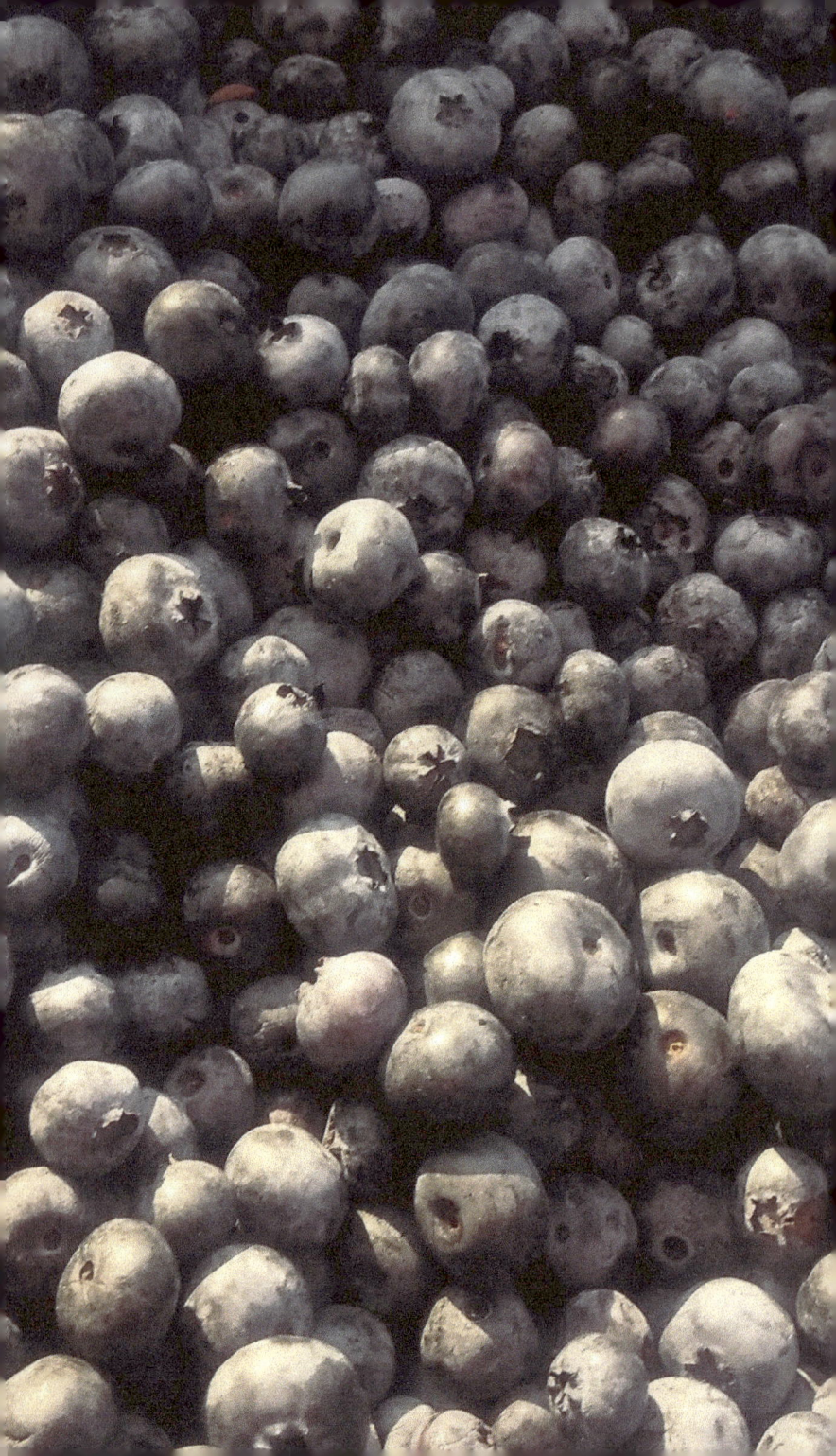

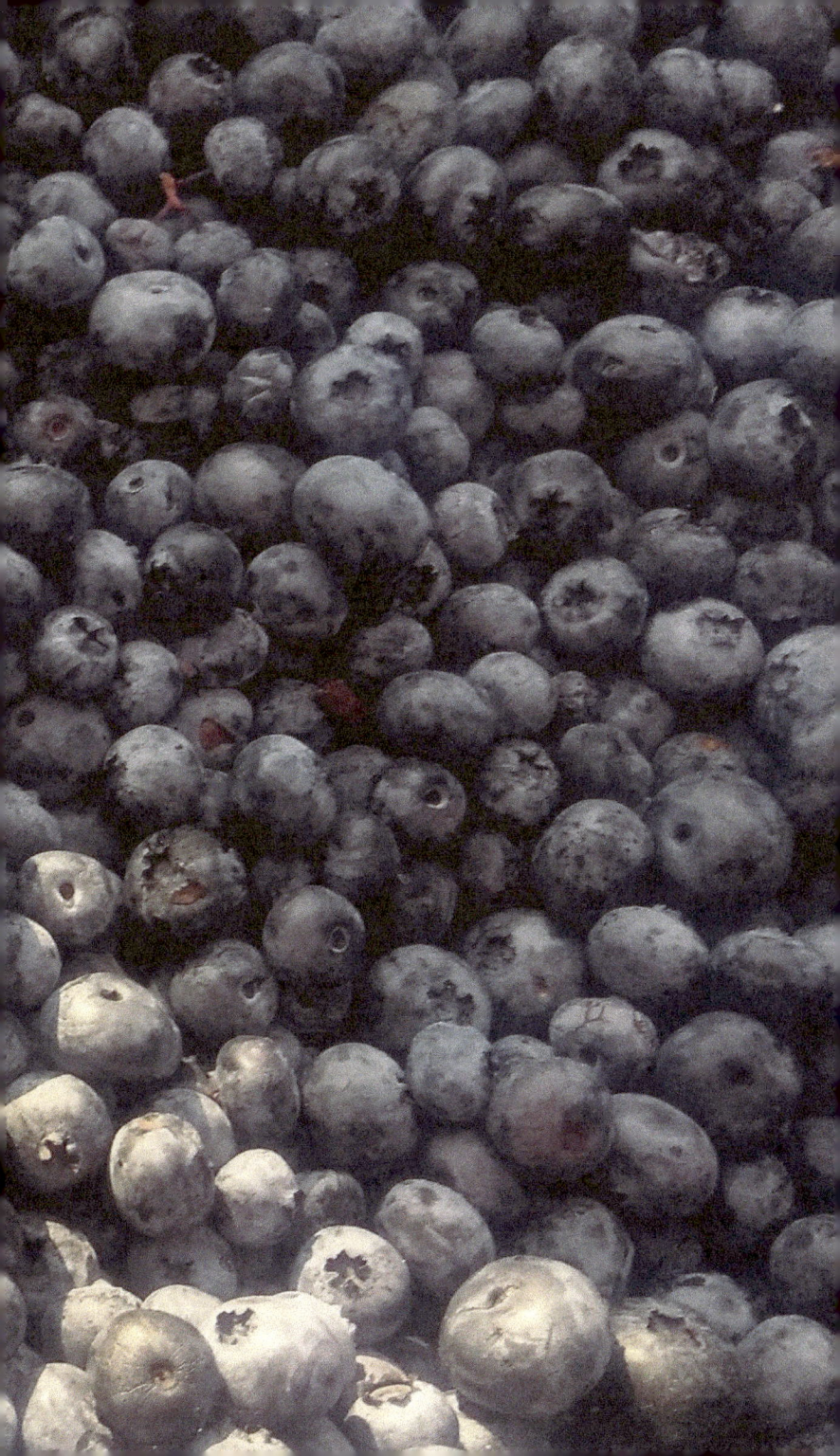

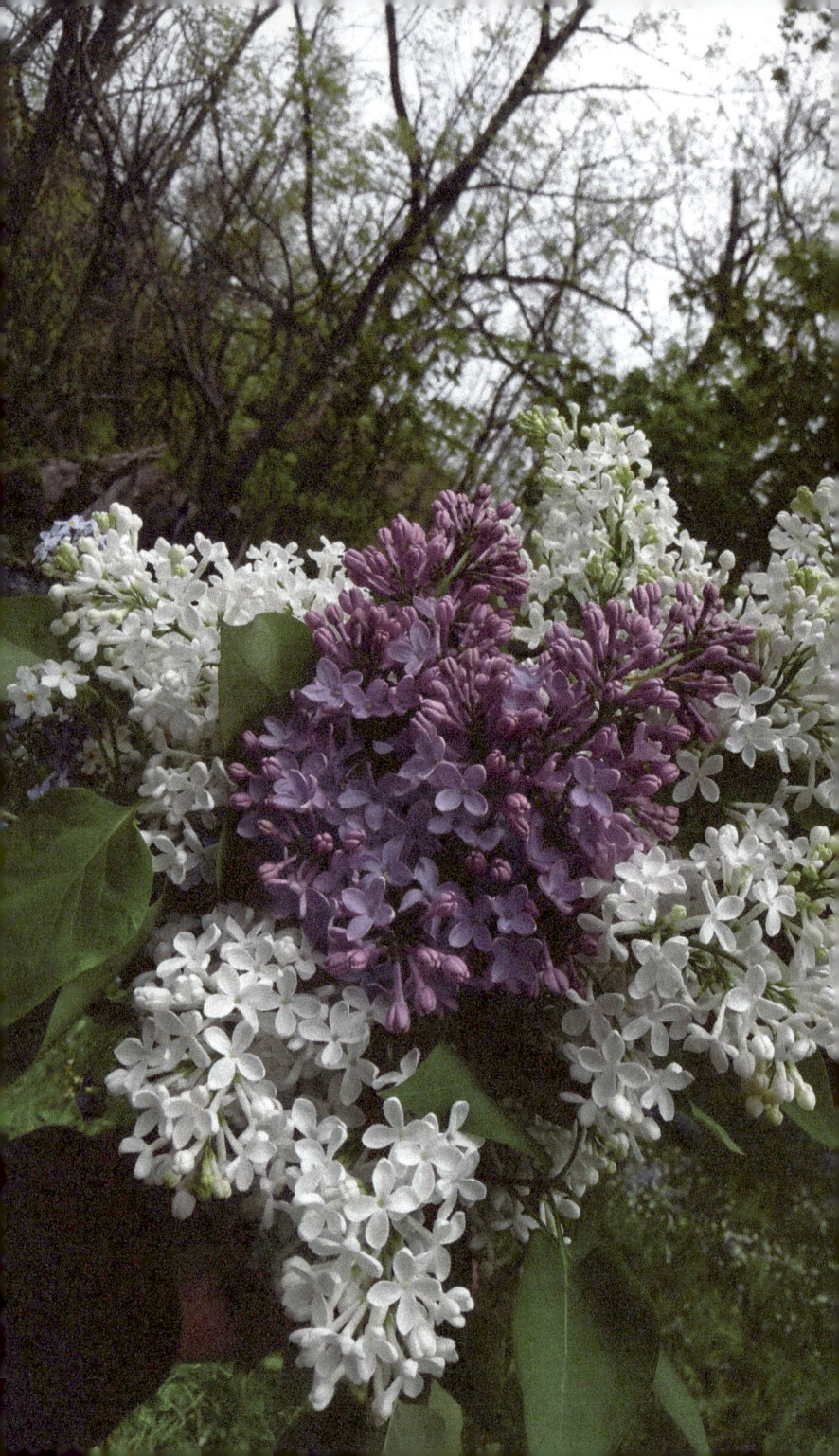

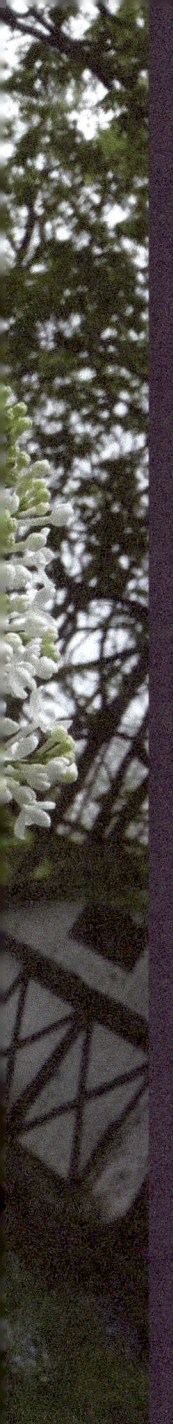

lilacs

white wicker furniture on old wooden porches

hand spun and hand dyed yarns of every tint and shade

pink and orange plaid

curling up in bed with a dog at your feet

rocking chairs

lace curtain shadows on the dining room floor

waking up in a tent

the smell of campfire on your clothes

bushels of apples

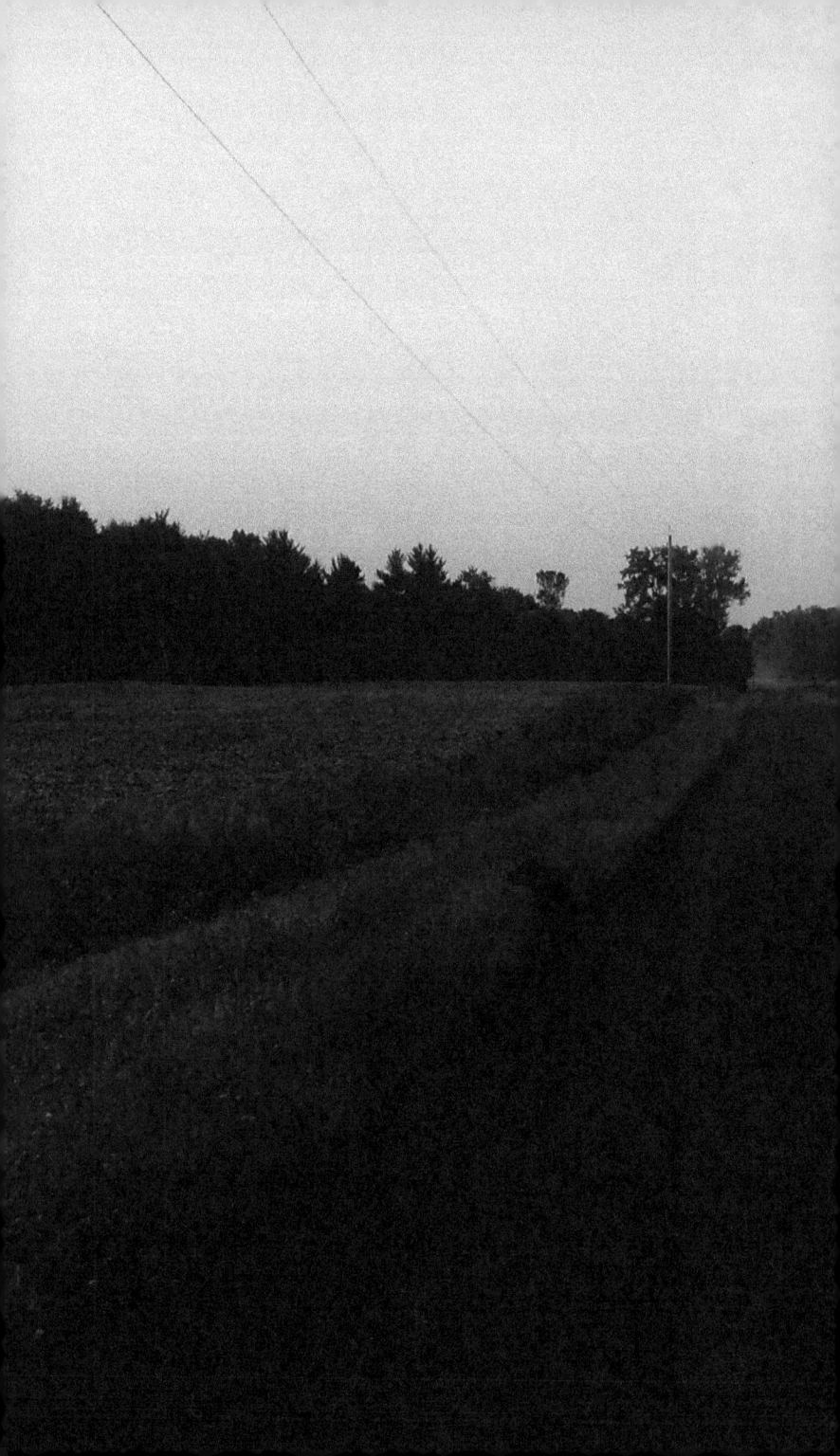

farmers markets

fruit in faded blue/green quart baskets

the end of August

roadsides overgrown with wildflowers

baby raccoons

thunderstorms that rattle old farmhouse windows

the first sighting of fireflies

firewood stacked on the porch

field mice

vintage oil paintings of farms

homemade soap

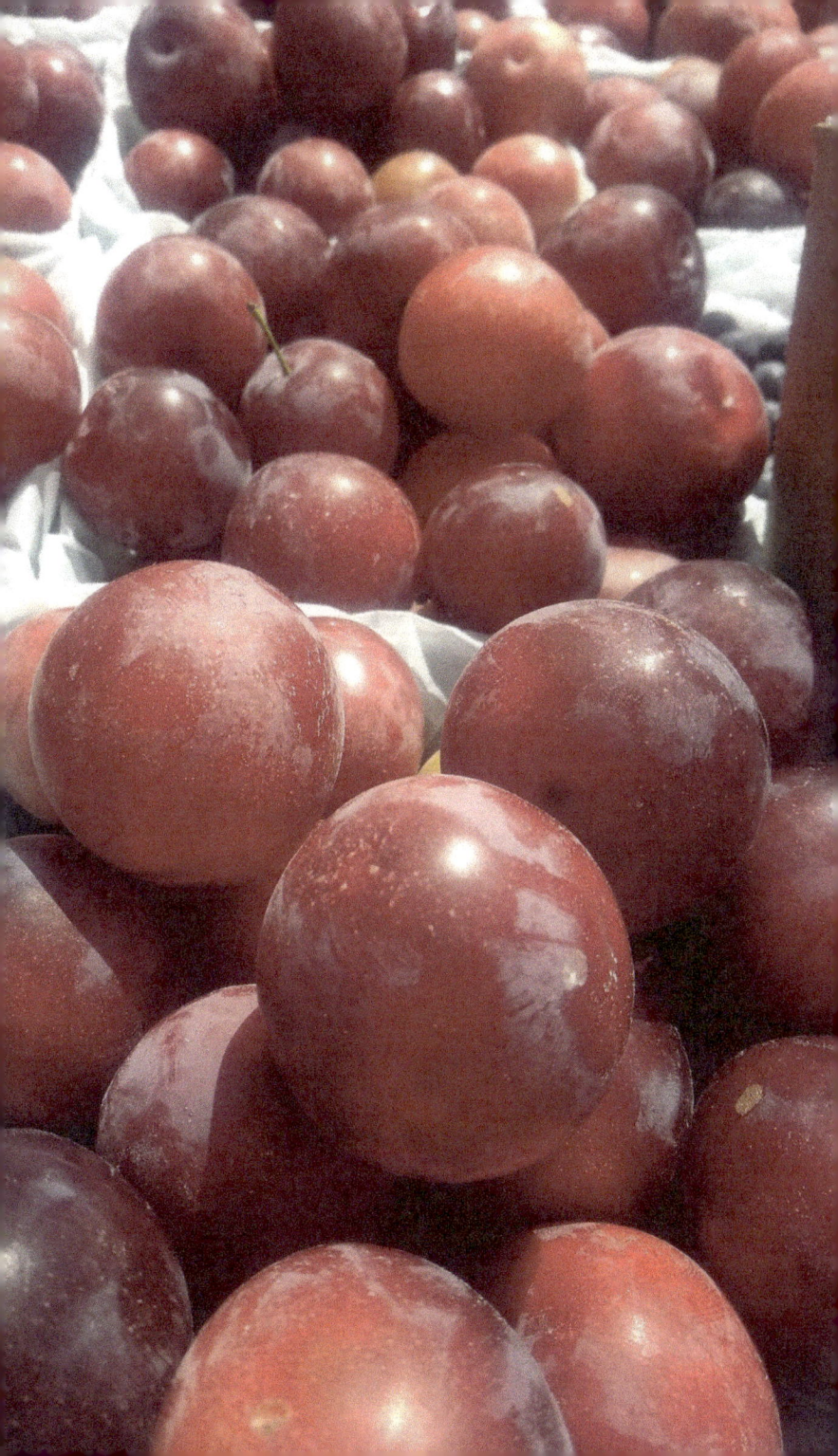

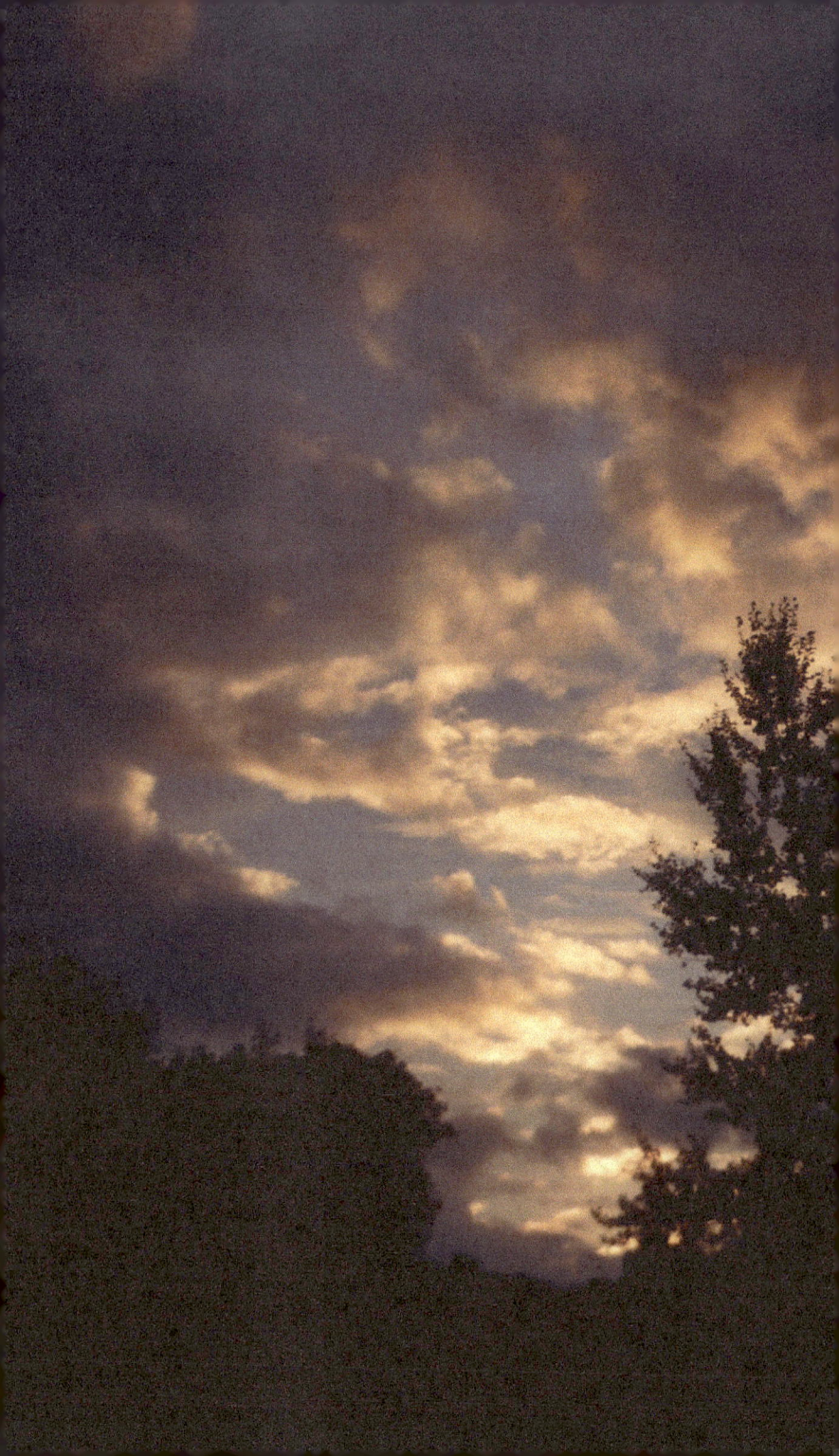

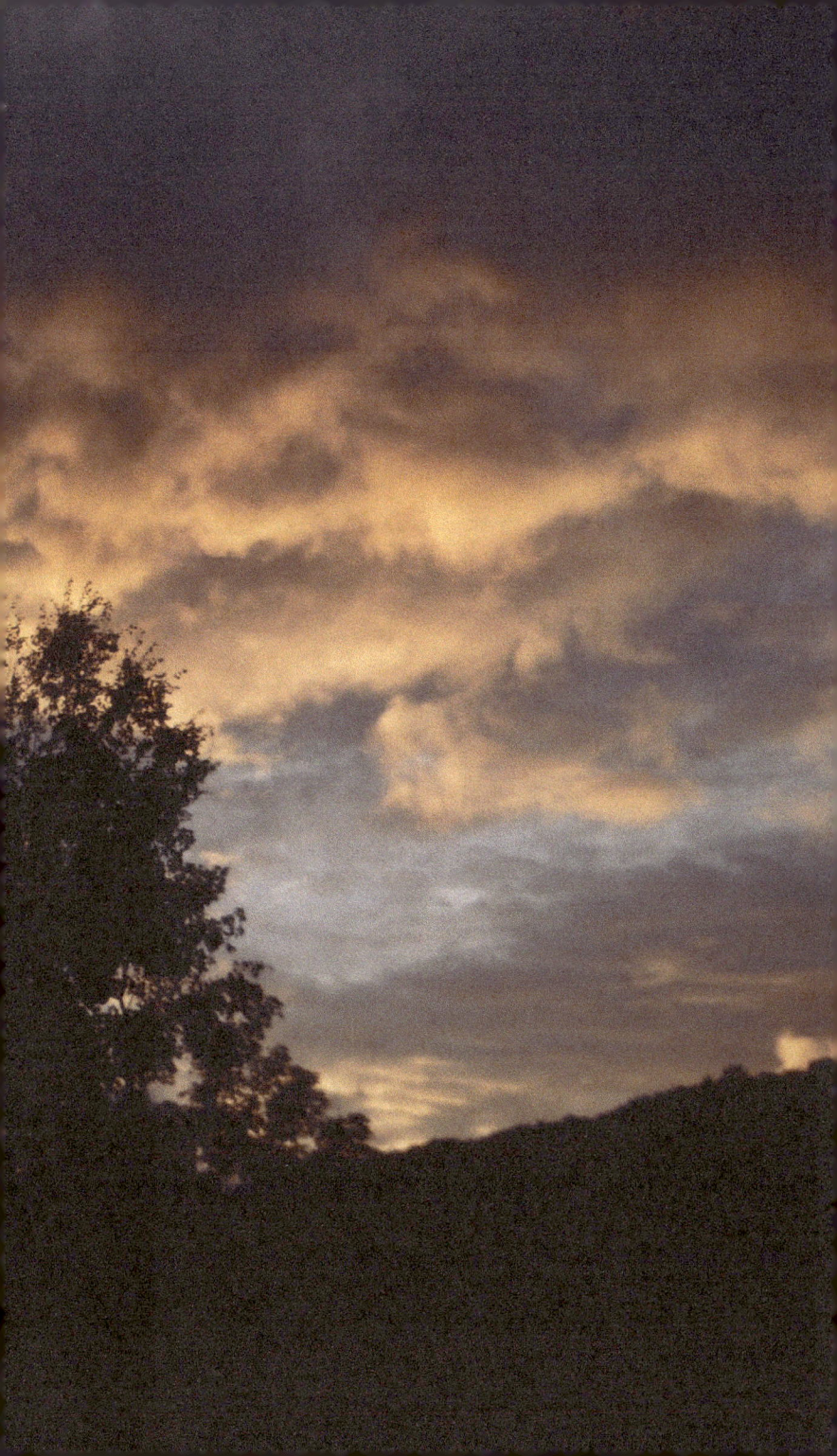

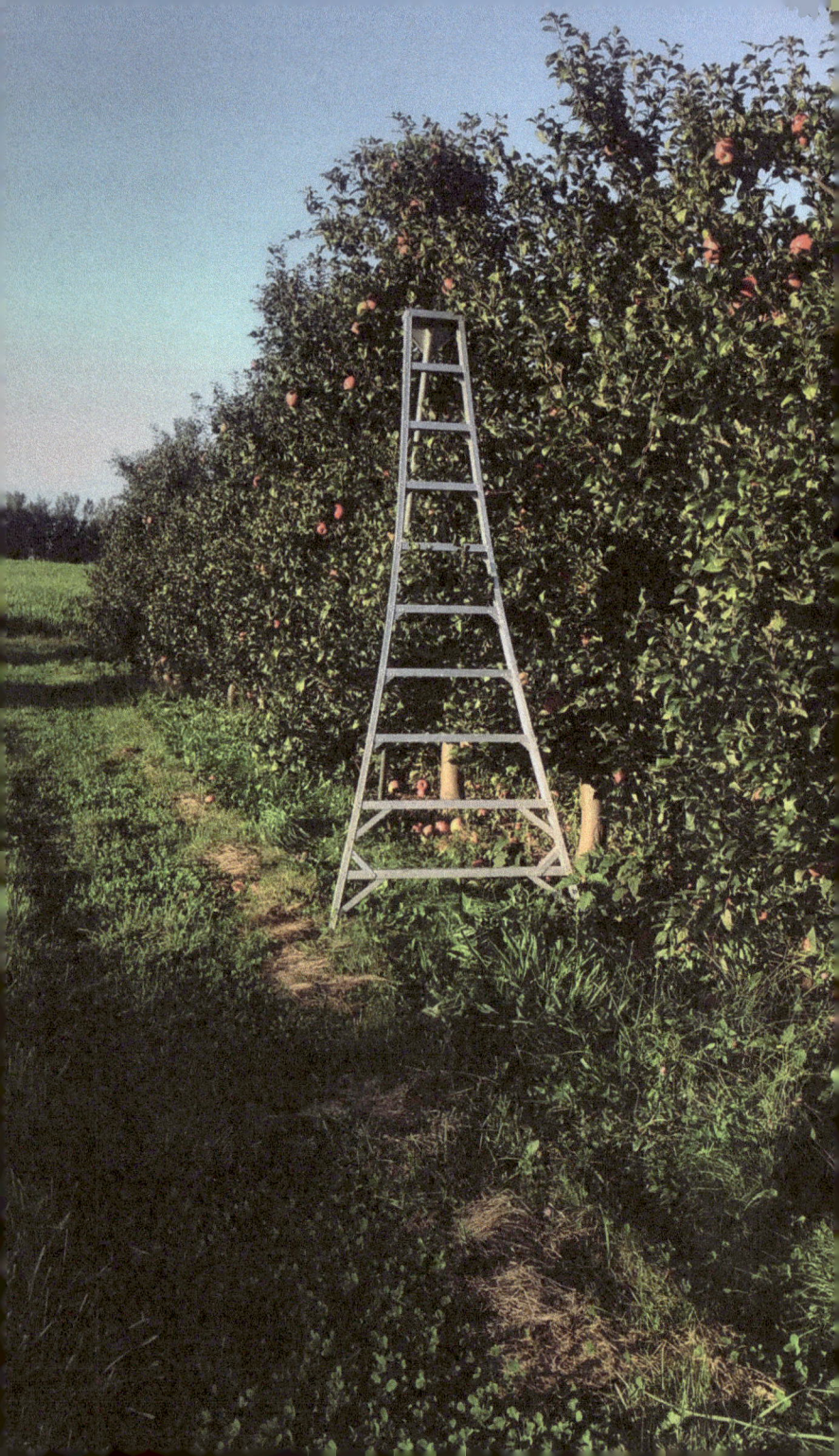

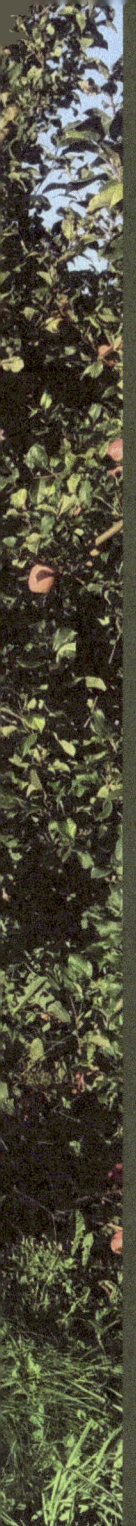

salmon and pink sunsets

riding in the back of a truck through an orchard

wooden wind chimes

broken coffee mugs full of paintbrushes

when the wind picks up

horses

the constellations

maple syrup in the springtime

root cellars

bookshelves full of advice on gardening and homesteading

popcorn over the stove

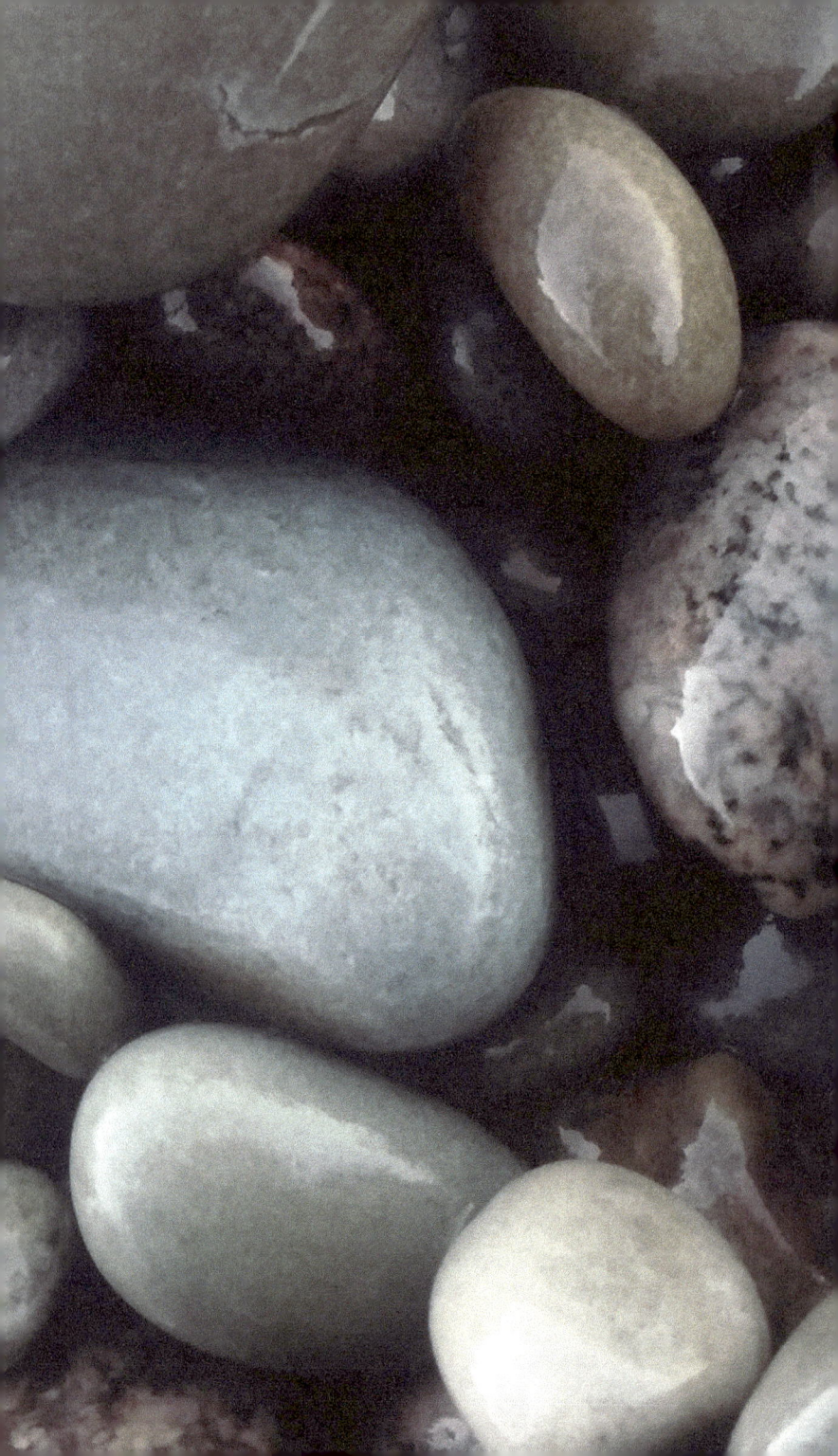

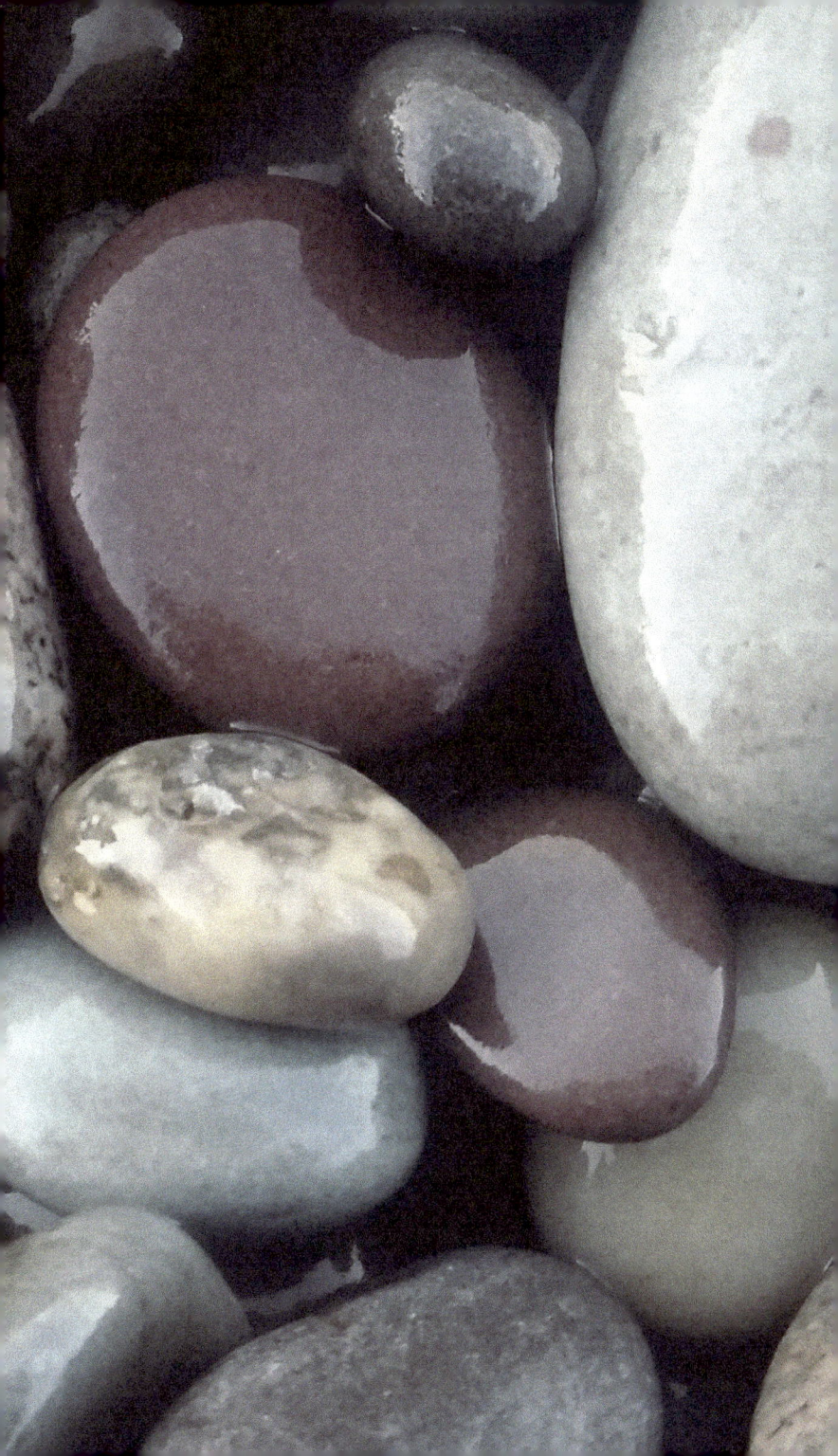

hanging lavender to dry in the kitchen

nectarines

geese flying south for the winter

VHS movie collections from the thrift store

rocky lake shores

coffee in handmade ceramic mugs

a full moon over the corn field

wild pink daisies

morning sunshine through the windows

vintage postcards

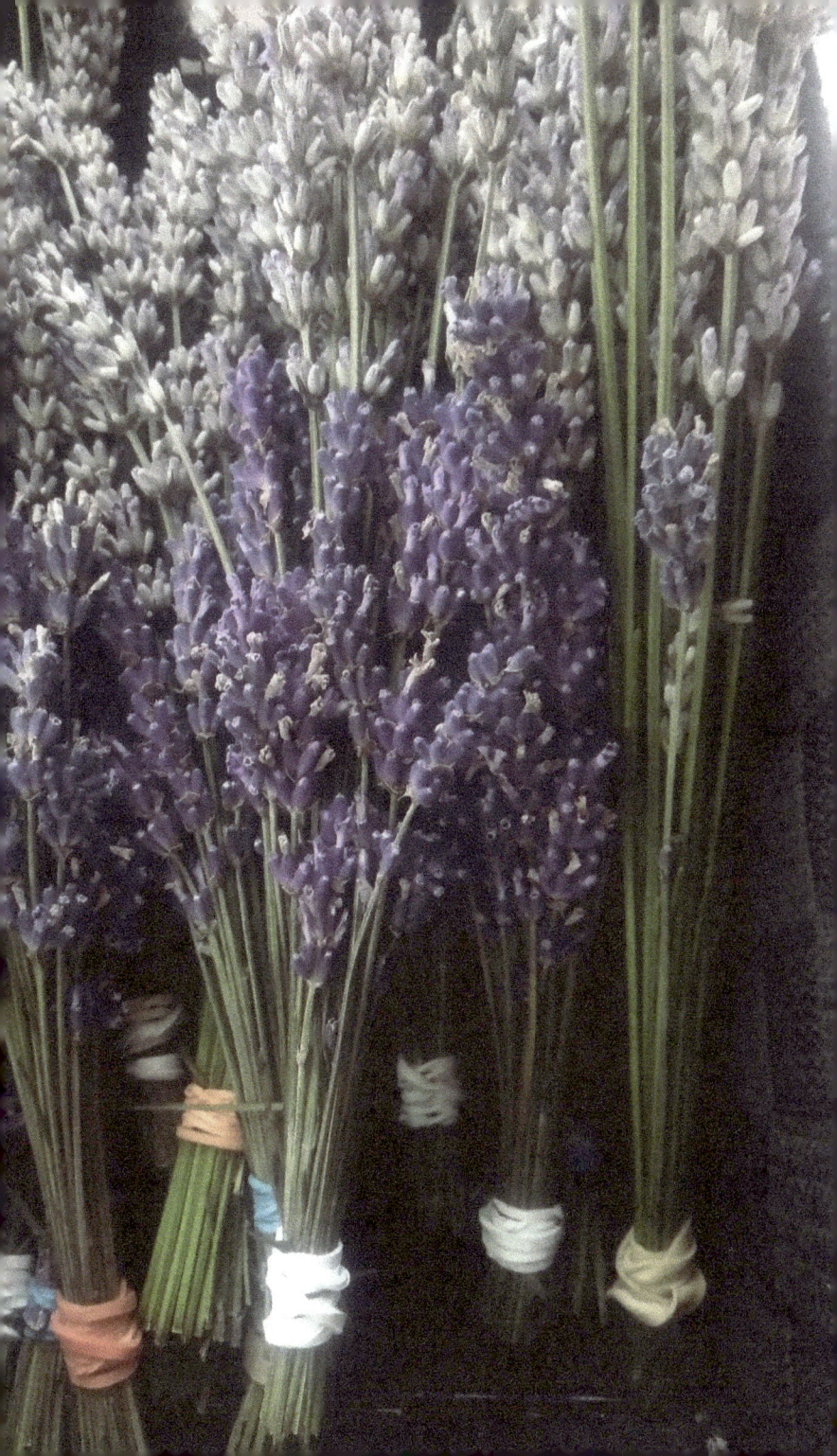

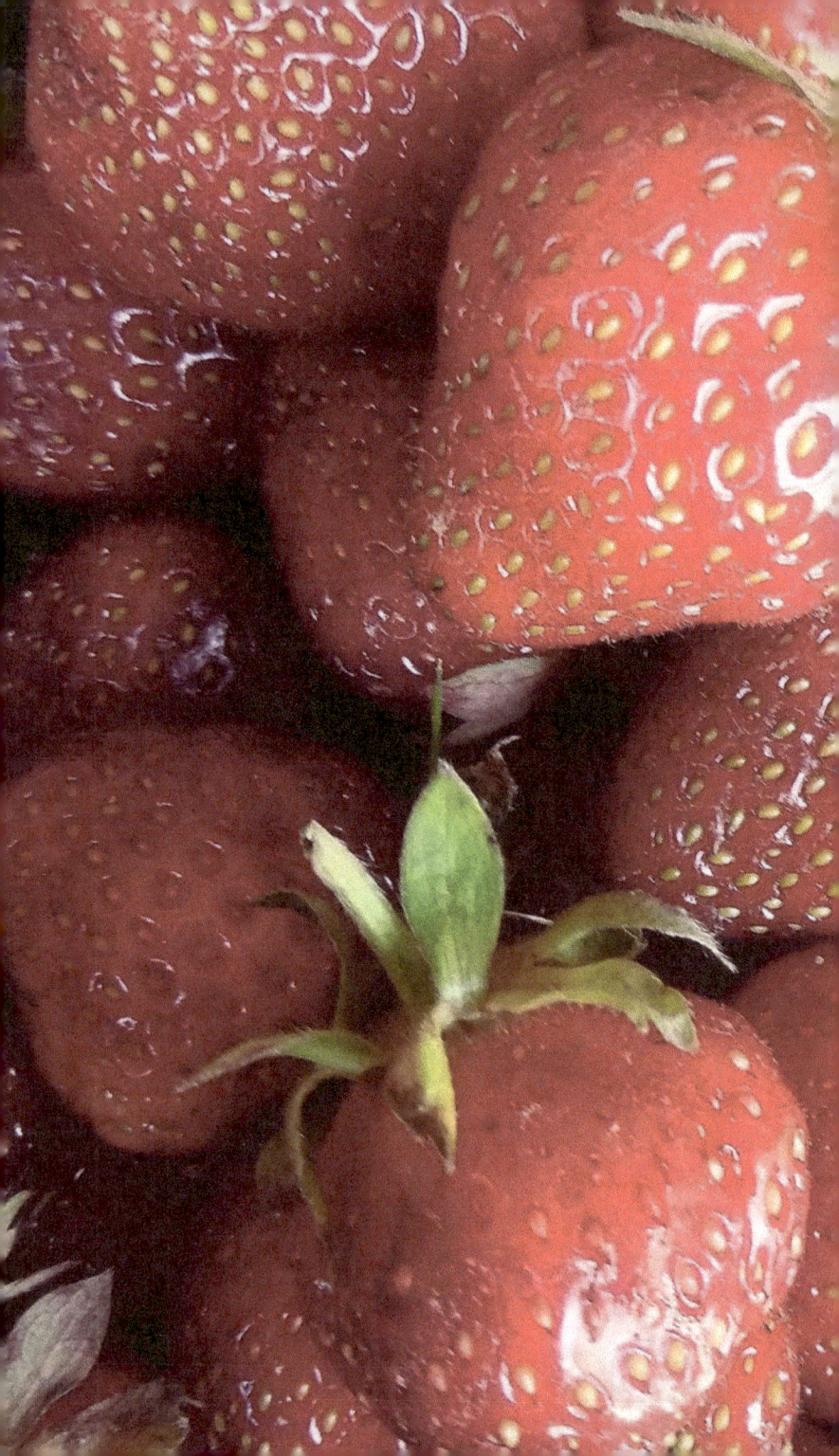

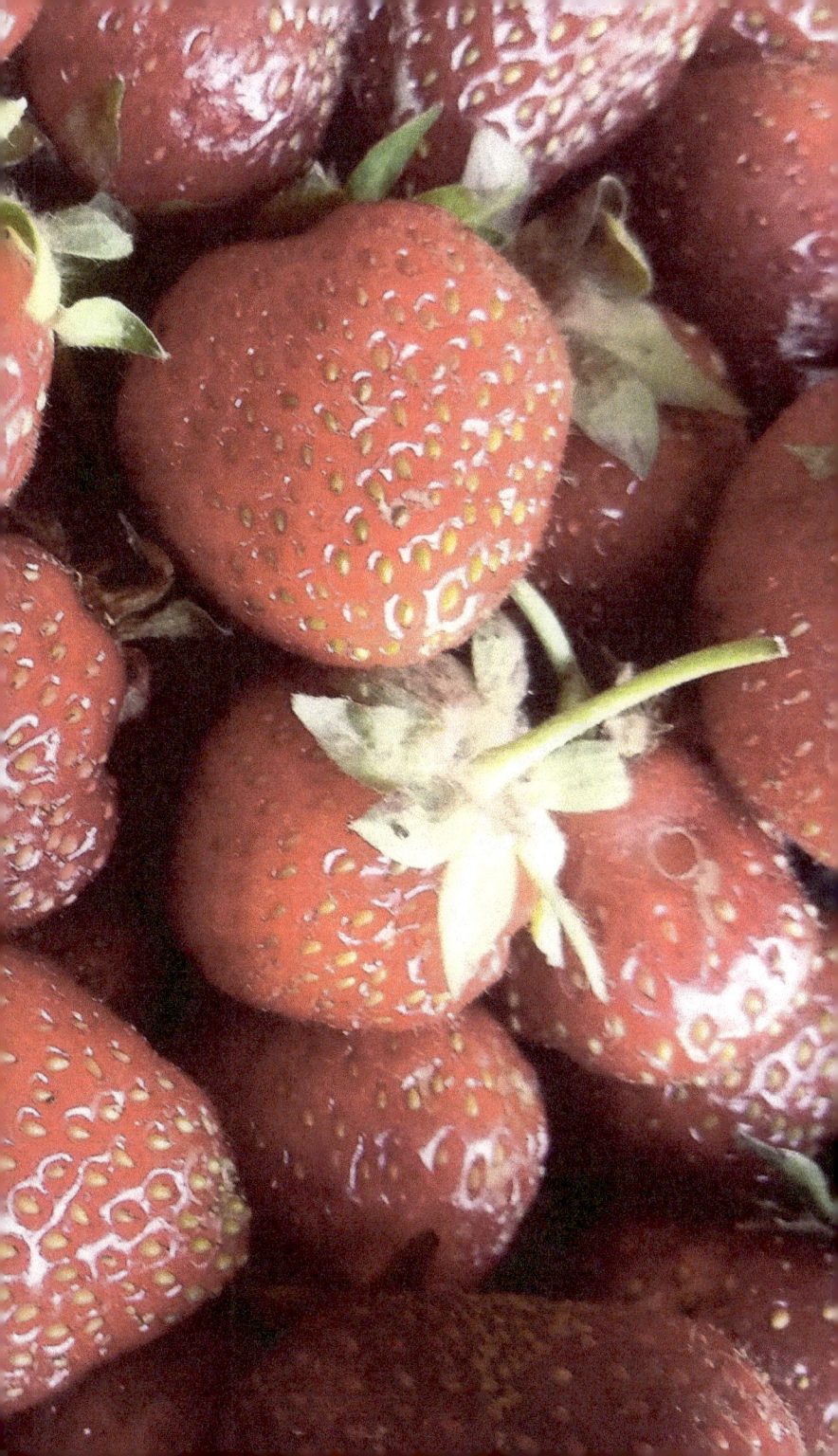

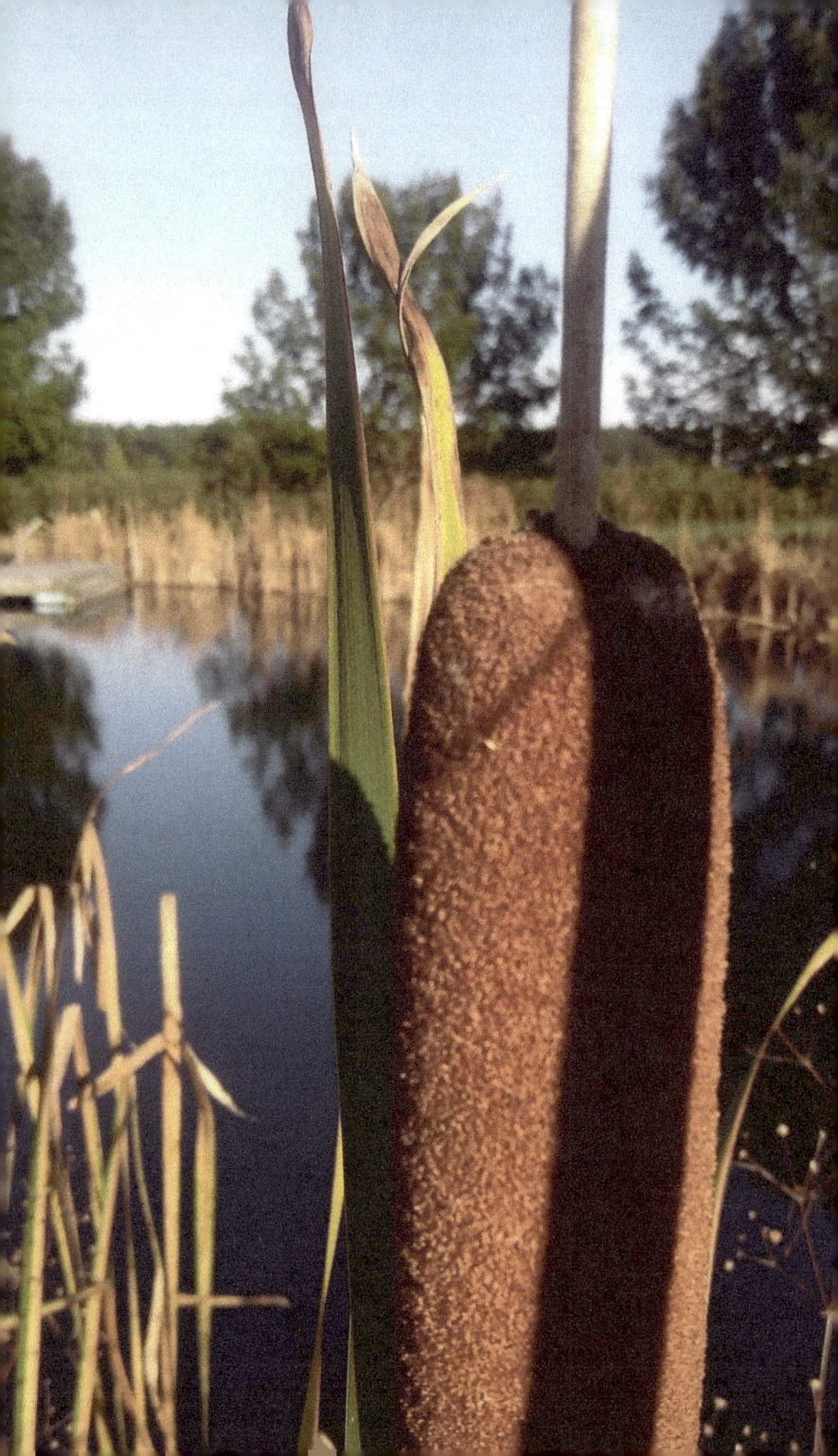

cat tails

old barns with chipped and weathered red paint

lace doilies under photo frames

polaroid photos hung on the fridge

buttercups

sugar snap sweet peas fresh from the garden

hands dyed purple with blackberry juice

hot cocoa and toast

shooting stars viewed from the corn field

the view from a grain silo

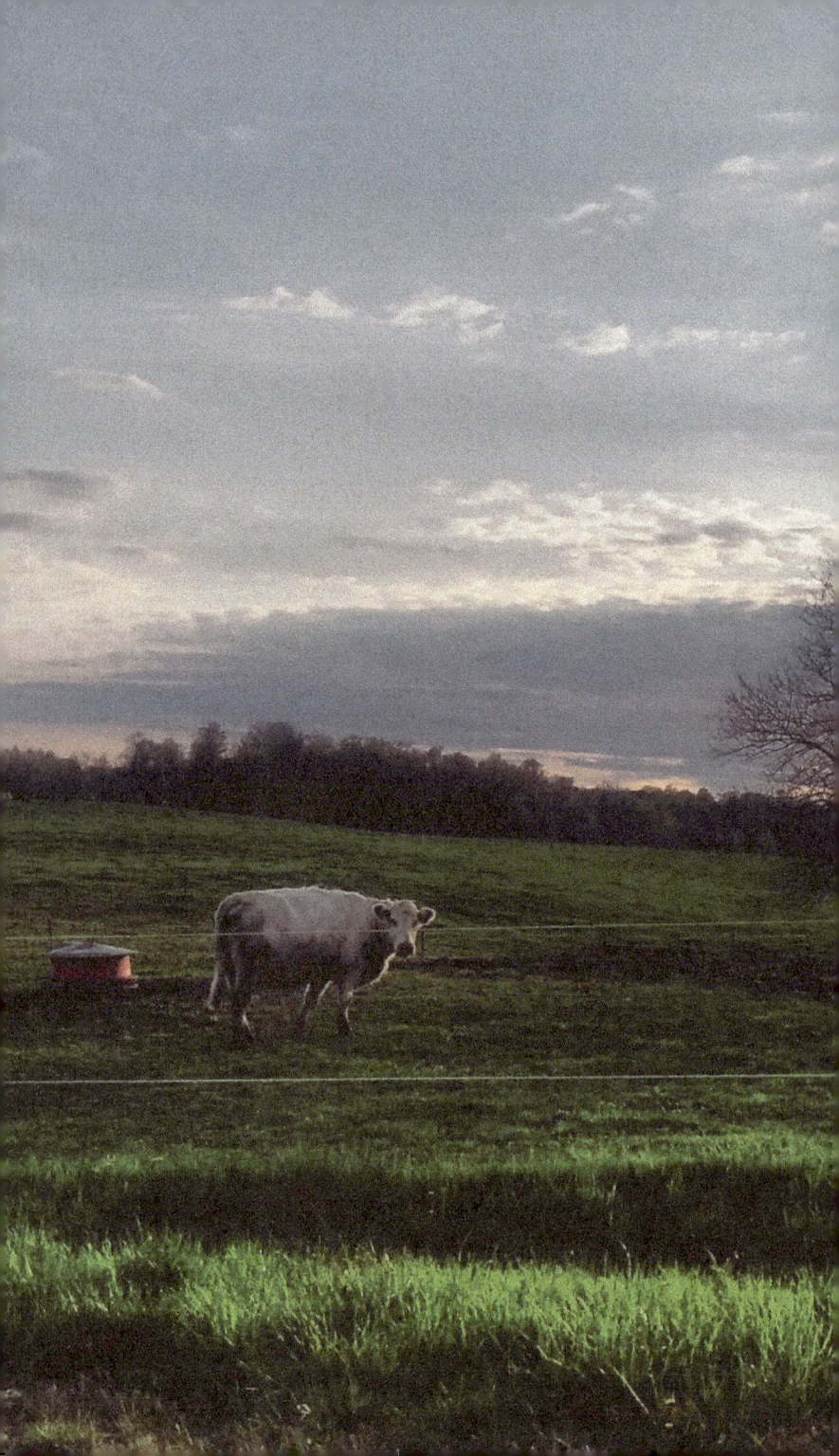

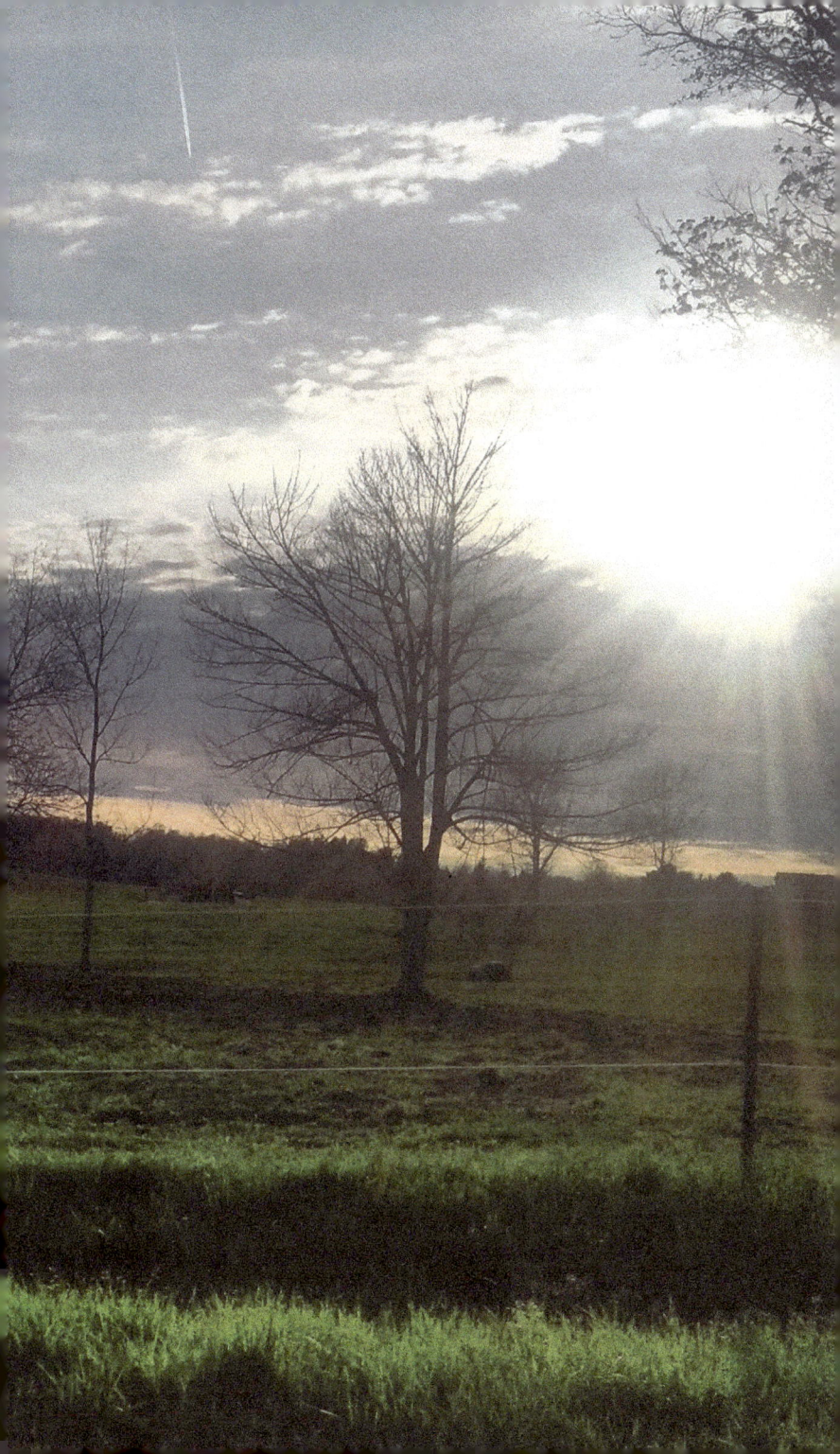

finding fossils in rocks

small town harvest celebrations

red fox

wooden clothespins on the laundry line

luna moths

spotting the first springtime daffodil on the side of the road

the old farmers almanac with the nail hole in the left hand corner

fall equinox

glow in the dark stars on your bedroom ceiling

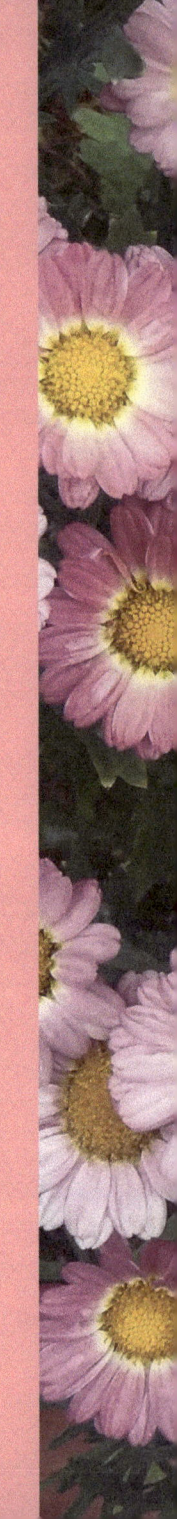

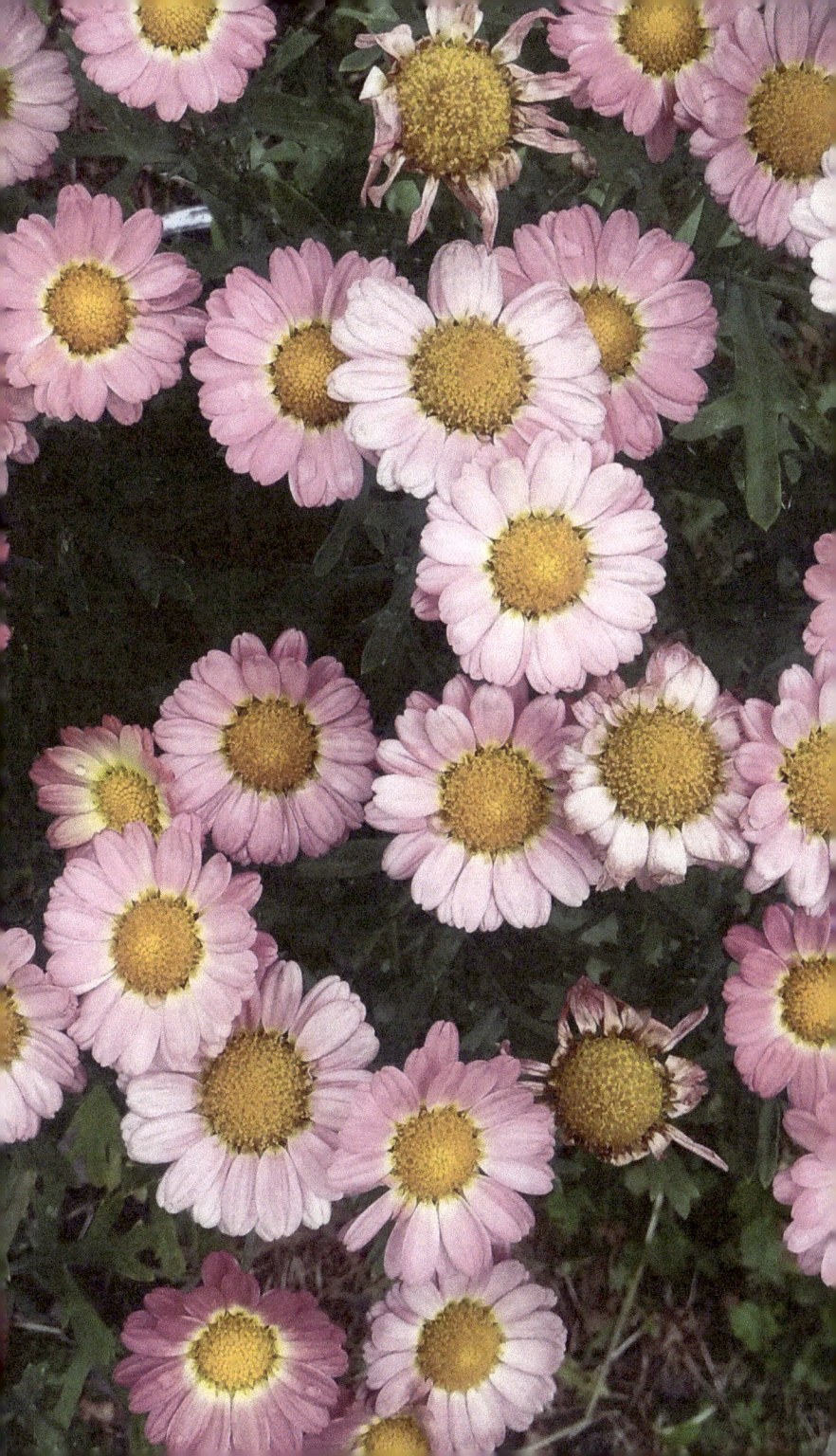

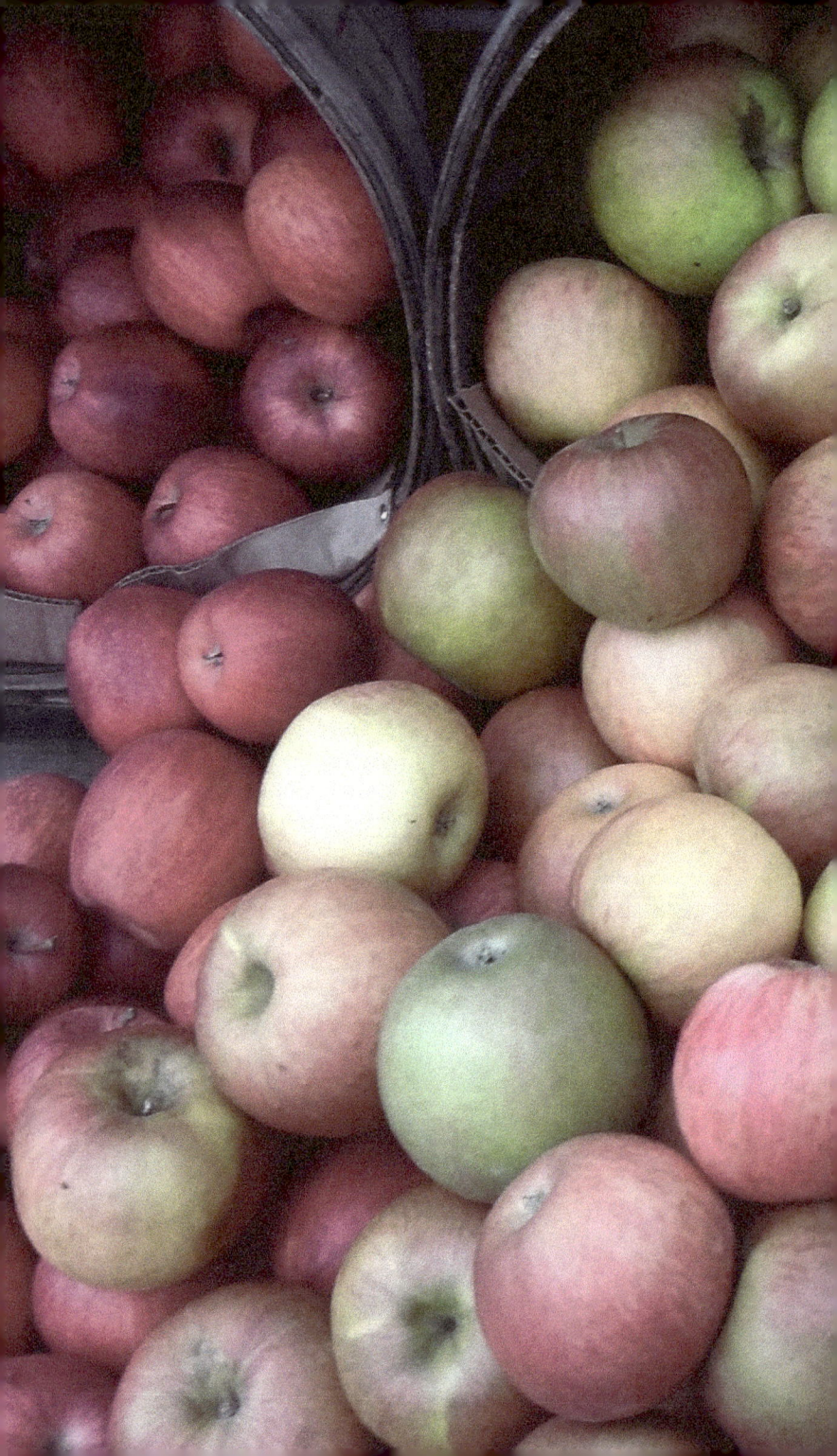

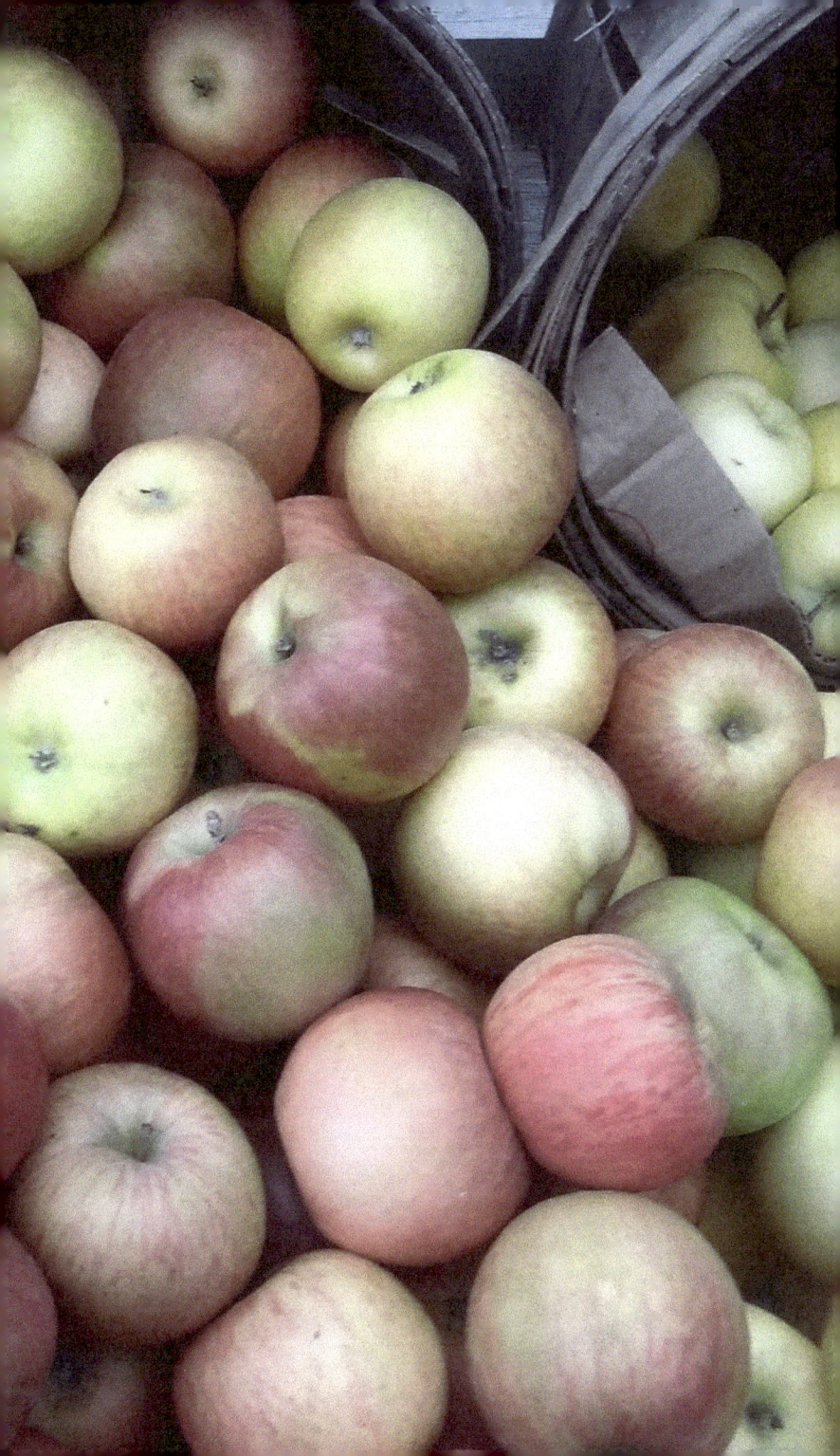

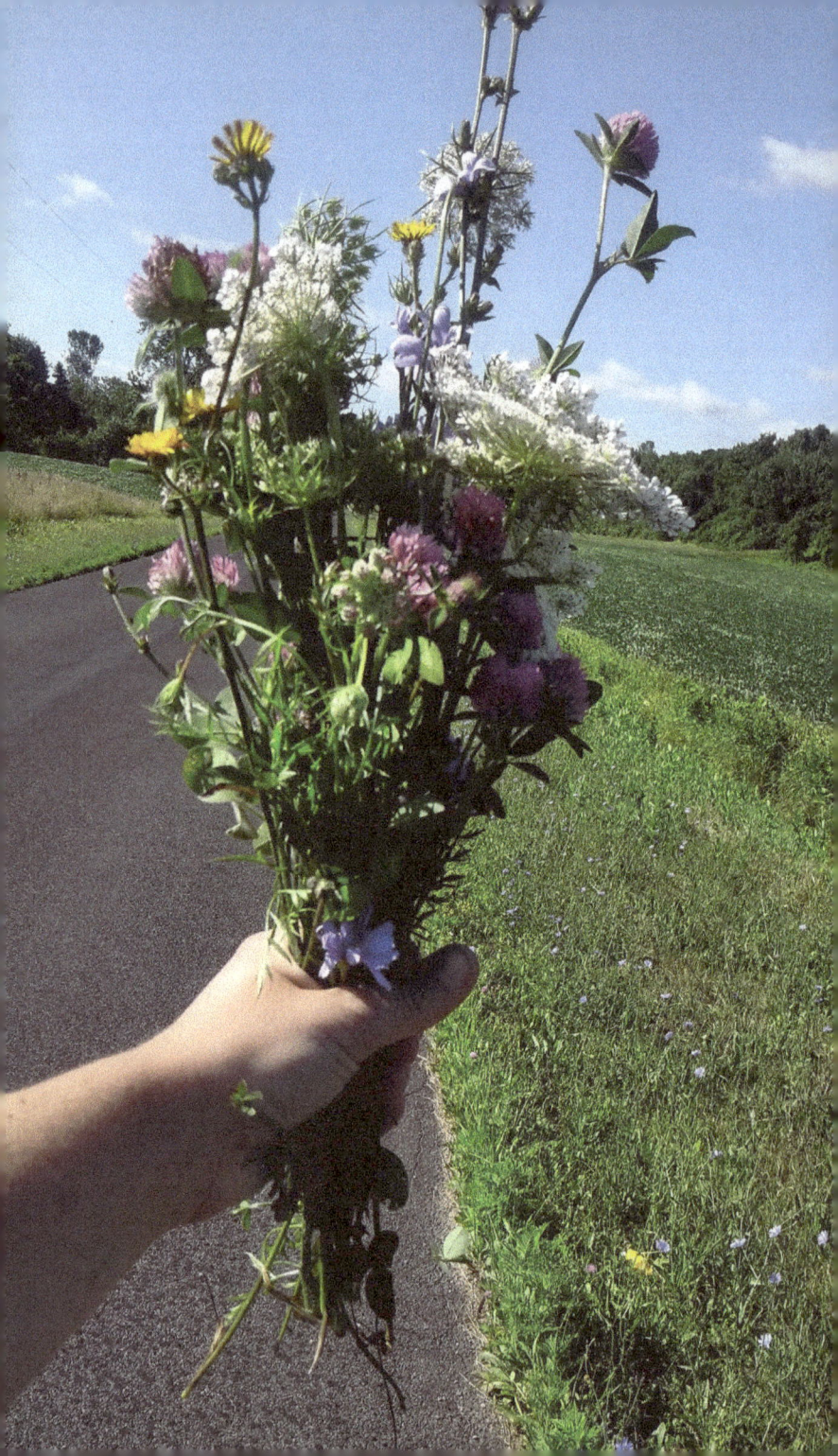

queen annes lace, blue chicory and red clover

tree trunks after it rains

vinyl records playing old time music

old metal washboards

hand embroidered tea towels

hanging crystals in the windows to create rainbows

stained glass

gardens edged with rocks

paper birch trees

potatoes freshly dug from the garden

planning weekend getaways

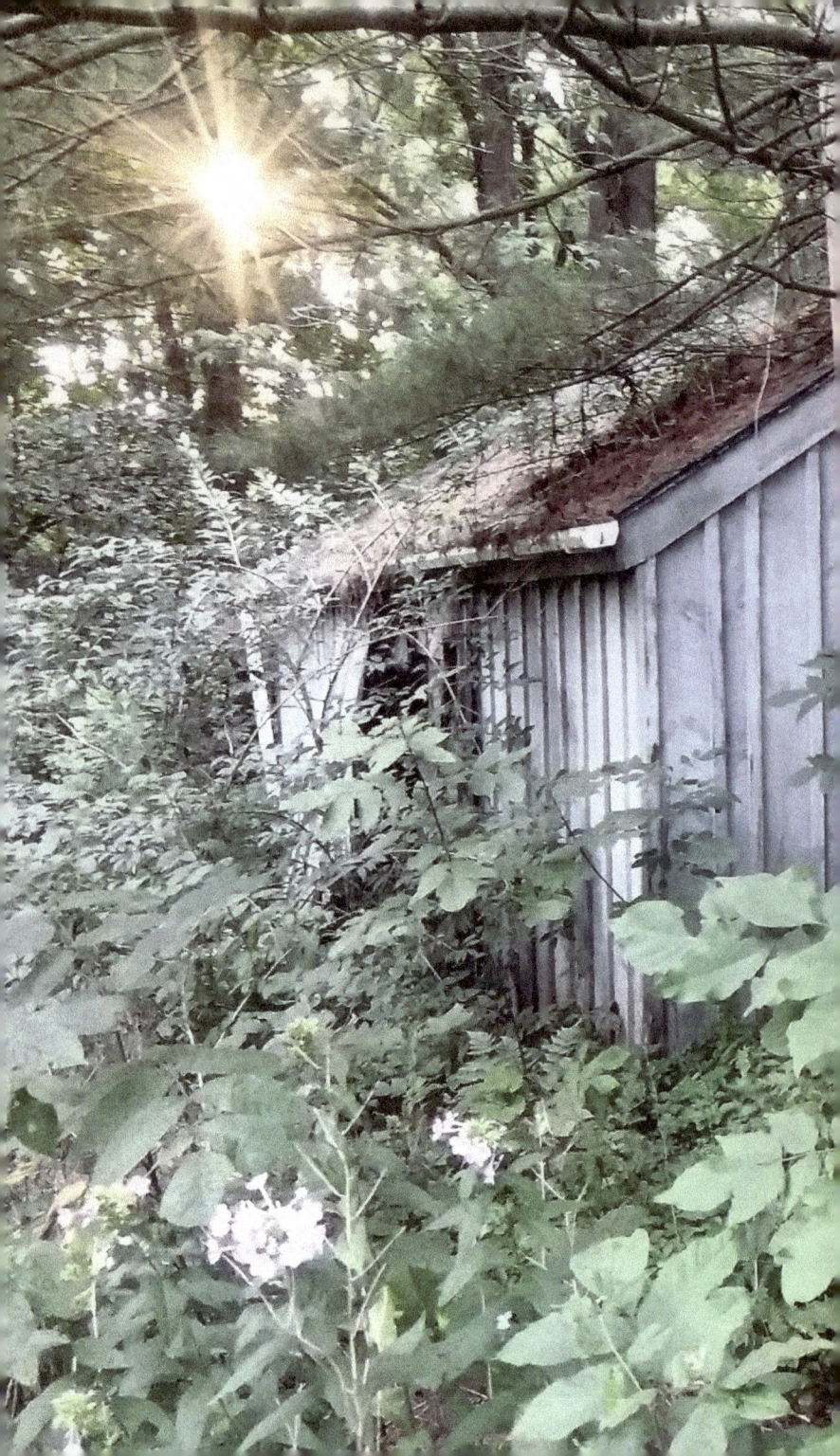

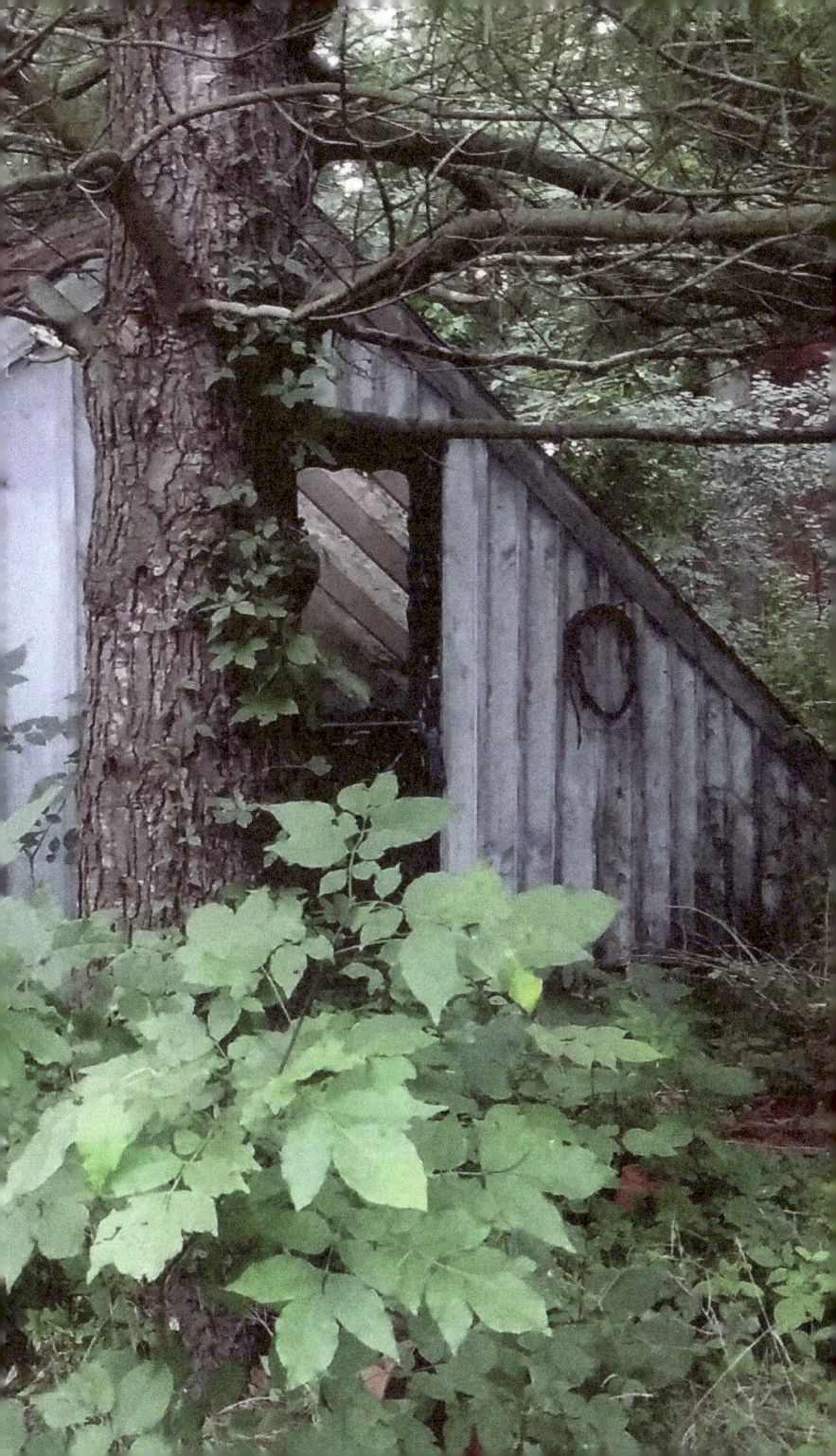

power outages during
summertime thunder storms

worn in work boots

puppy paw prints on the
pavement

pink rock salt crystal lamps

seed packets with artwork
on them

chicken coop fencing

midnight Christmas eve
services by candlelight

tadpoles

tiger lilies blooming by
blackberry bushes

cut off shorts

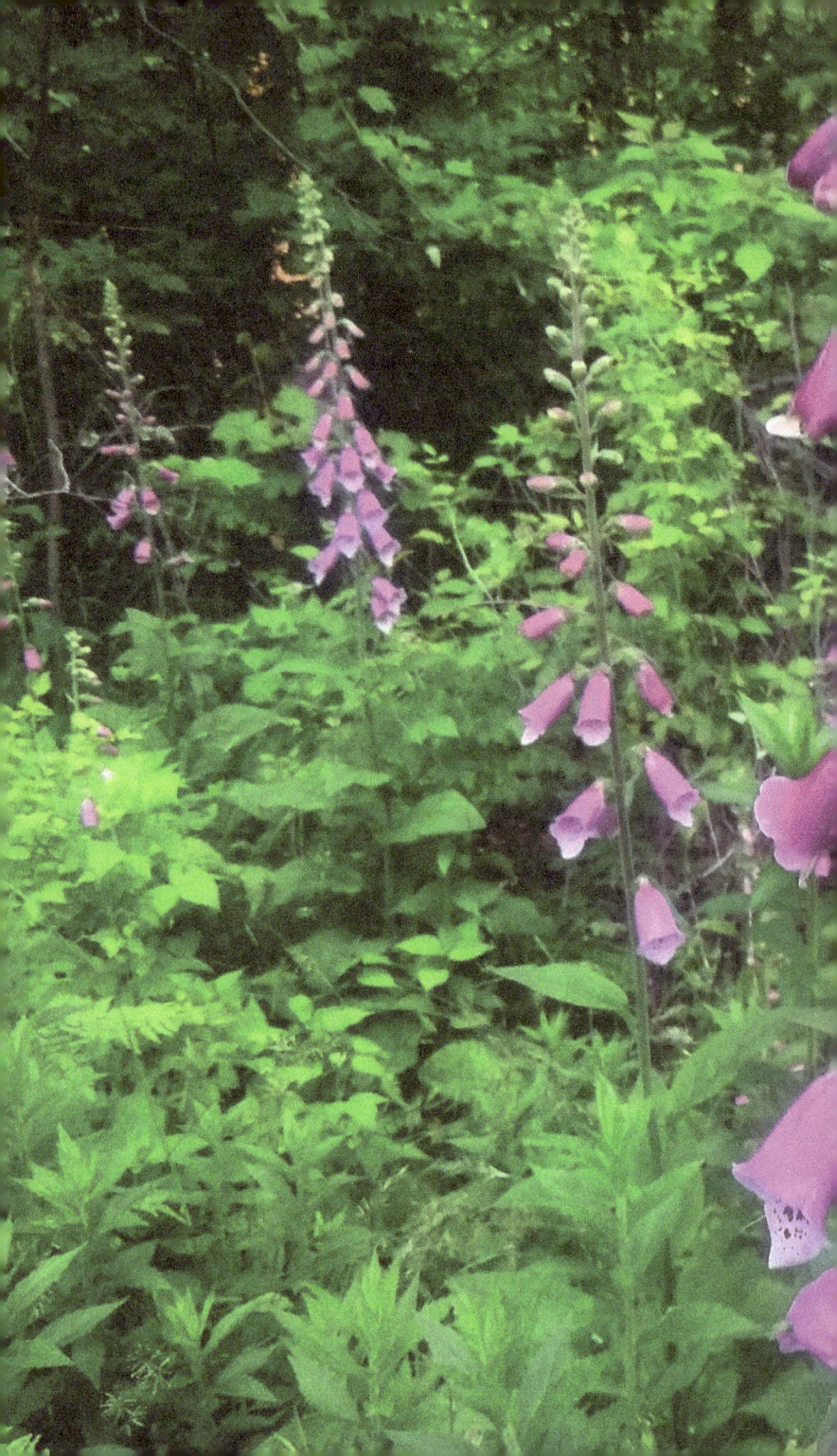

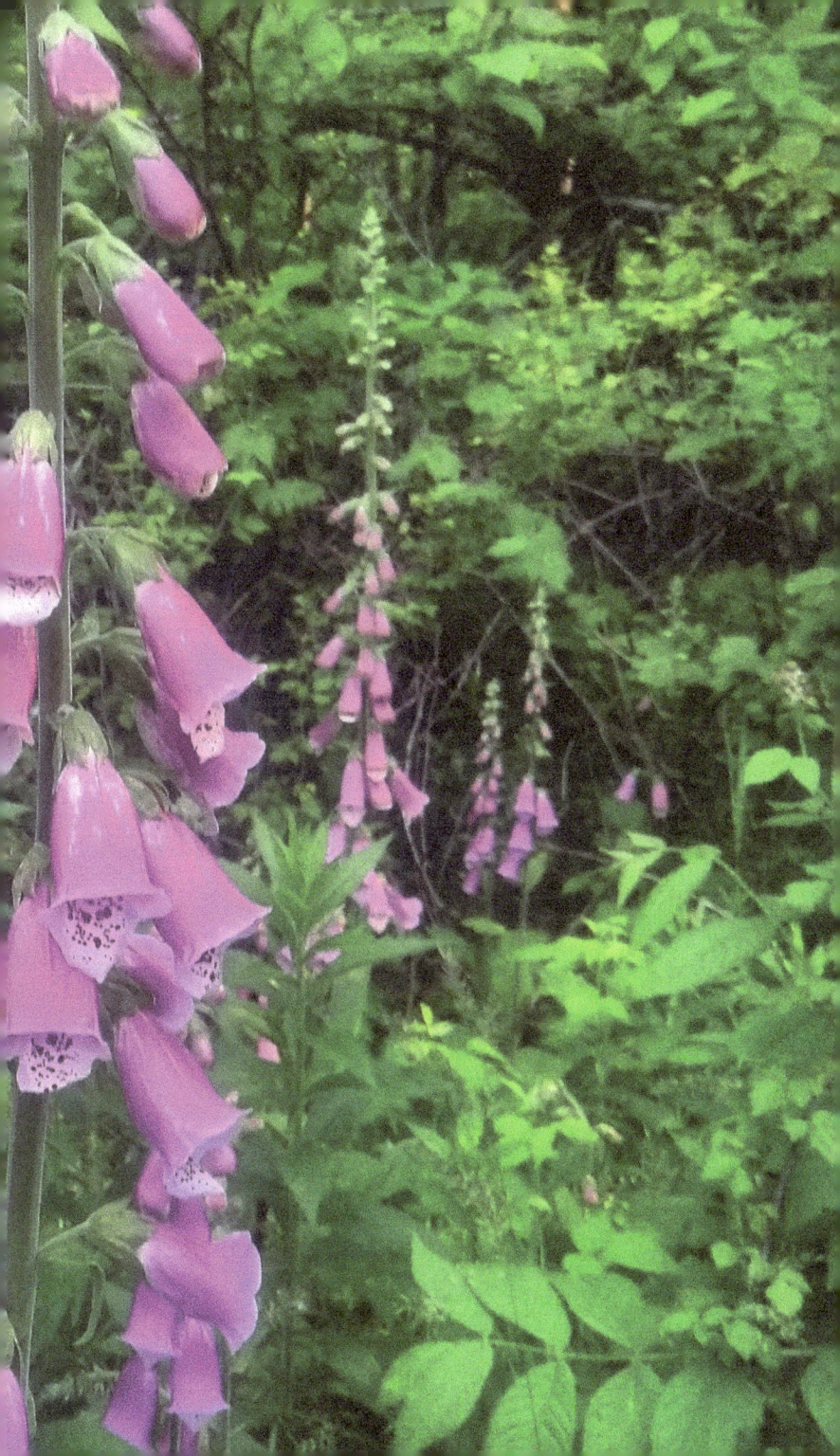

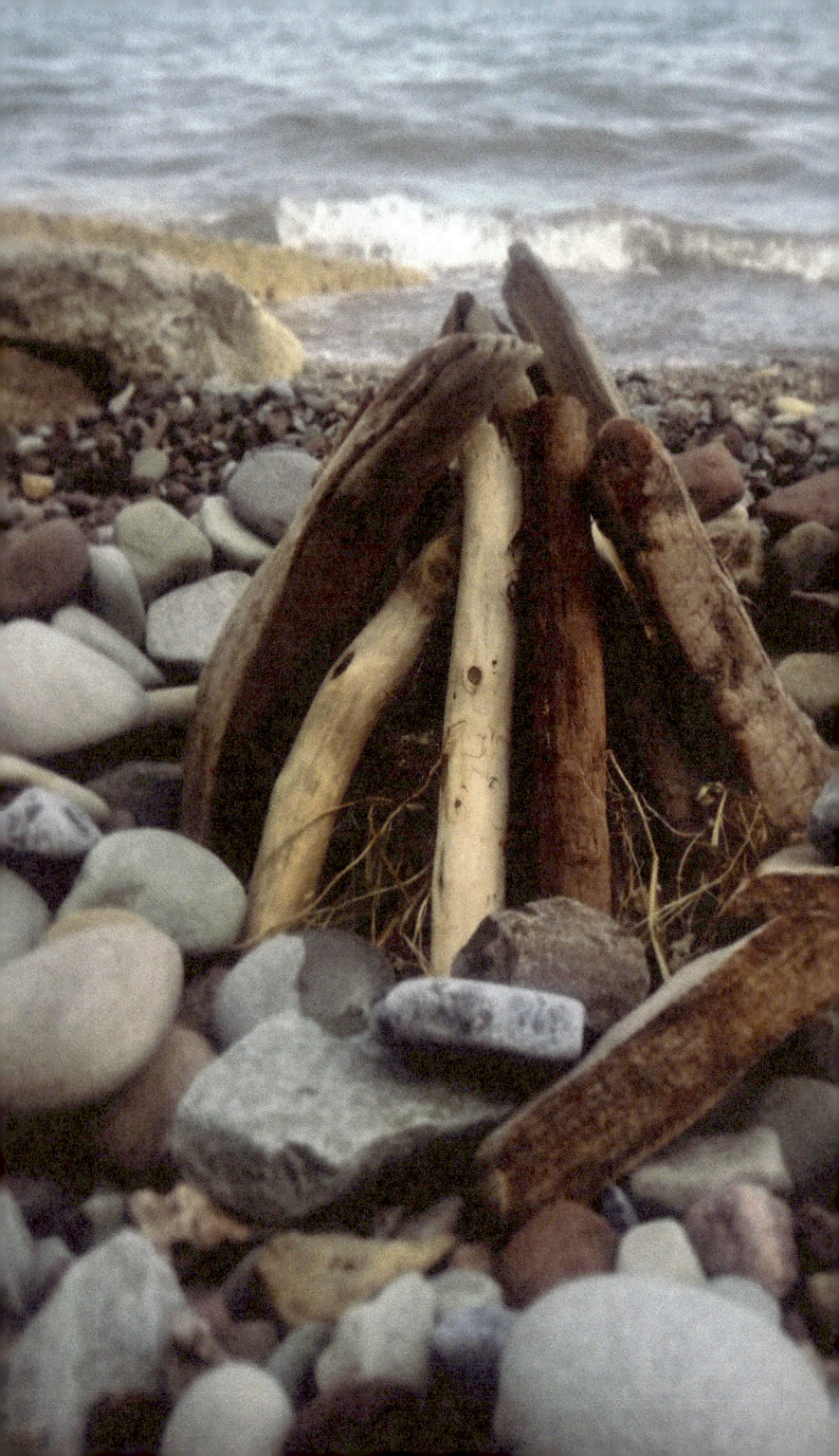

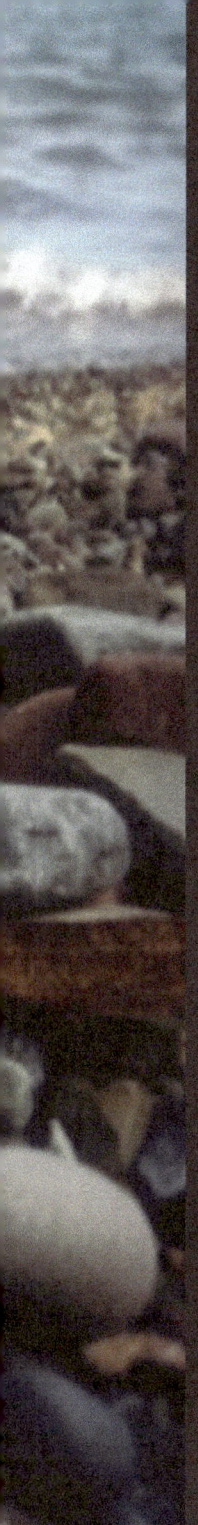

foxglove meadows

homemade sage and lavender smudge sticks

little country grocery stores

zucchini bread with chocolate chips

back roads with no lines

finding a four leaf clover

the creak of old wooden staircases

canning

the sound of rain on the tin roof

coffee shop holiday concerts

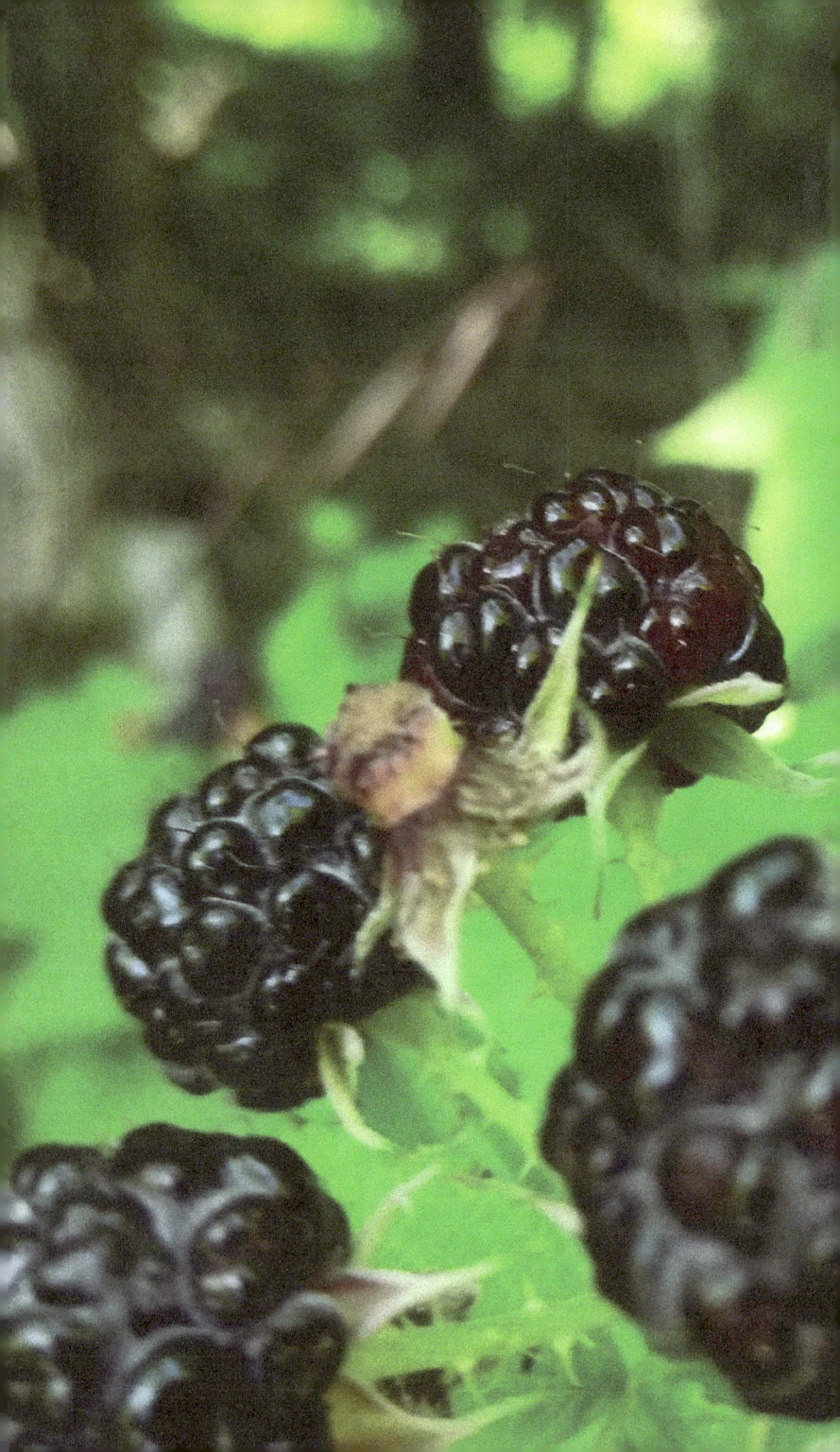

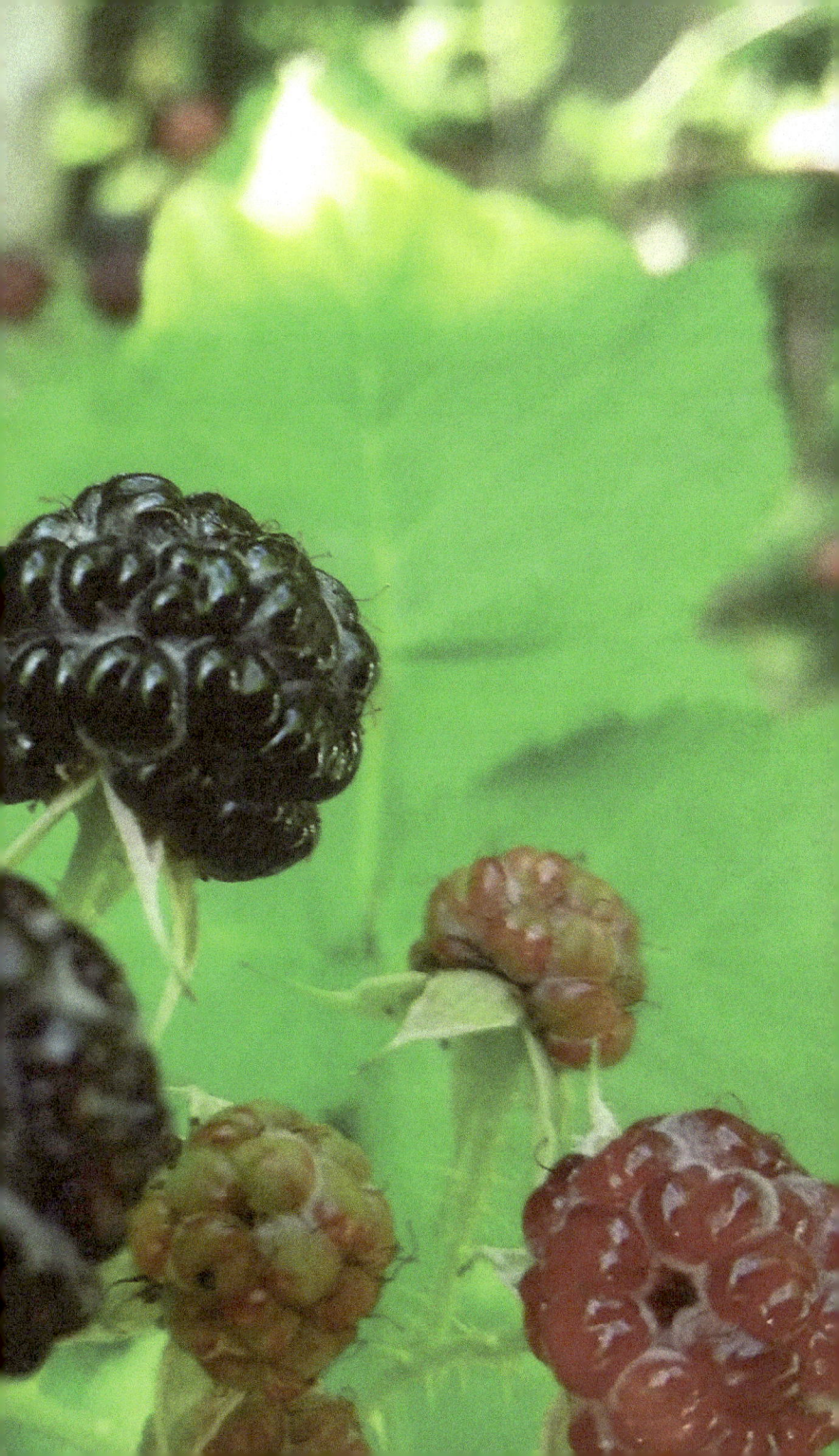

old outhouses

taking midnight walks to see
the firefly magic

grapevine wreaths

skipping stones

the sound of wind rustling
through the trees

the Adirondack Mountains

wheat fields waving in the
breeze

grackles

the crispness of air in the
wintertime

pumpkin patches

the month of October

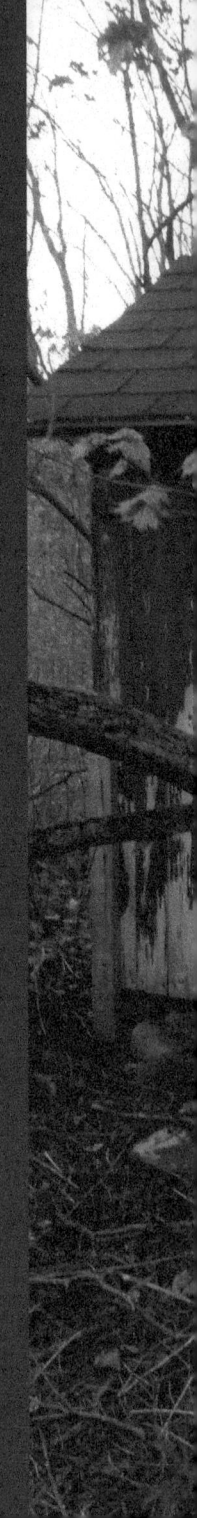

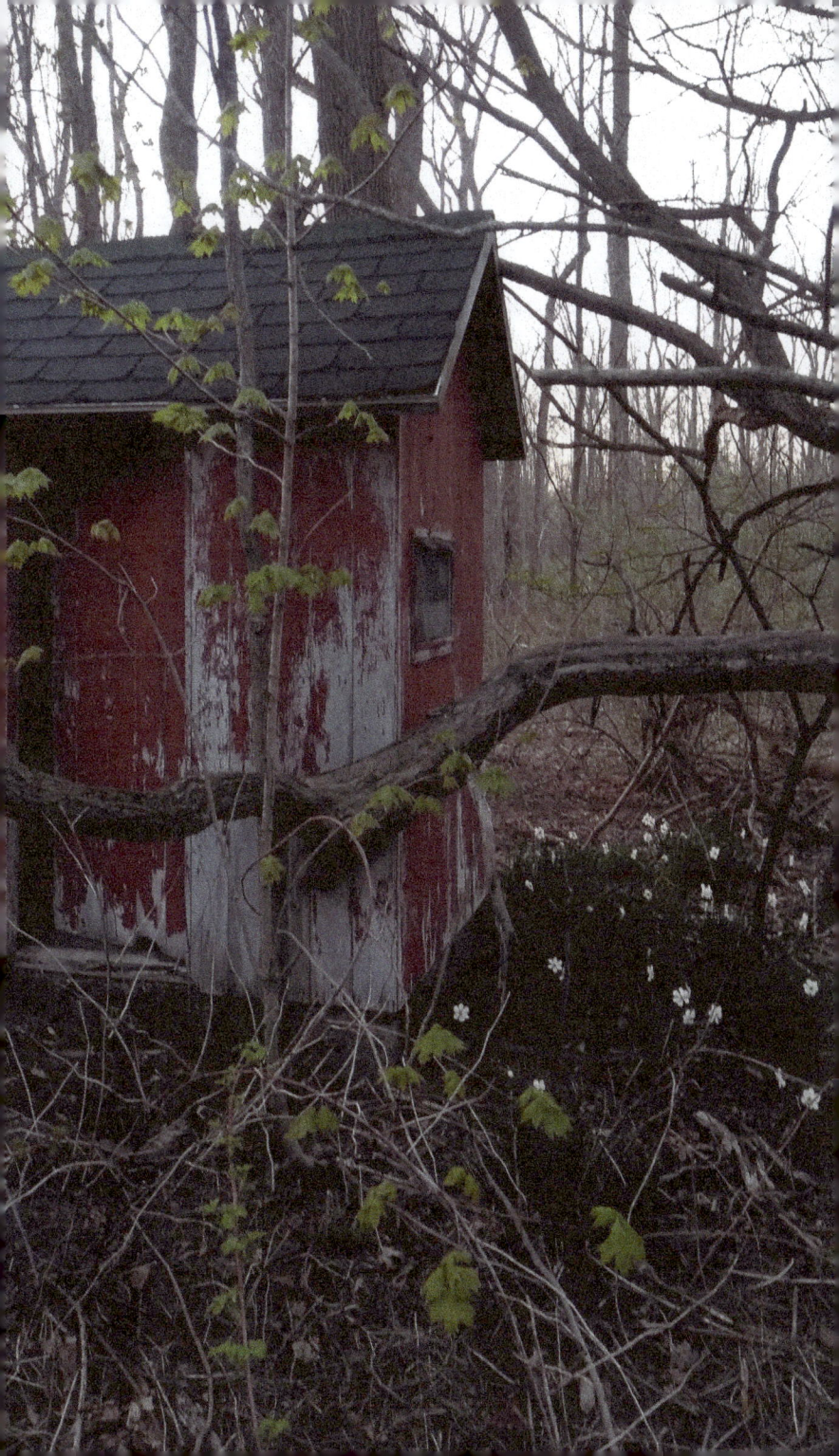

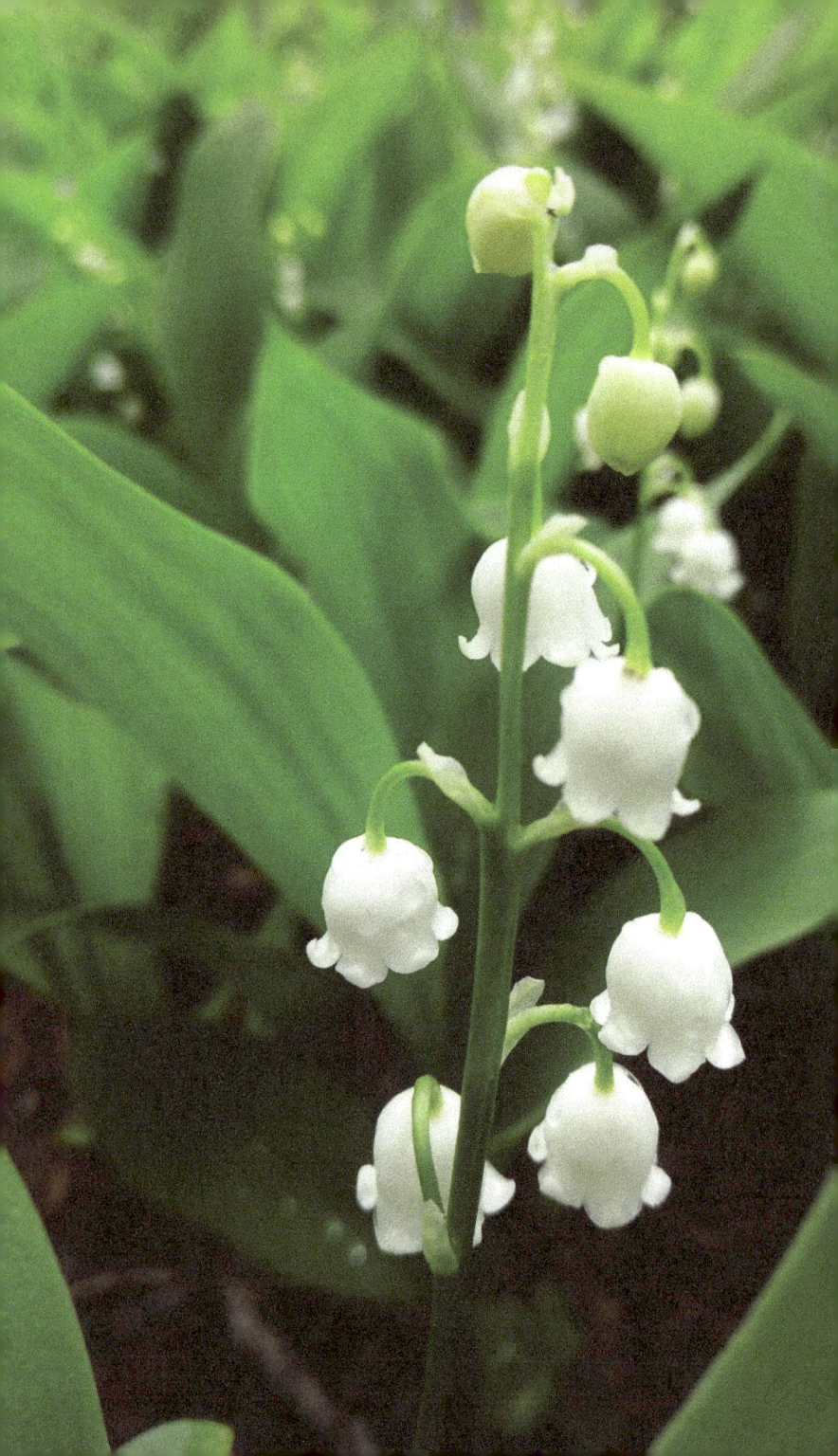

lily of the valley

falling asleep to the sound of the waves at night

braided rugs under dining room tables

punched tin chandeliers

s'mores around the campfire

houses that have history

baseball games when it starts to rain

canoe trips

mason jars that are tinted blue

living history museums

painting with coffee

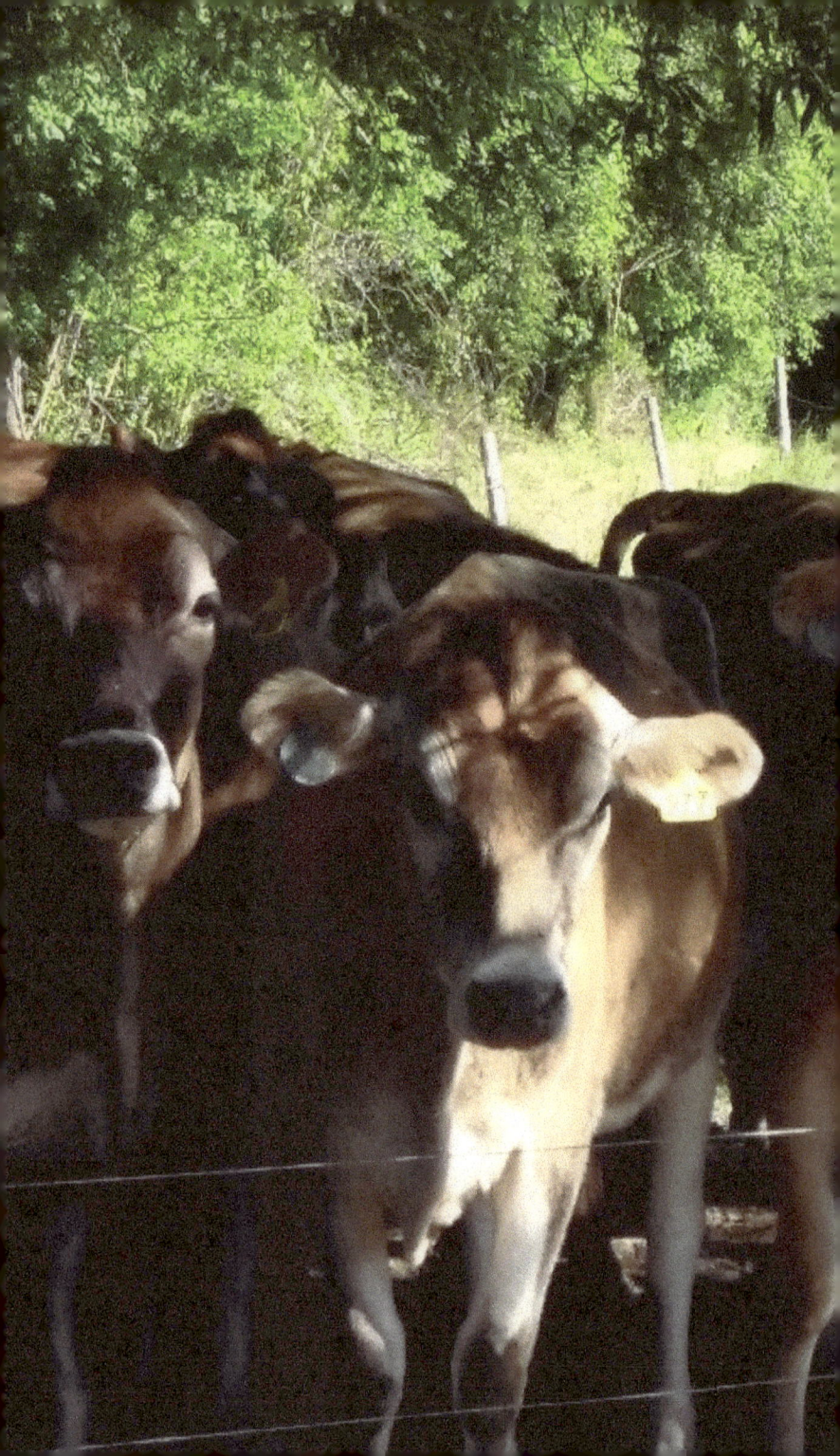

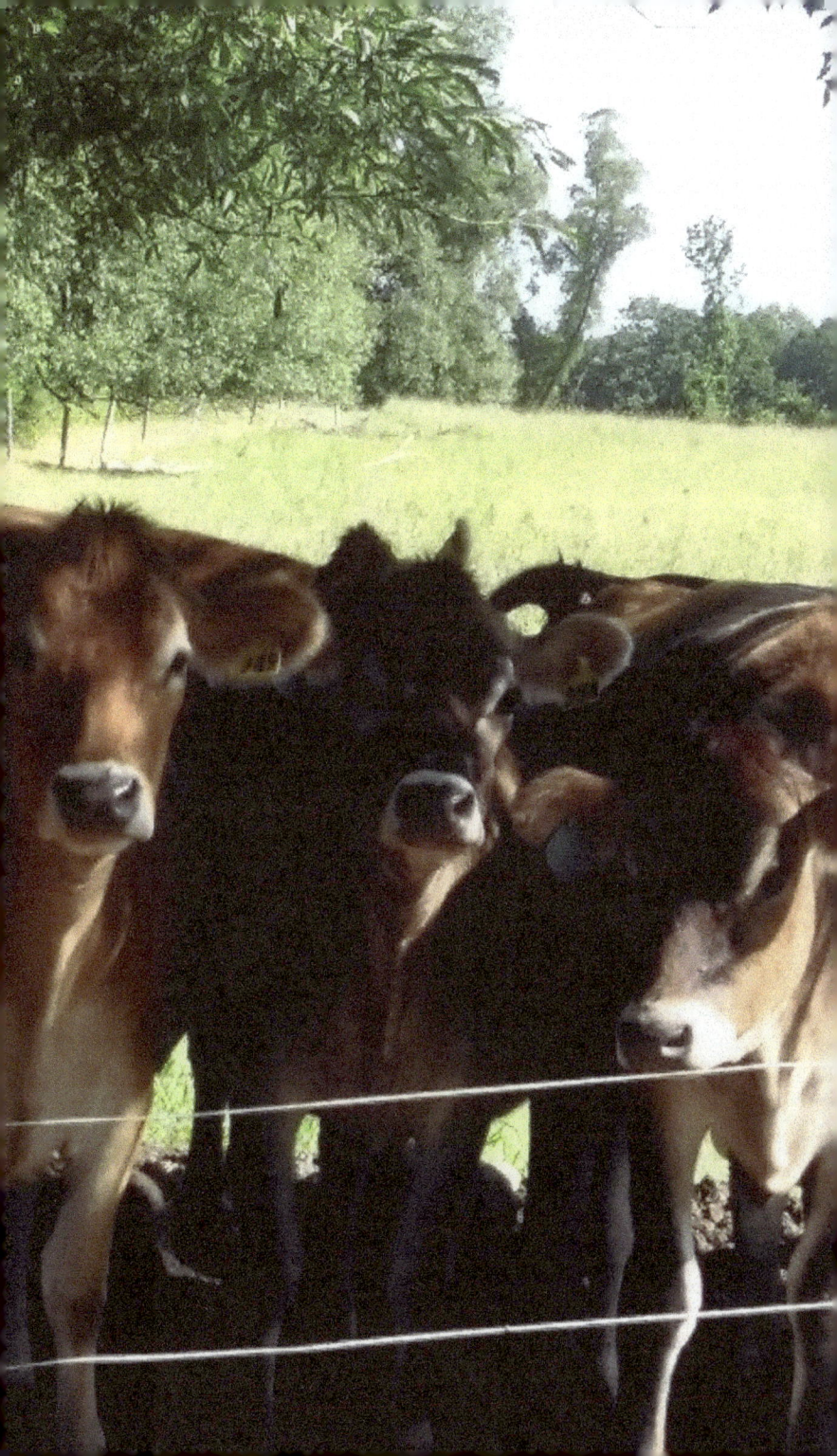

hay rides

parties at the lake shore

riding in a boat on the bay,
wind on your face

round bales of hay in the field

summer drives through the
countryside

foggy mornings

hayloft concerts in the fall

suntanned faces, shoulders
and hands

lavender lemonade

wishing stones

when the leaves start to turn

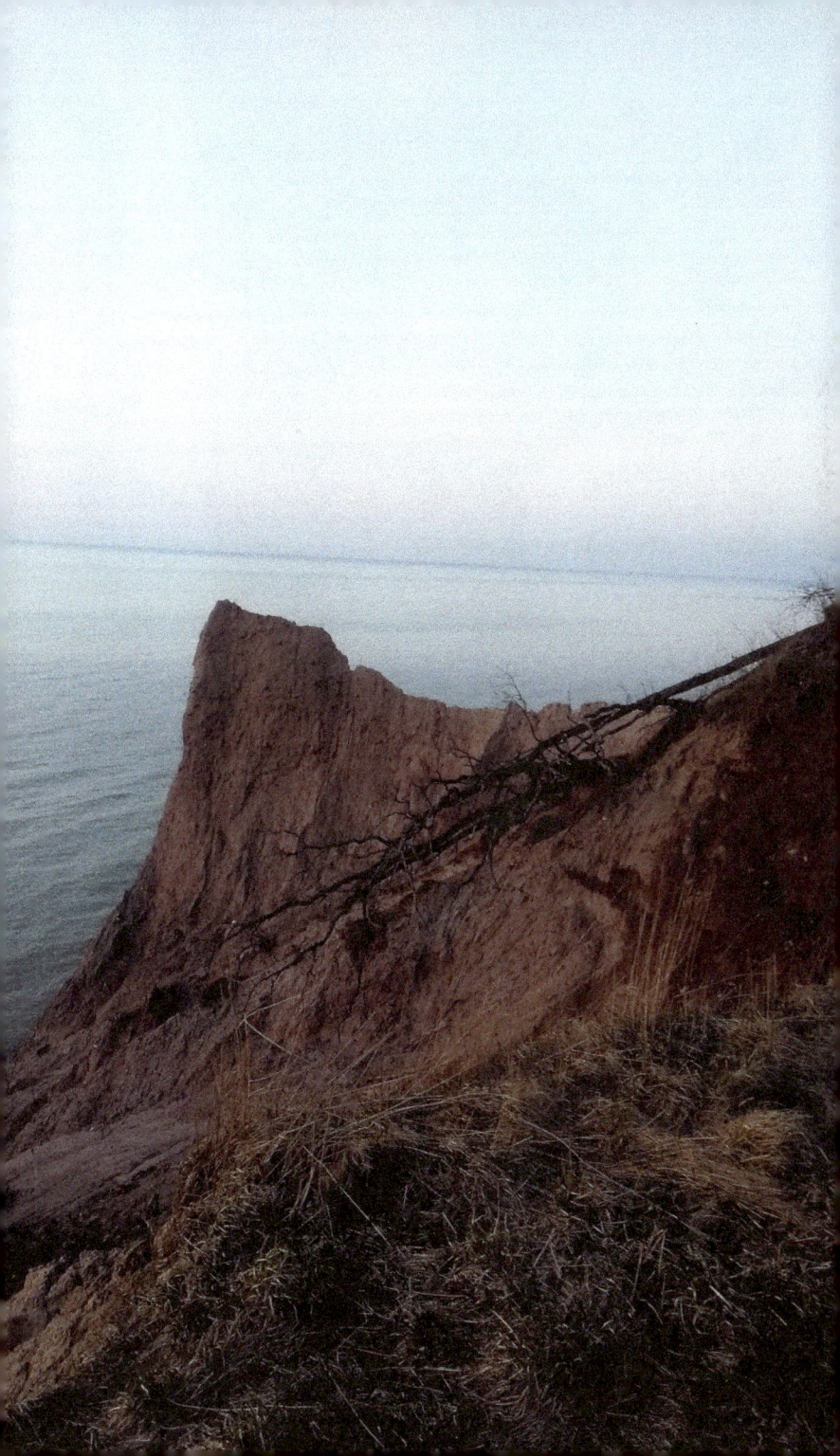

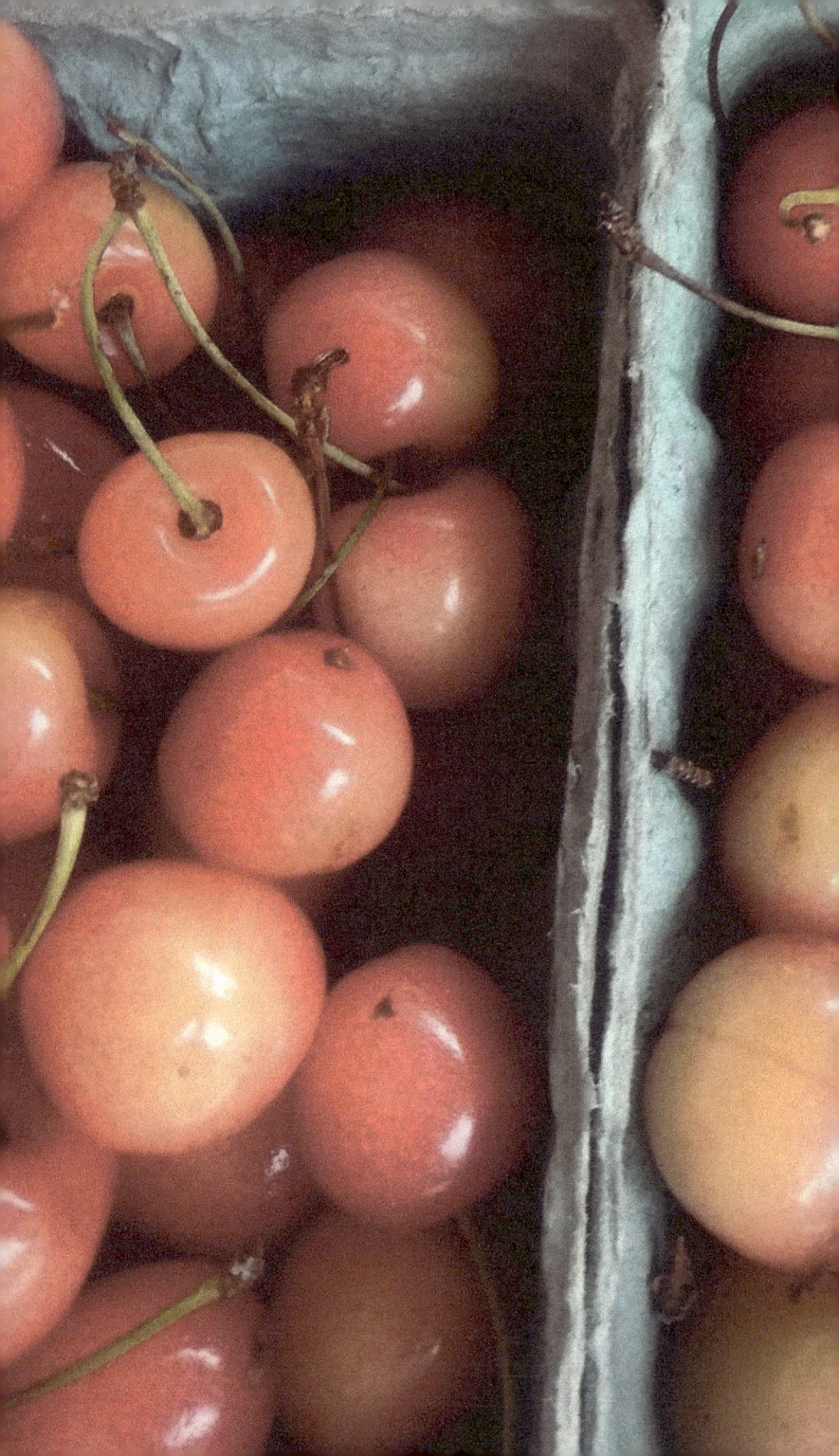

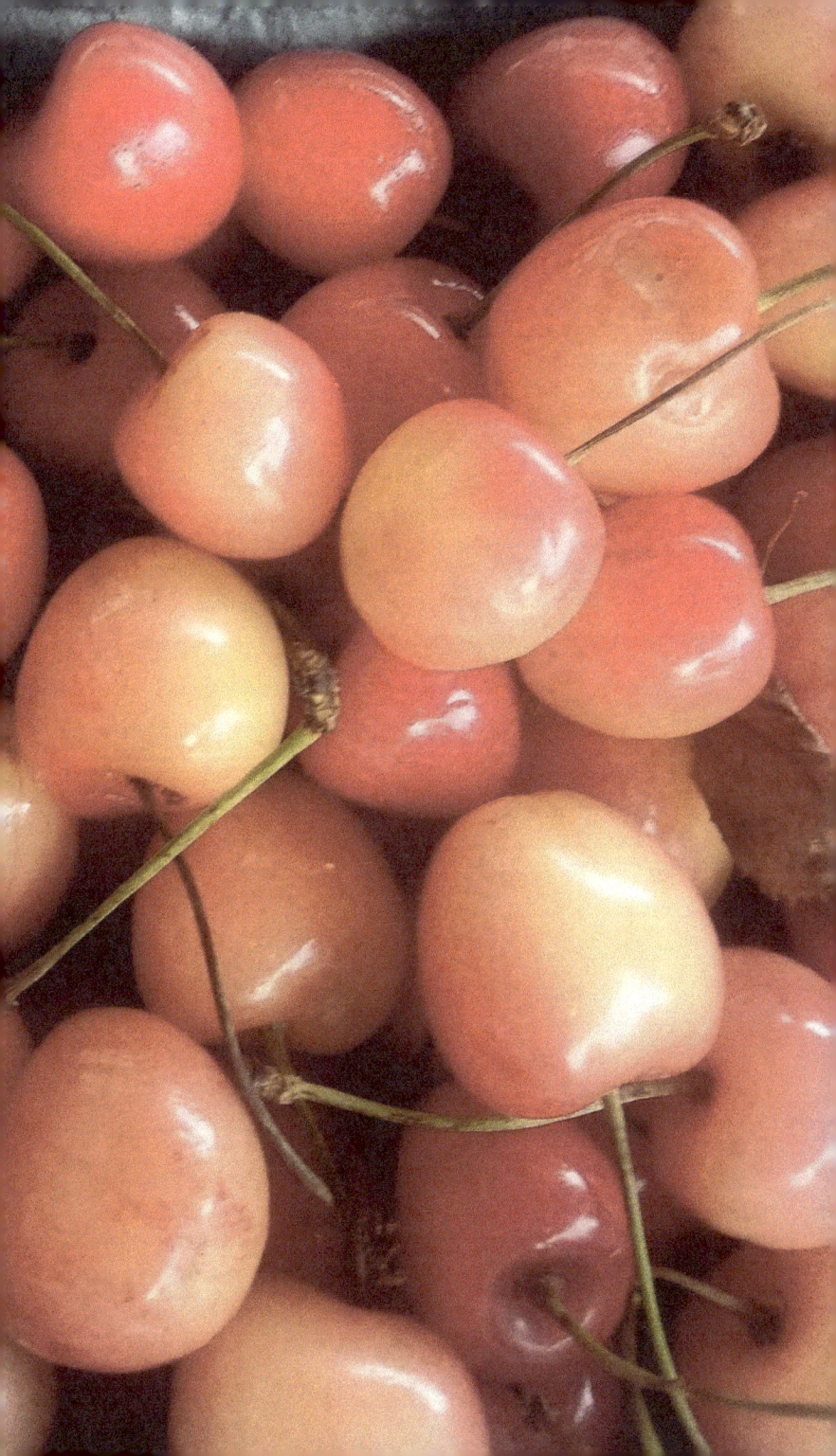

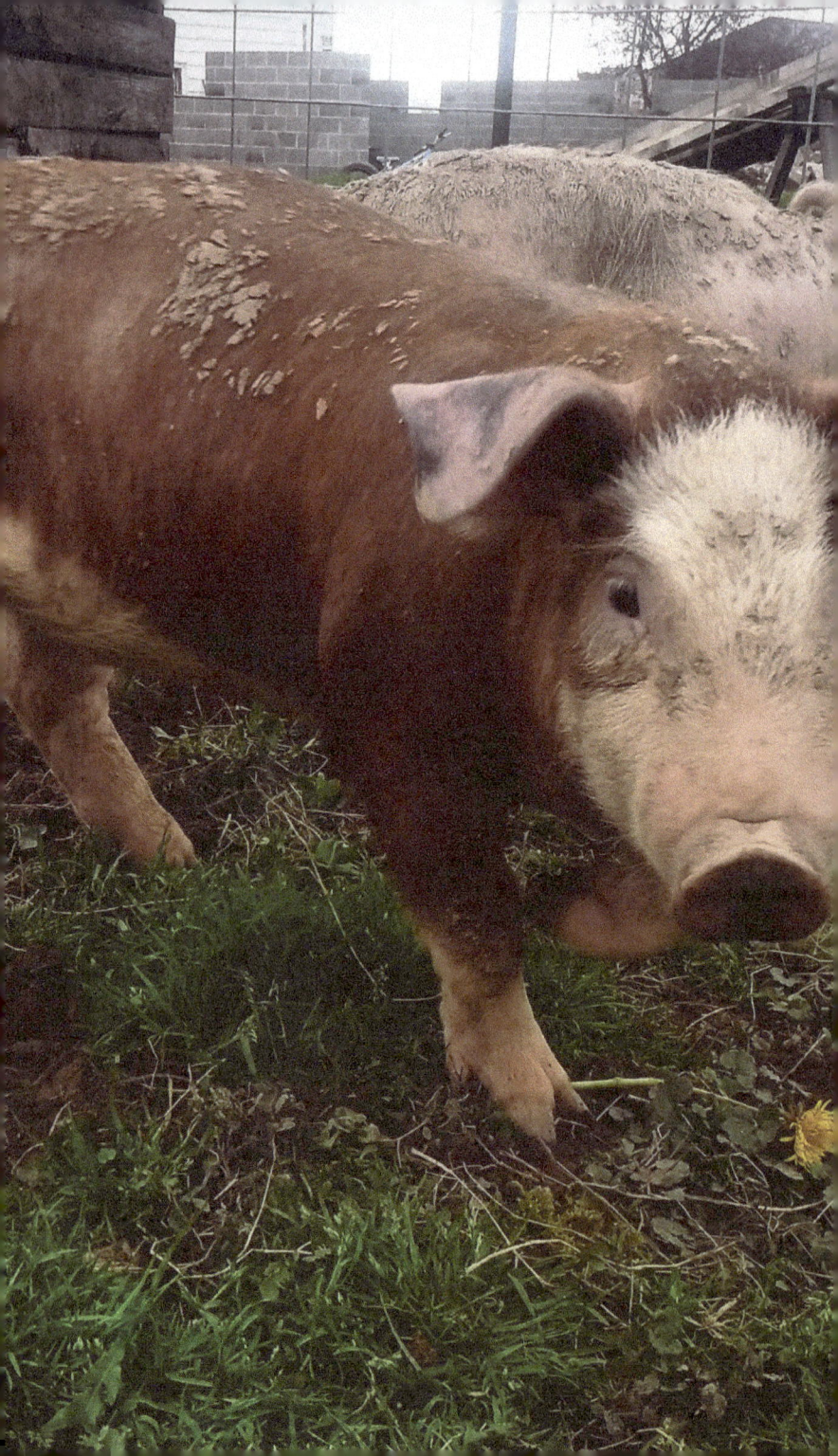

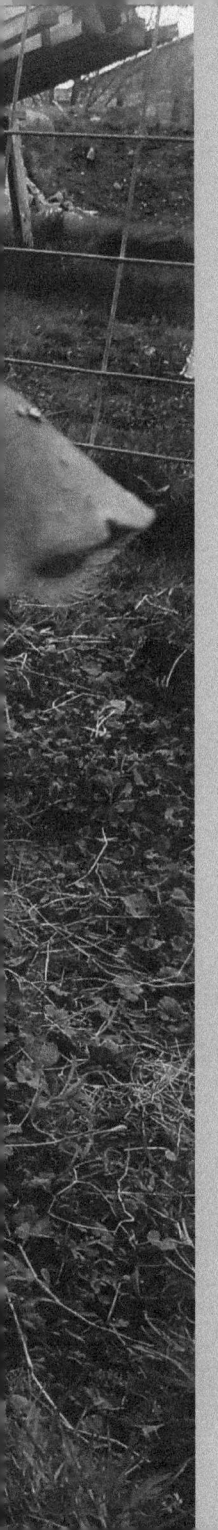

piglets

overgrown greenhouses

walking down railroad tracks

smoke curling out of farmhouse chimneys

orchards ready to be picked

when it starts to get cold in the fall

silver tinsel on evergreen trees

gingerbread

pressing flowers in old hard covered books

1800's houses with lake stone foundations

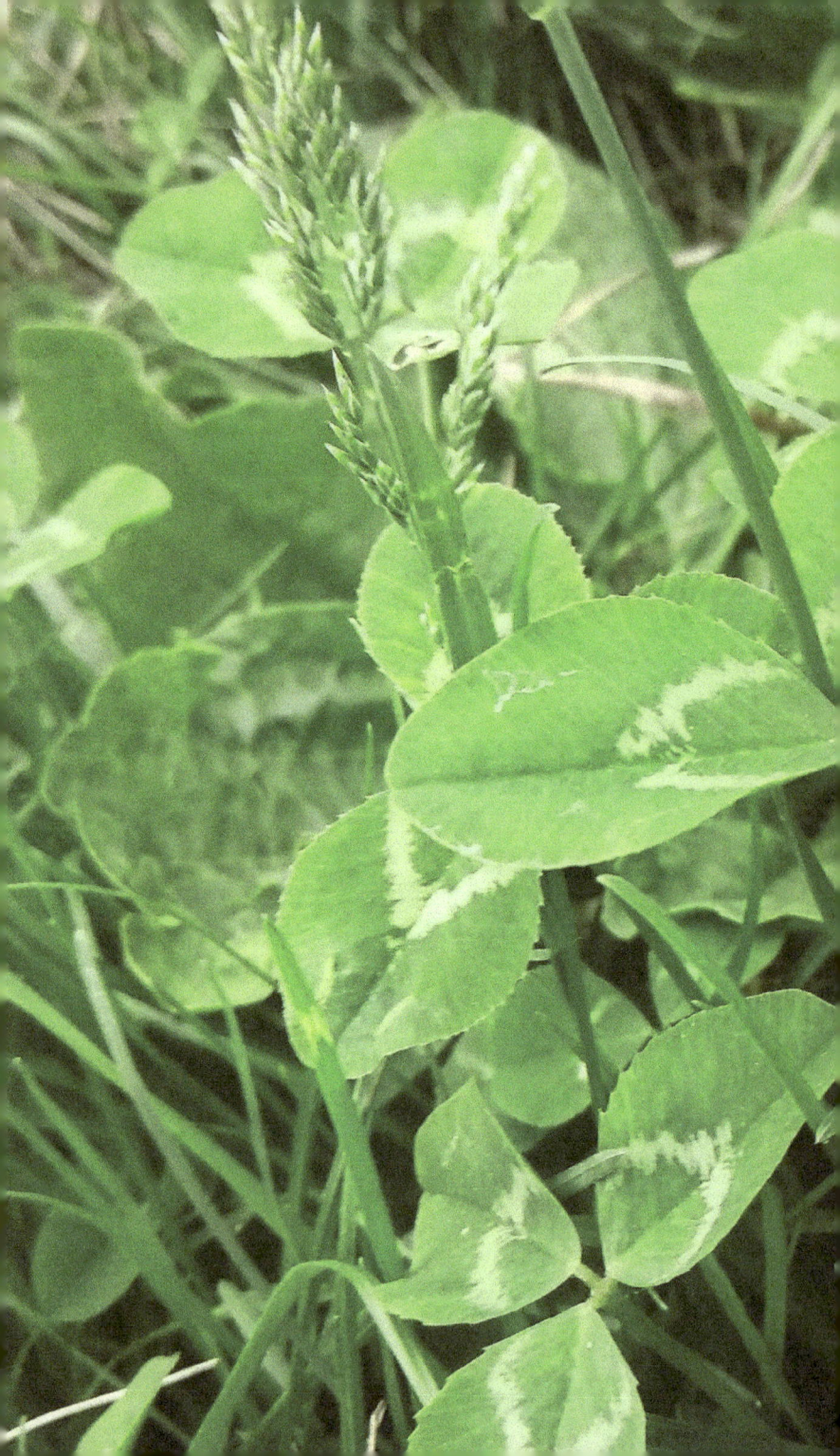

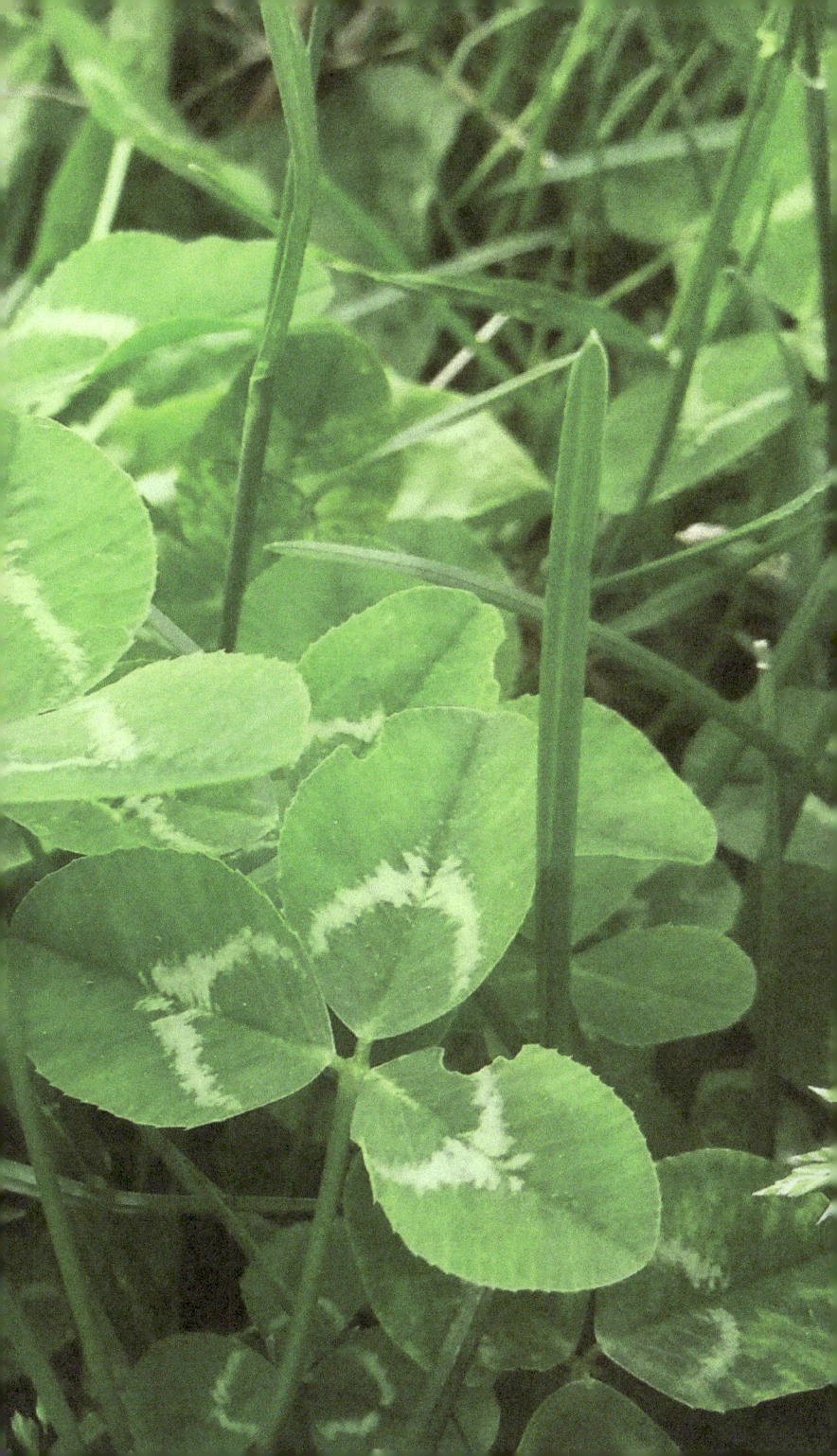

ice that coats every branch
in the forest

hot apple cider

handmade holiday cards
from kids

car shows that include
old tractors

strawberry festivals

stockings hung by the fireplace

old barns with one or two
panes of glass missing

basement cisterns

family bibles with generations
of birthdays and marriages

collecting rain water

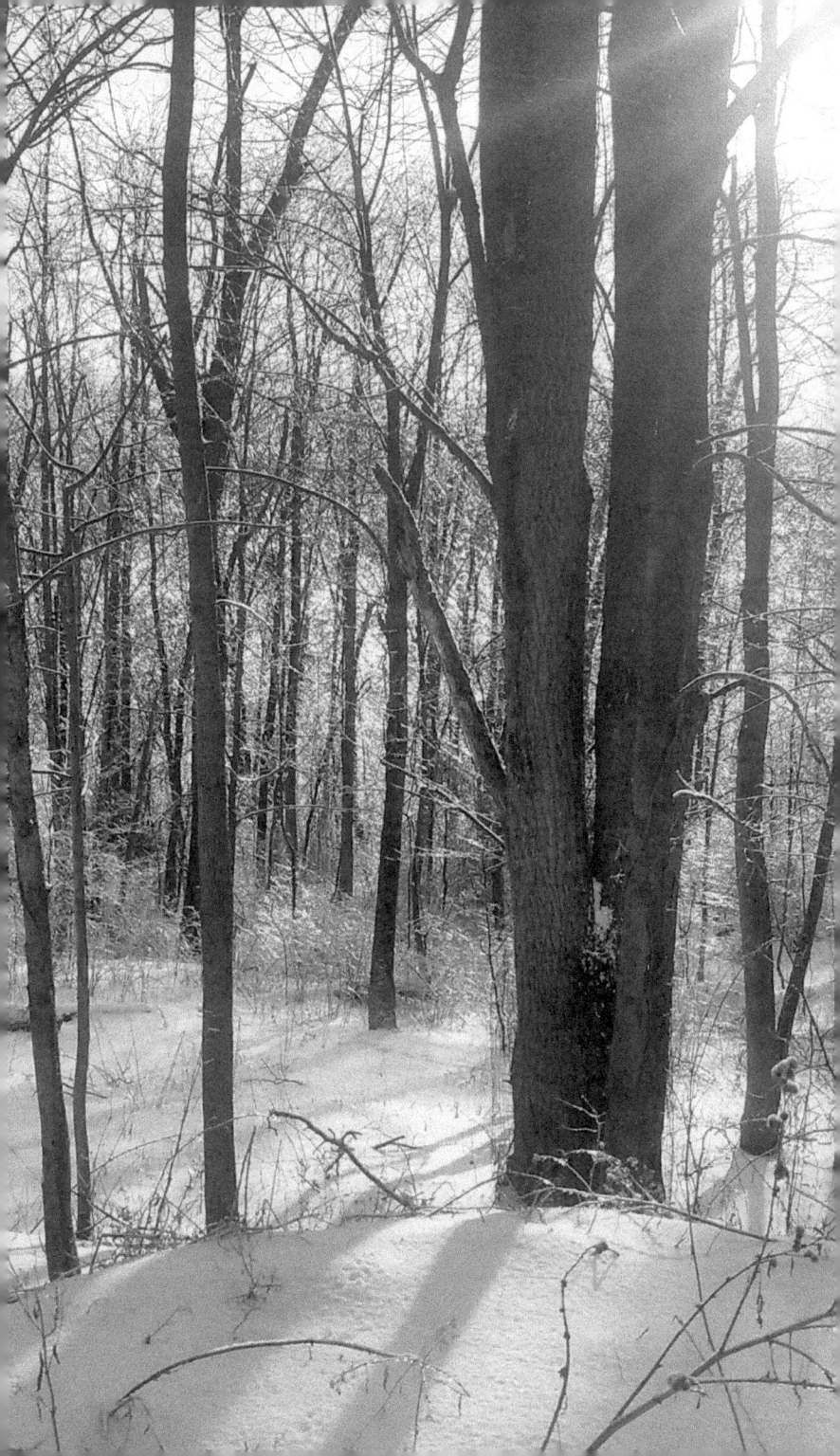

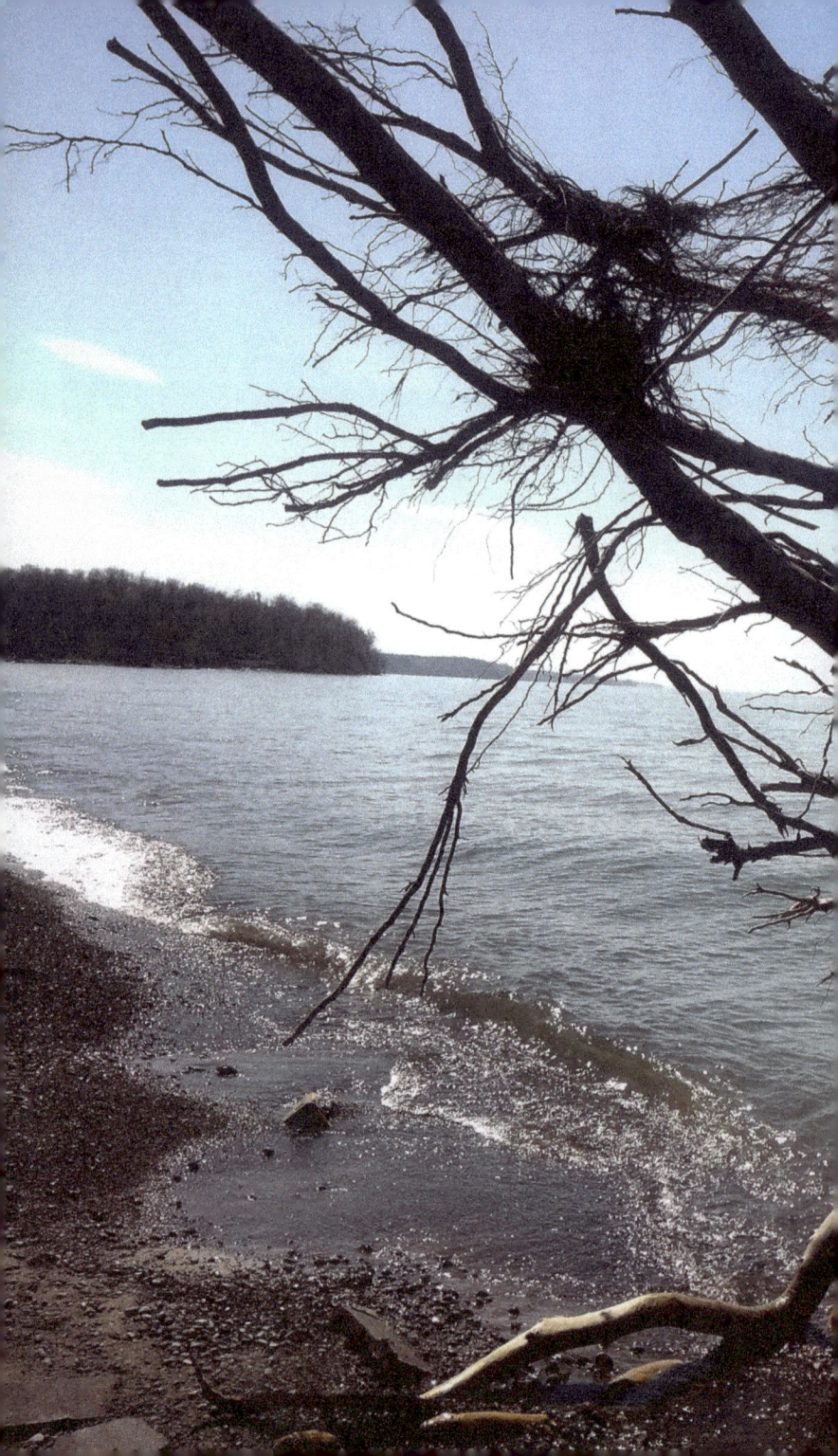

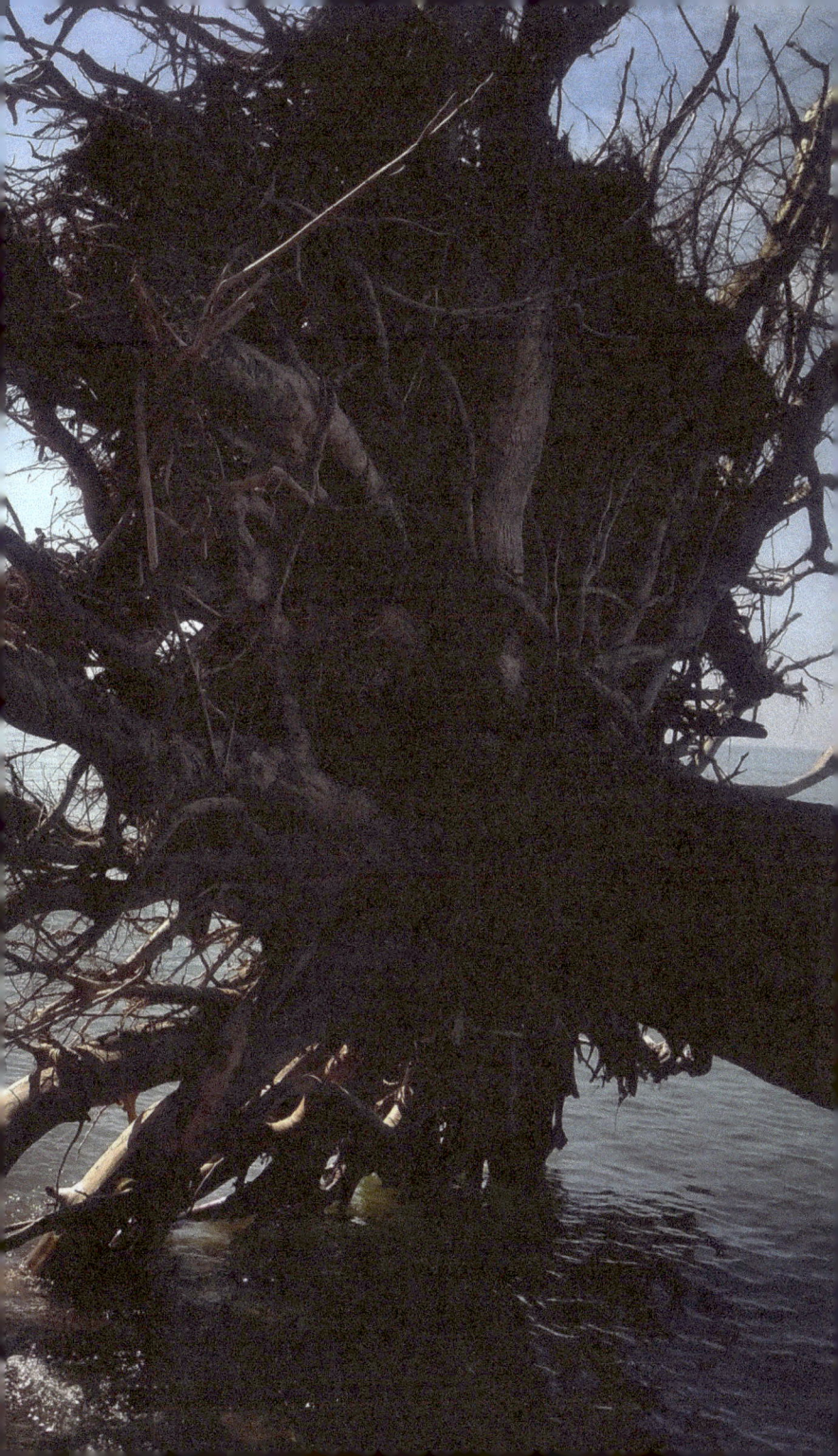

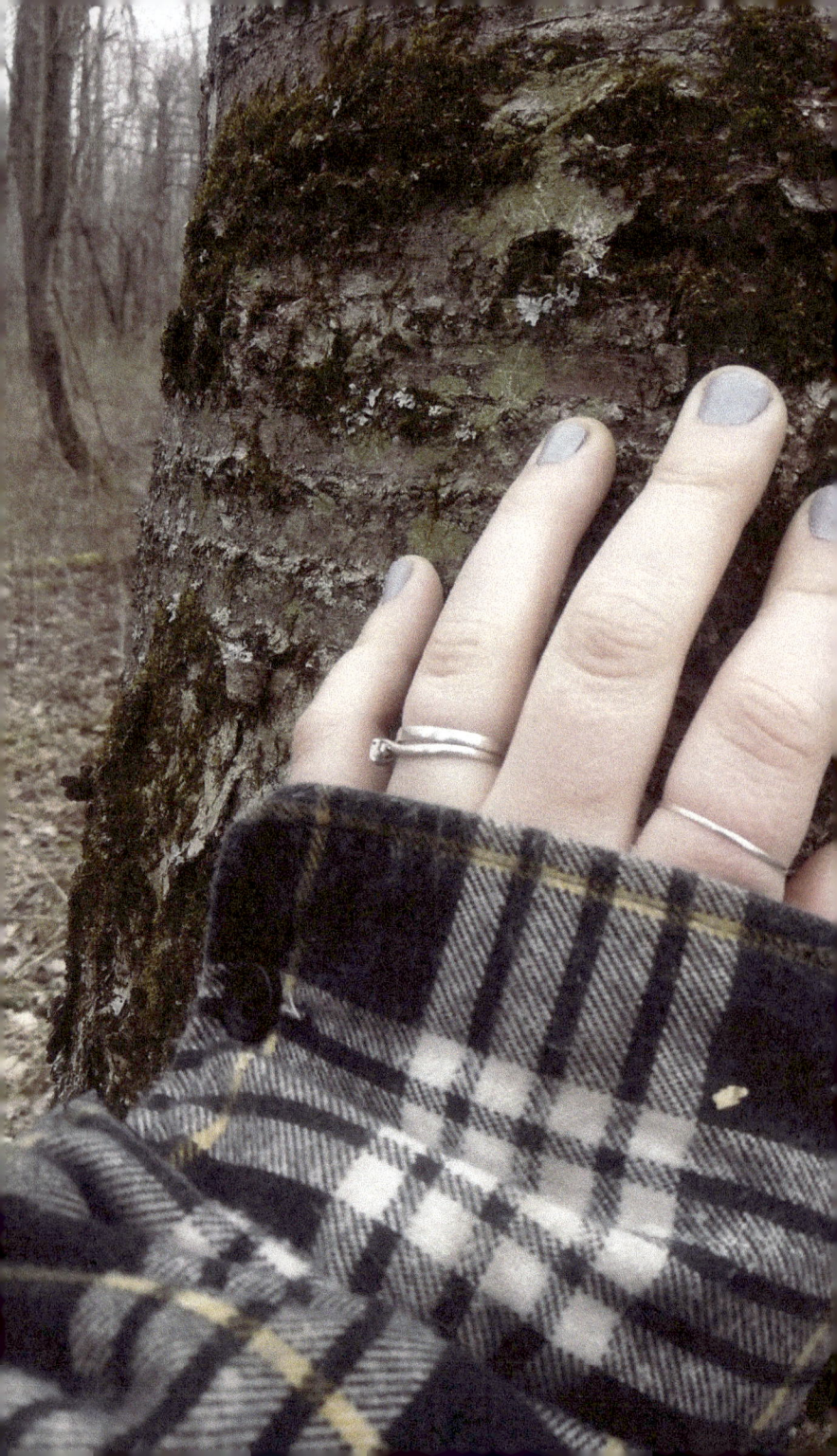

turquoise

bouquets of daffodils and grape hyacinth

coyote cries from the woods

heirloom flowers and vegetables

the phases of the moon

suspenders

the first snow of the year

cast iron frying pans

watermelon

handwritten letters from pen pals

apple crate bookshelves

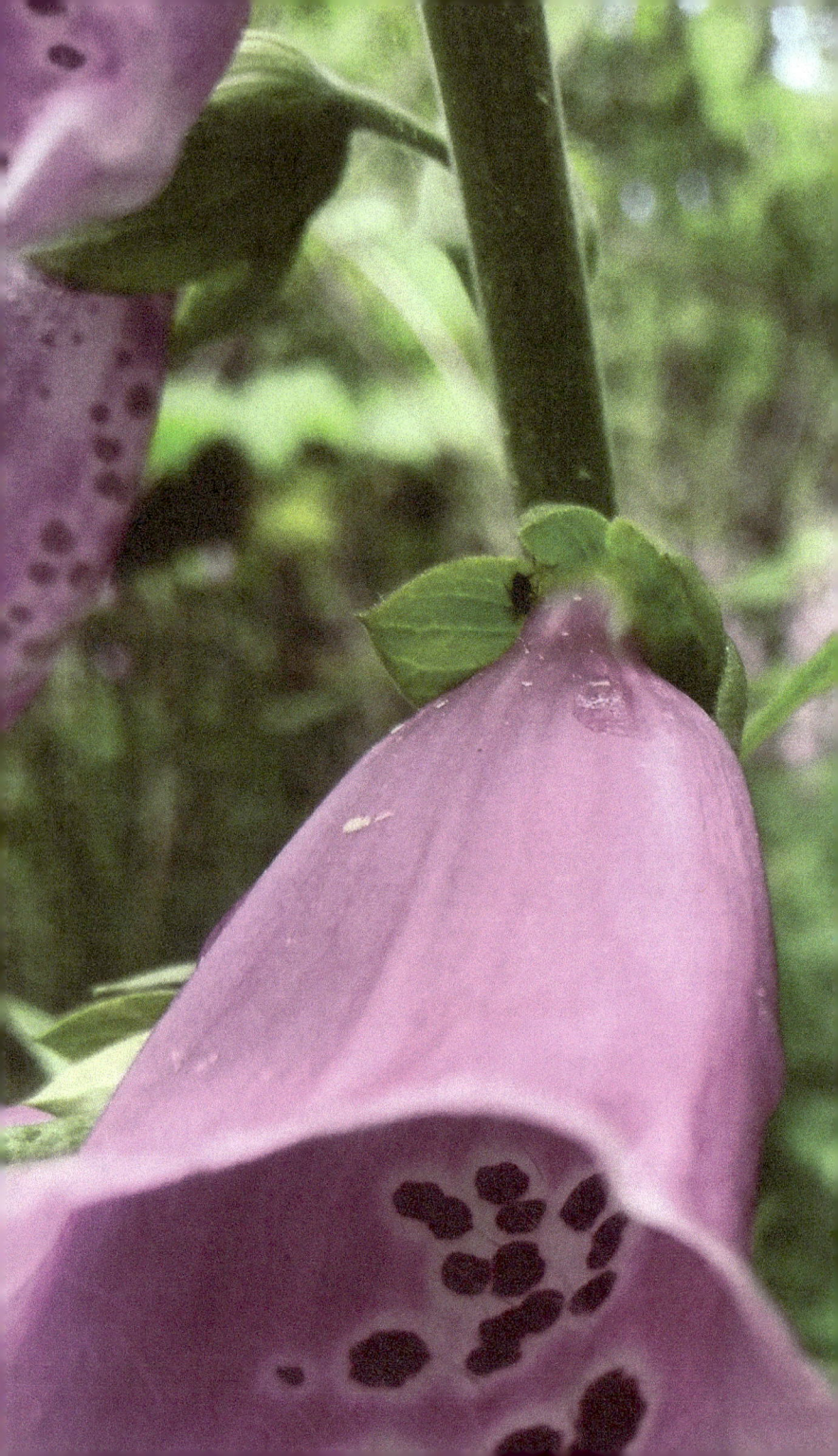

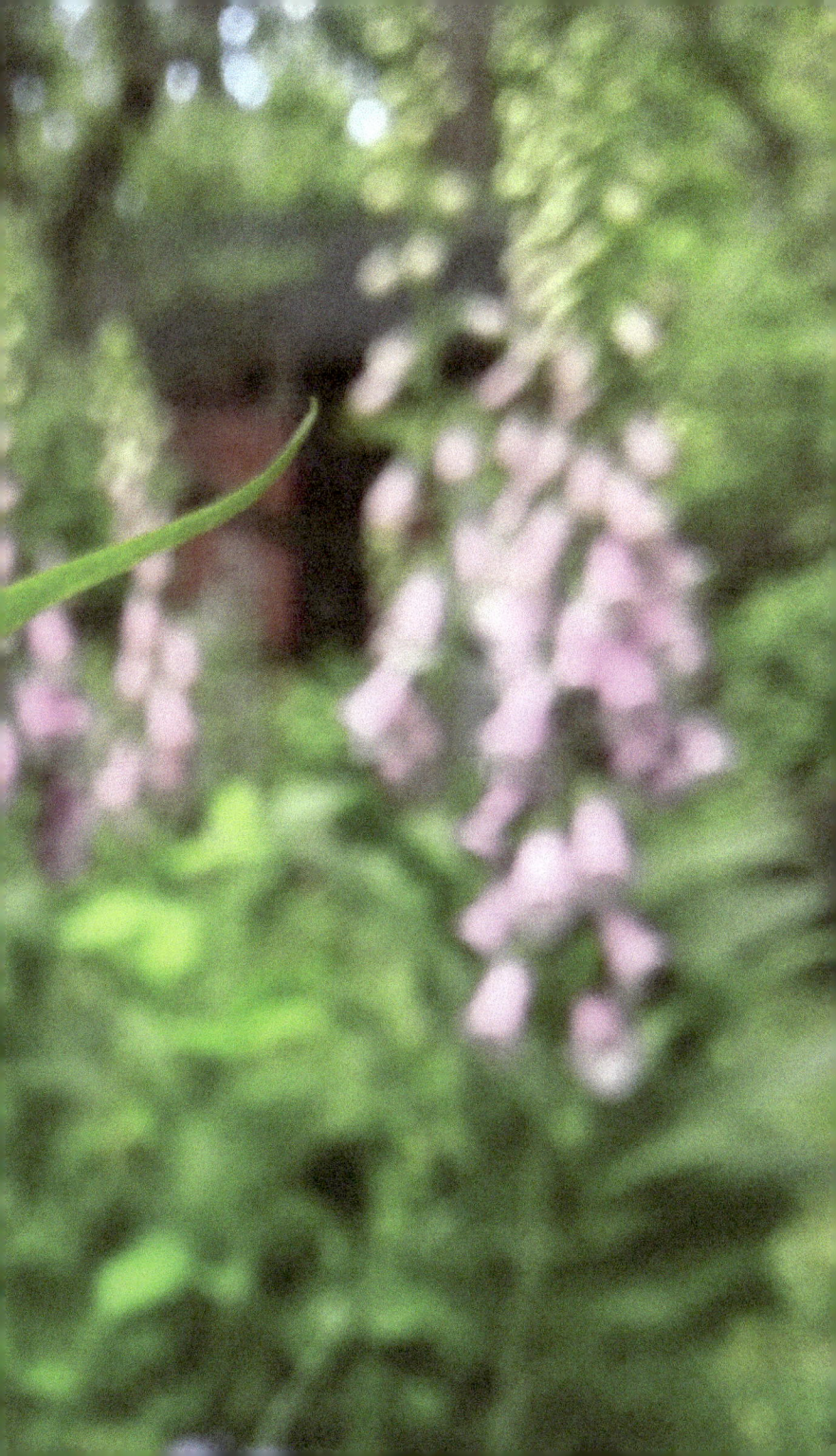

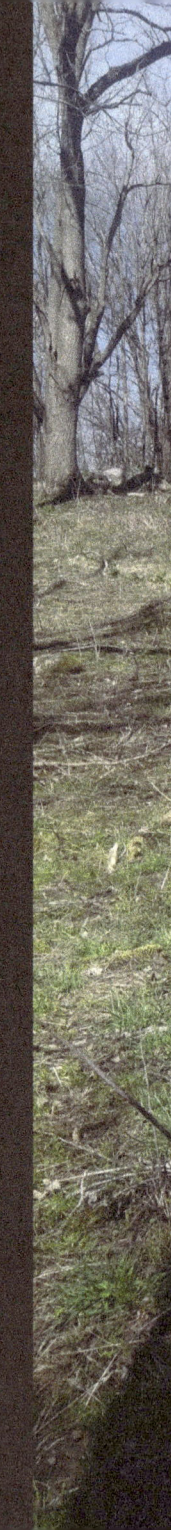

candlelight

intricate spider webs
glistening with dew

hostas

making black walnut ink

hand sewn bags of balsam
ceder to remind you of the
mountains

owls hooting from the trees

witches parades the weekend
of Halloween

seed catalogs that brighten up
dark February days

honey crisp apples

cinderella pumpkins

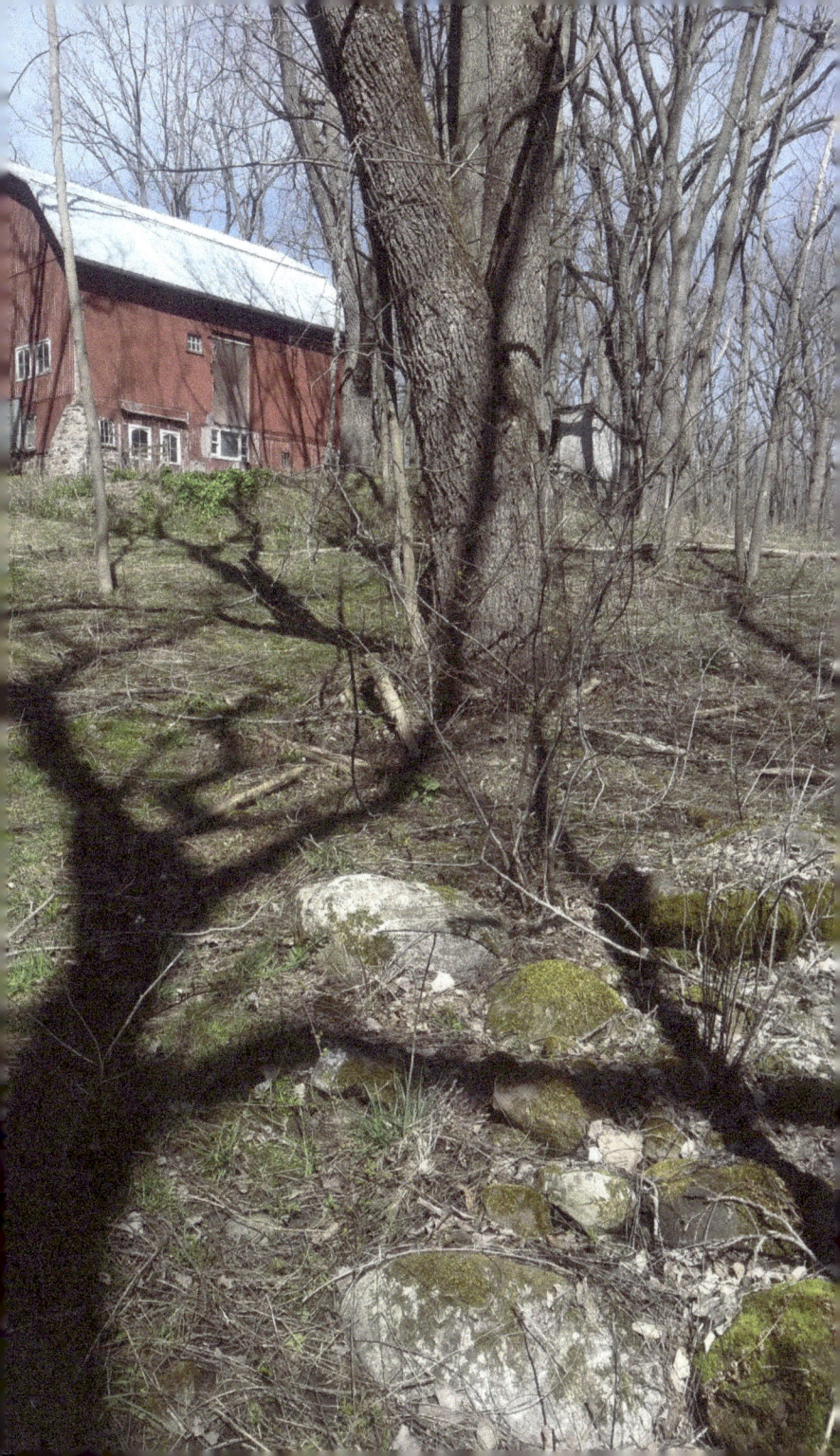

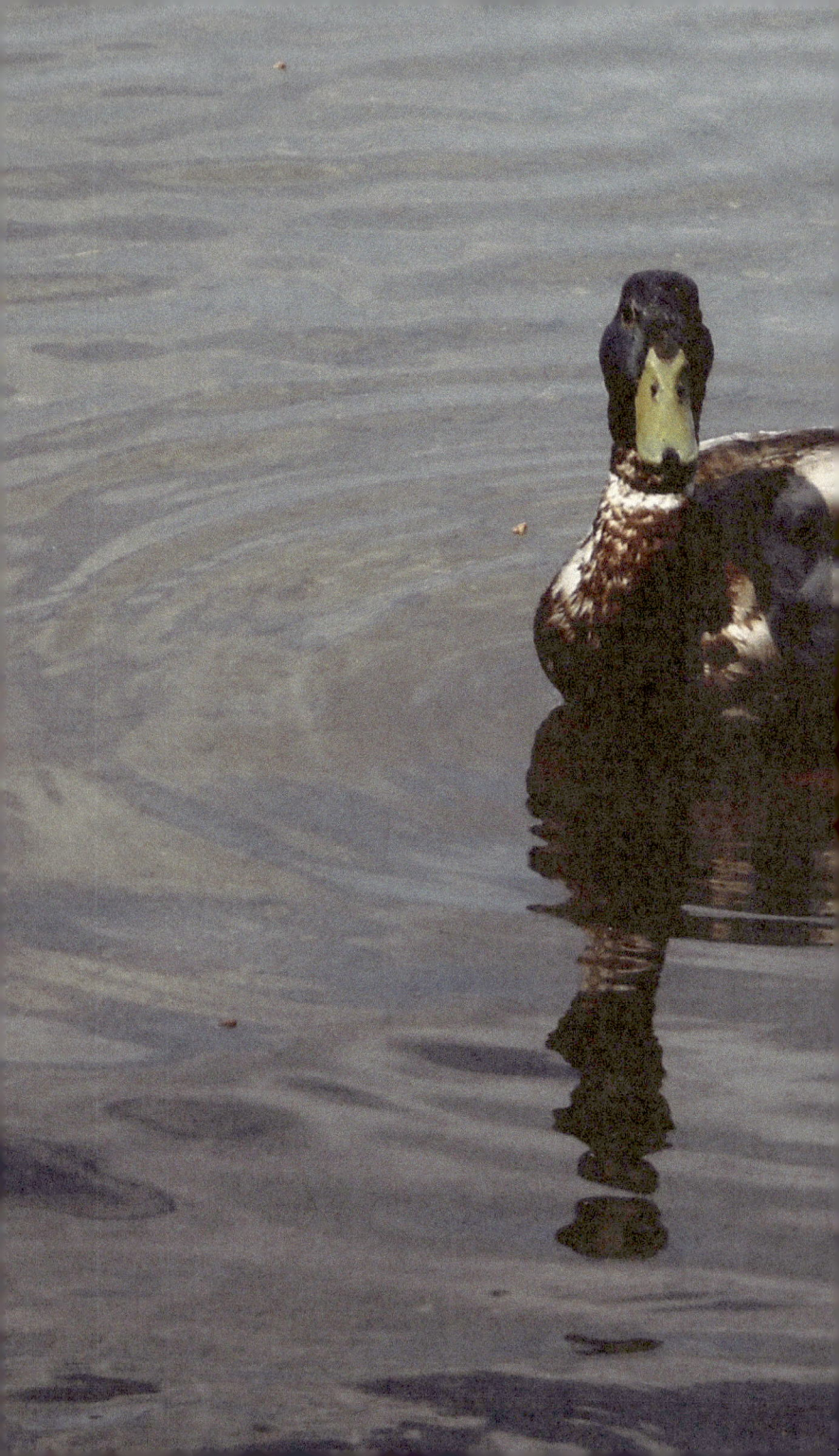

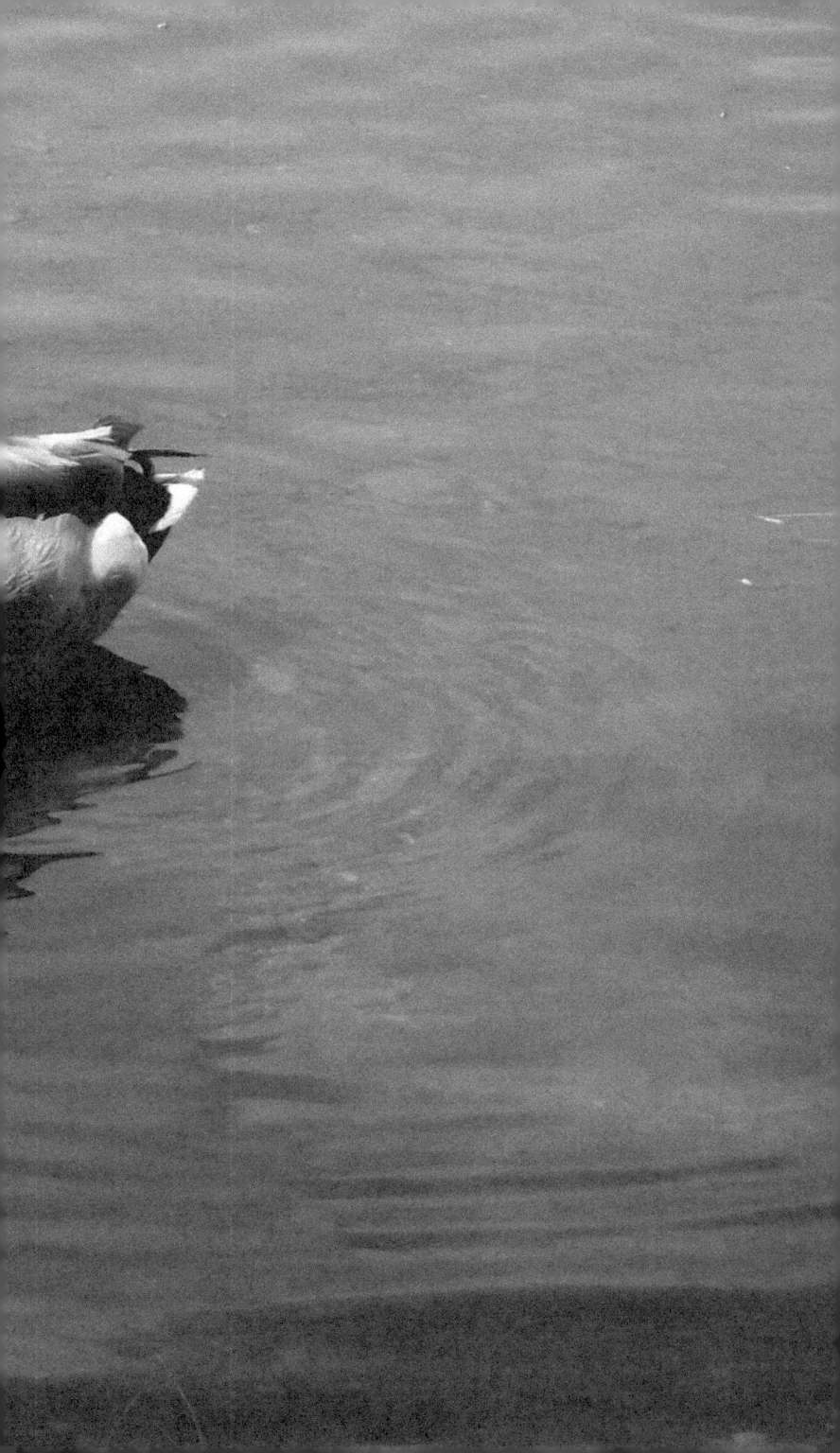

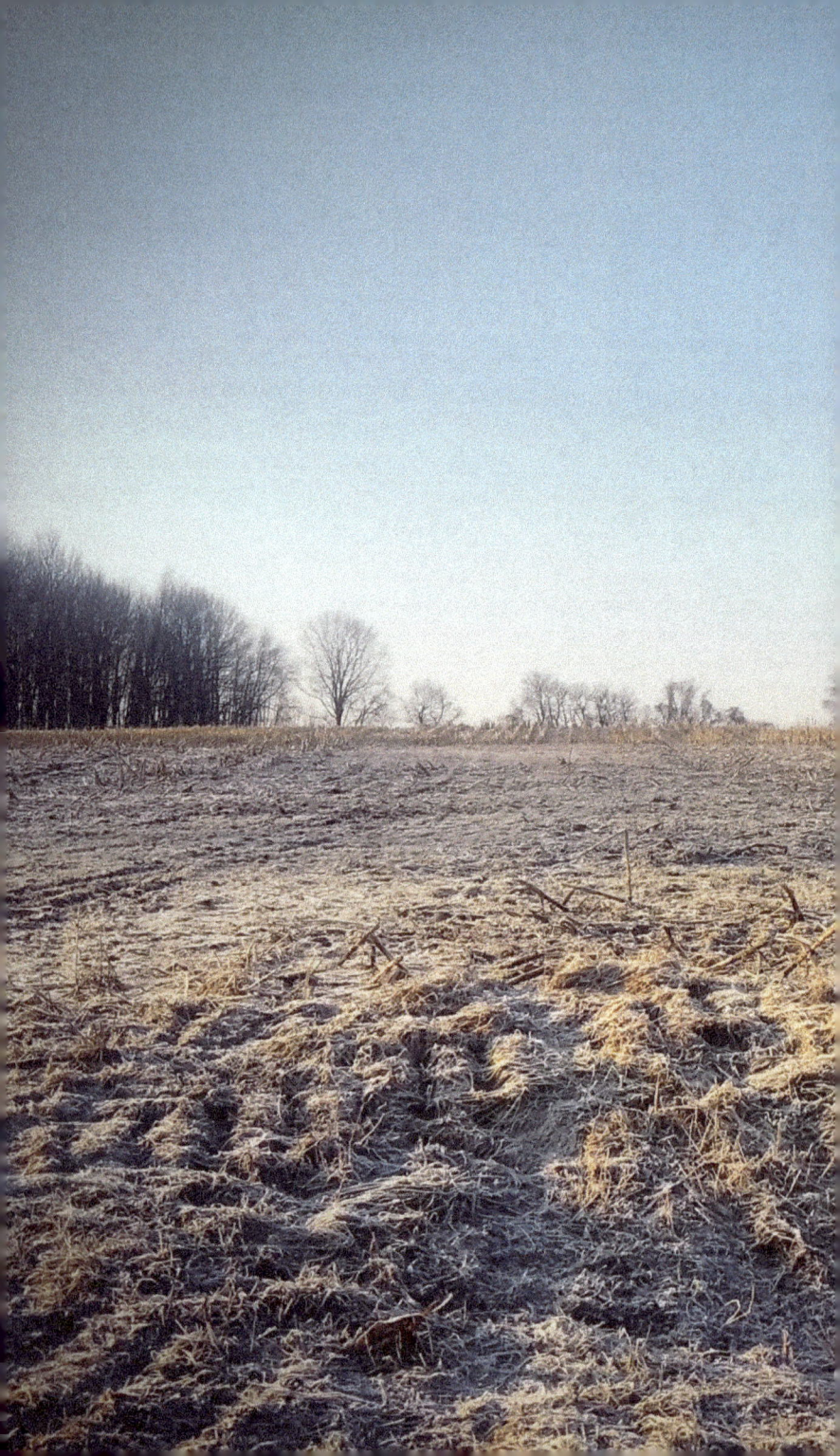

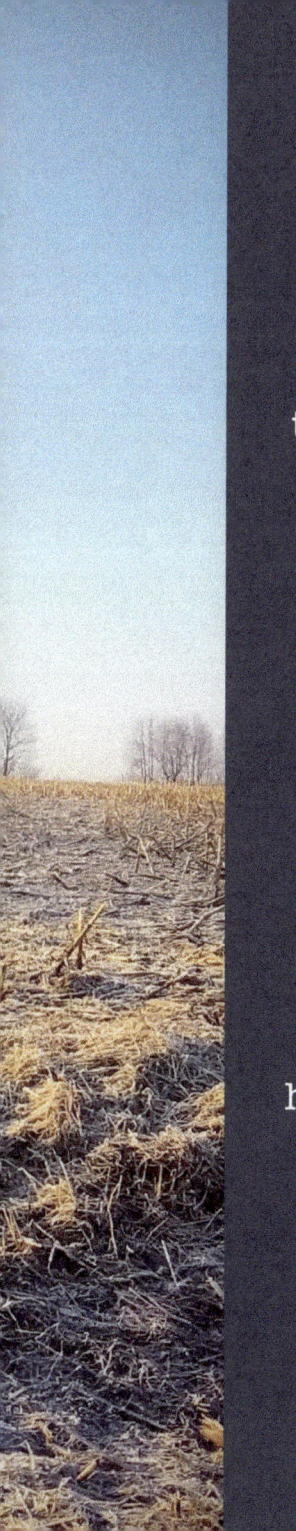

snowmobiling on open
frozen fields

weeding the garden

the feeling of coming home
after a week of camping

white wash paint

homemade apple pie

colorful canning shelves
full of food for the winter

crocheting

Christmas craft shows

hay wagon trick or treating

Harvest Moon

the illustrations in
children's books

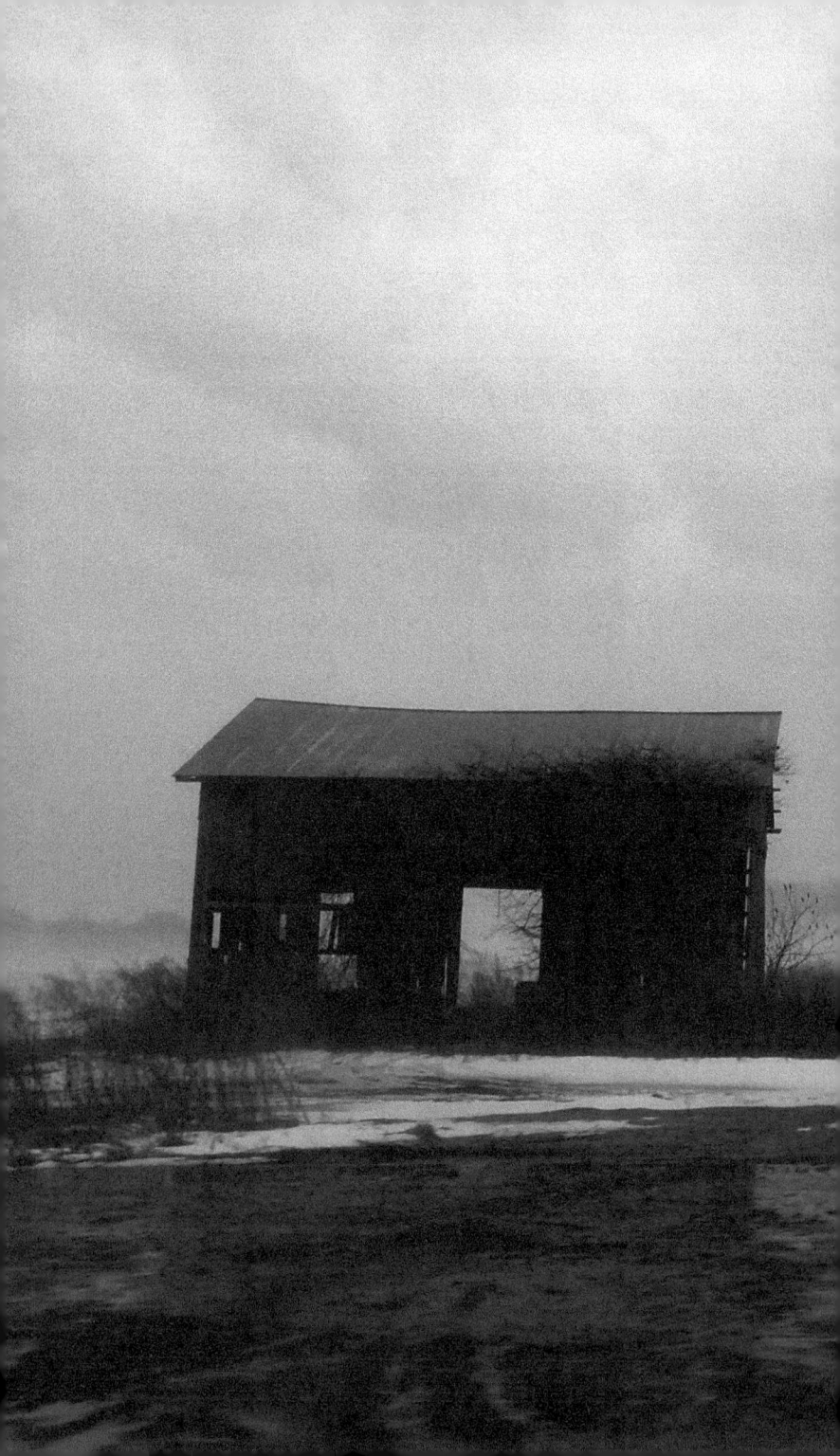

corn on the cob

the radio always on in the kitchen

twistable crayons

the sparkle of snow as it falls

watching lightning storms

dream catchers hanging above your bed

field guides

quilt rows laid out on the floor ready to be sewed

the wheel of the year

raspberries

wood cabins

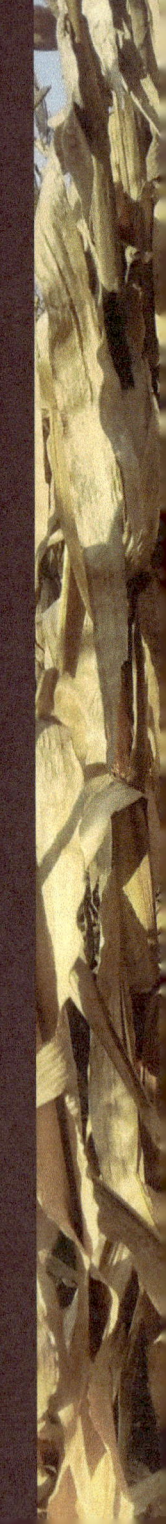

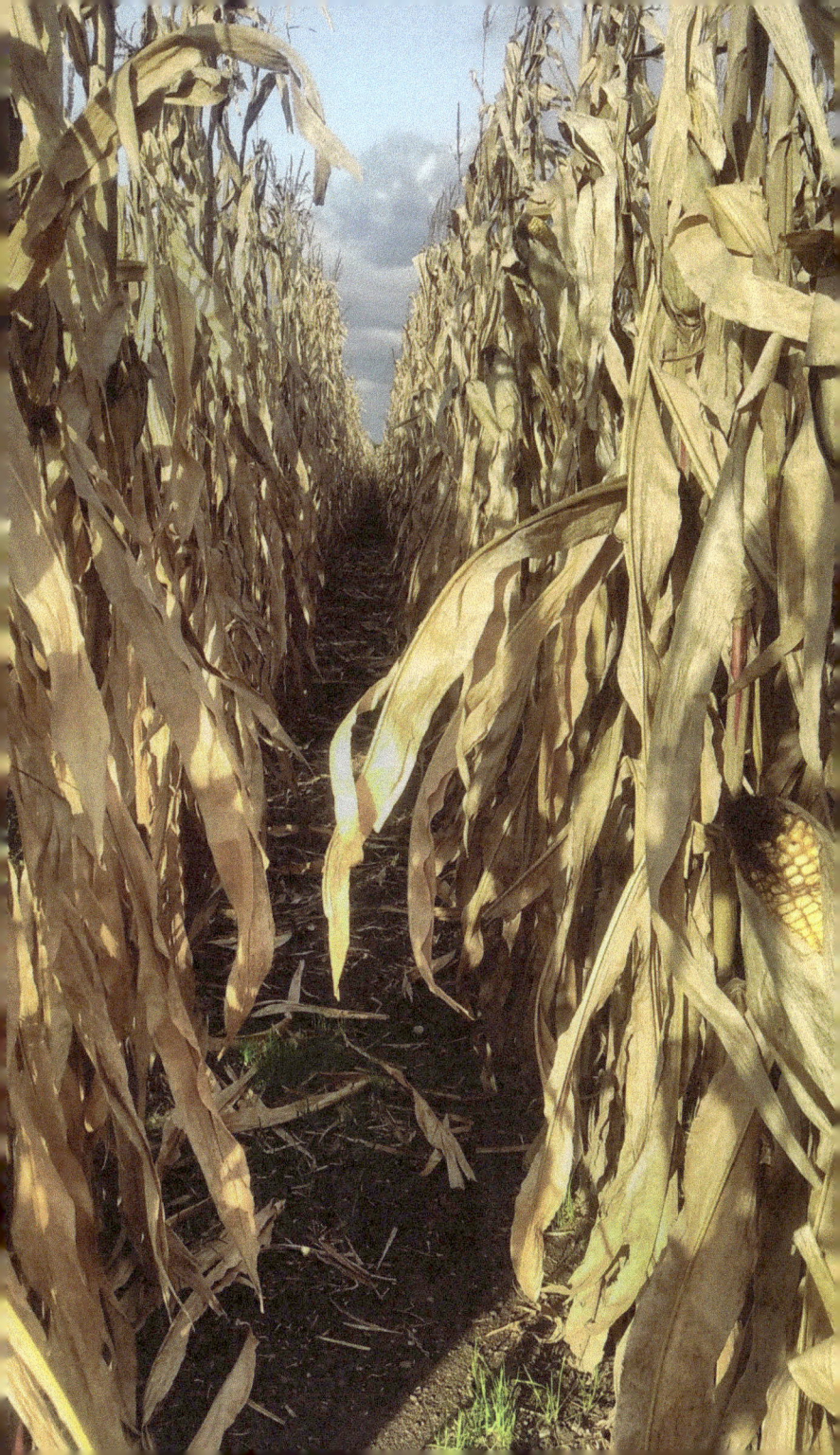

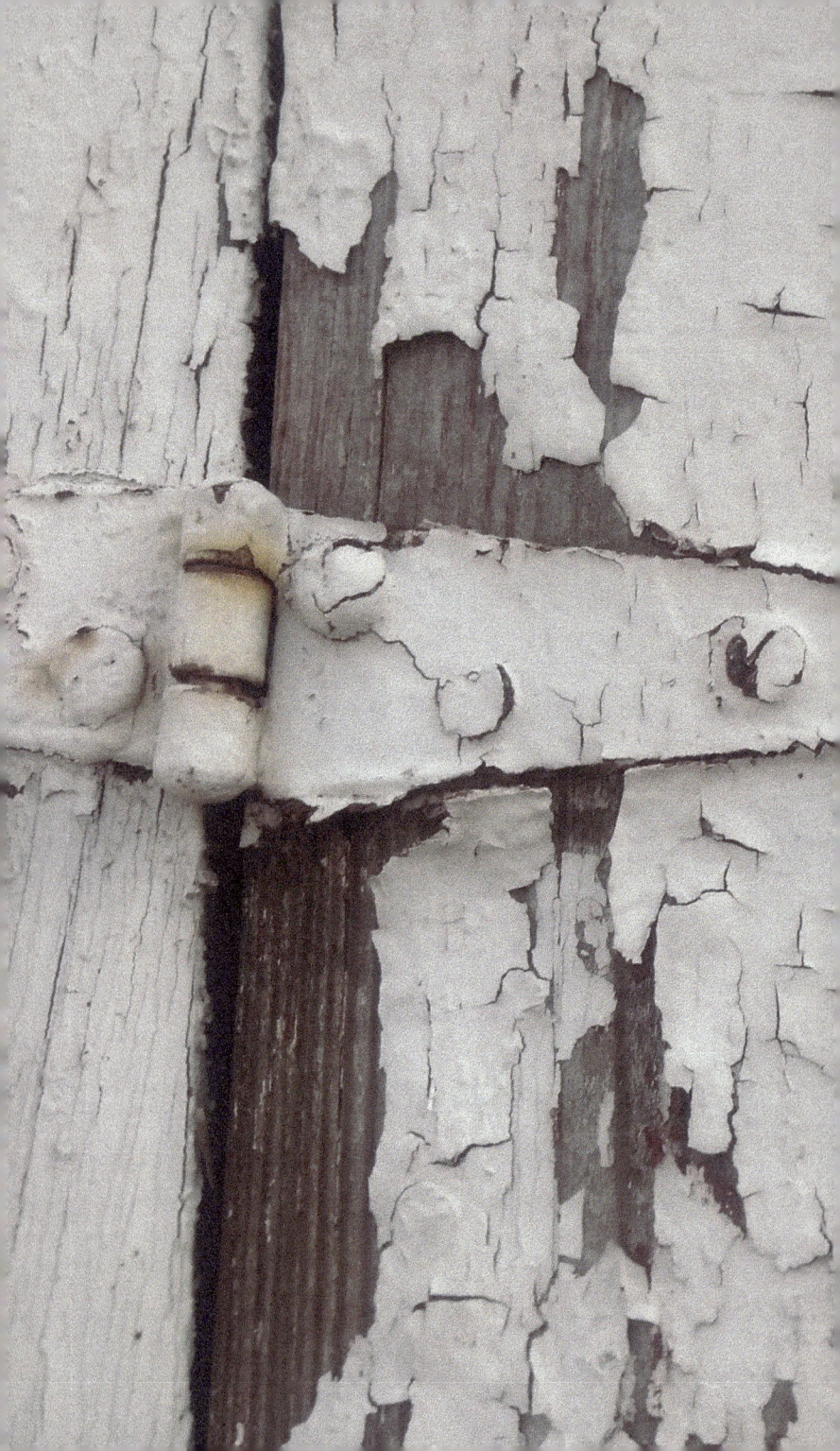

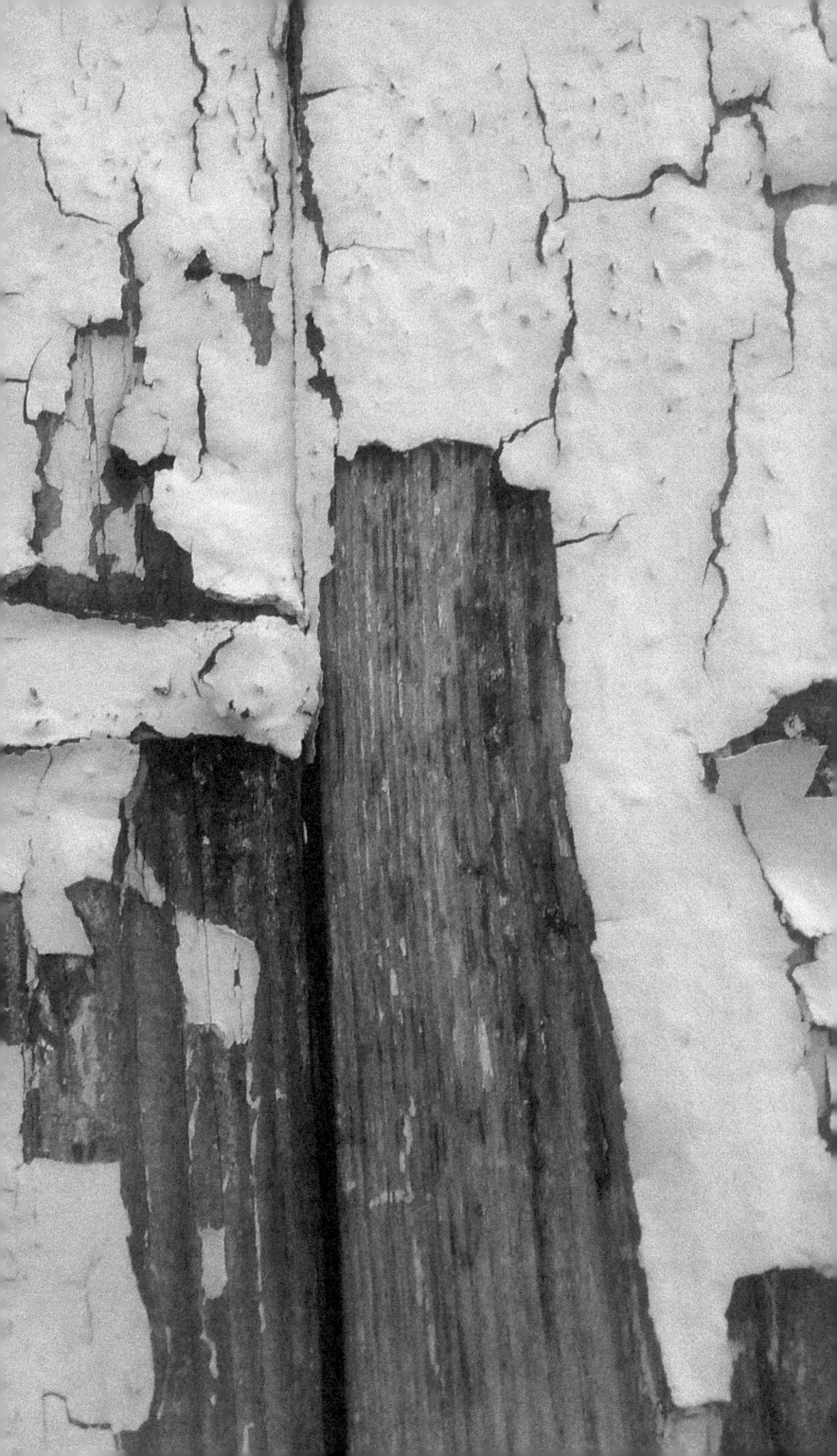

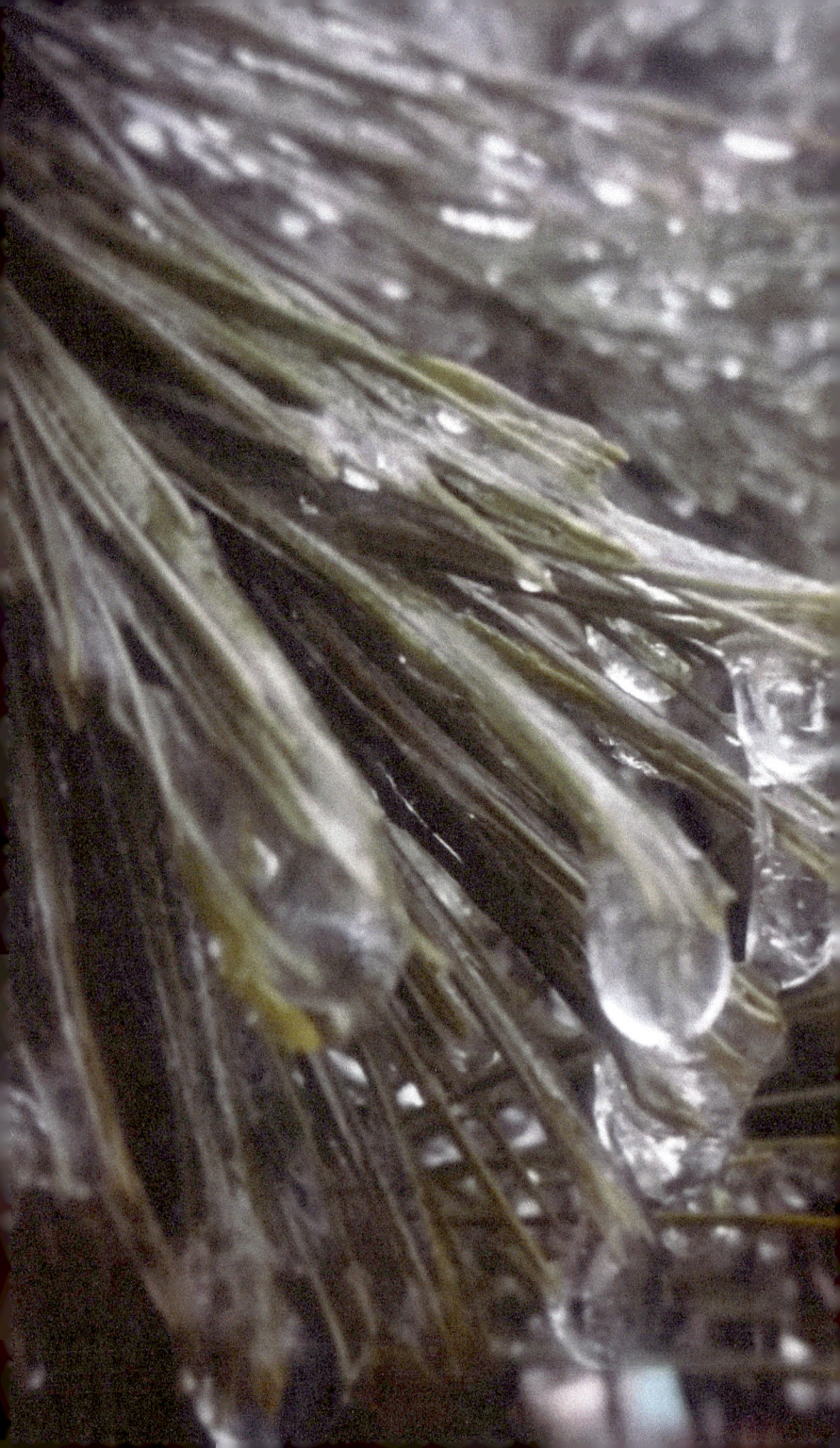

snow days

when your favorite song comes
on the radio

sea glass

hard cider made with
local apples

acrylic paint tubes of every
color and shade

new construction paper

handmade birthday cards
and happy birthday banners

mountain music with banjos

sun printing

rainbow moon stone

black cats

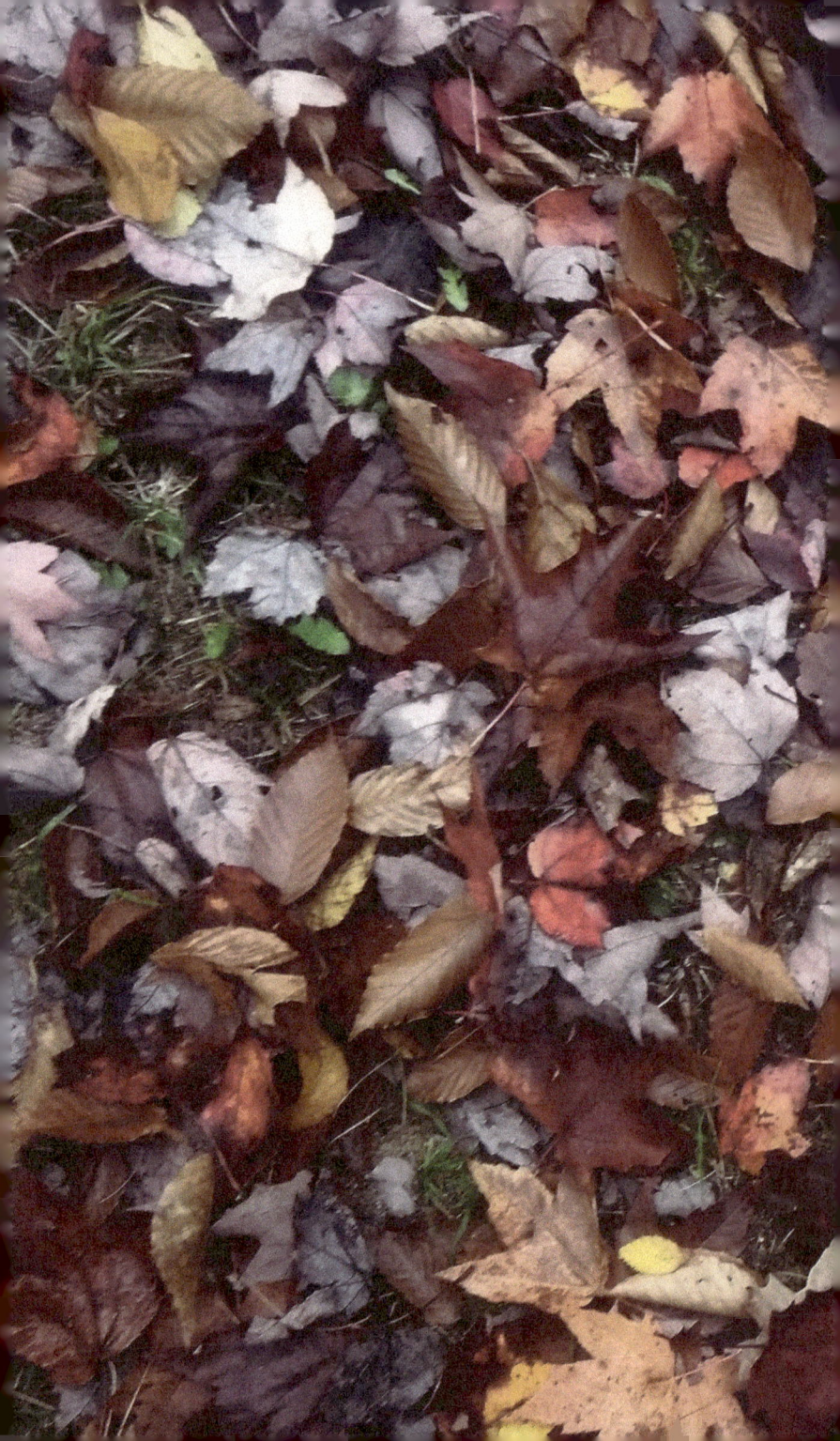

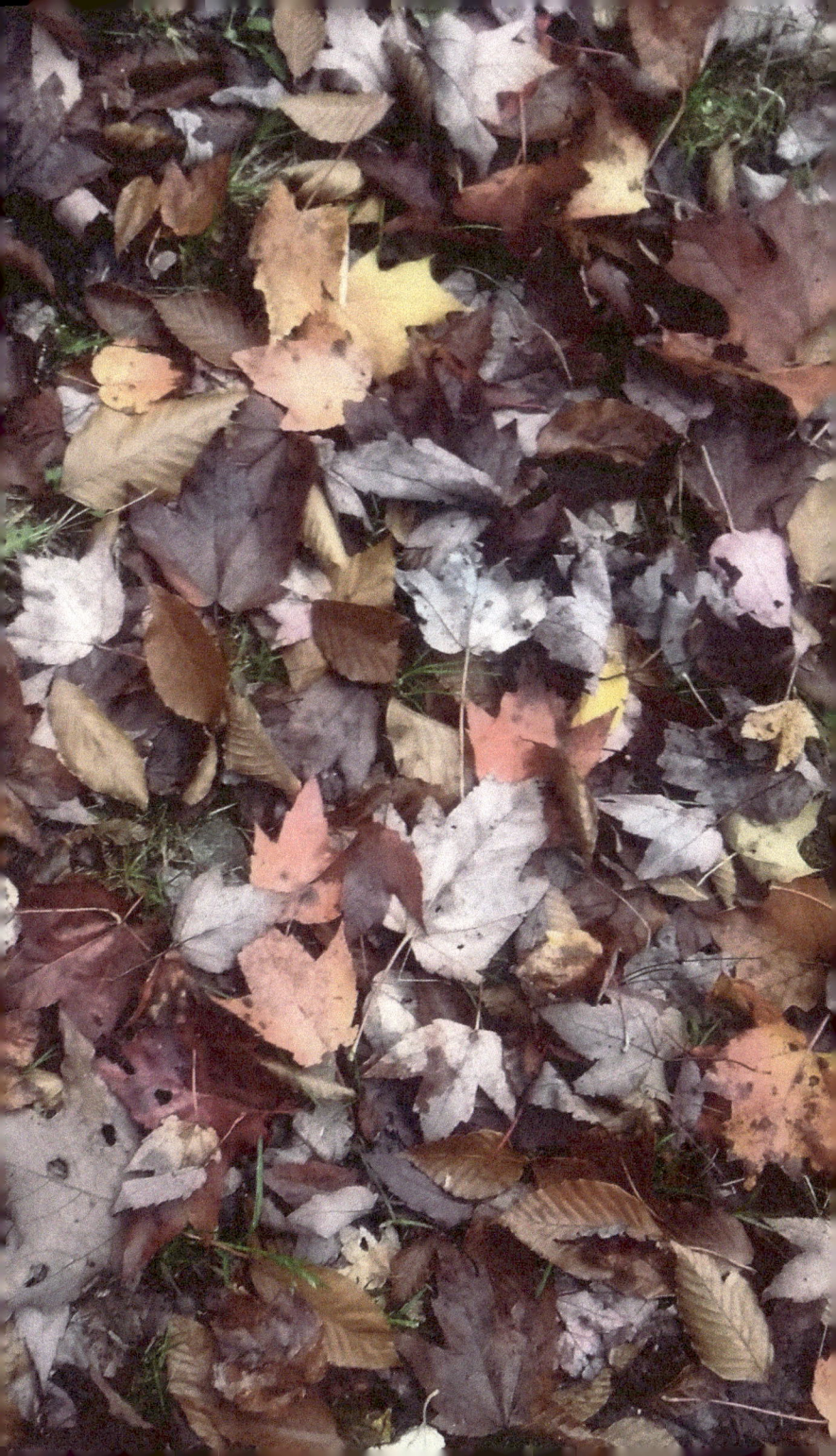

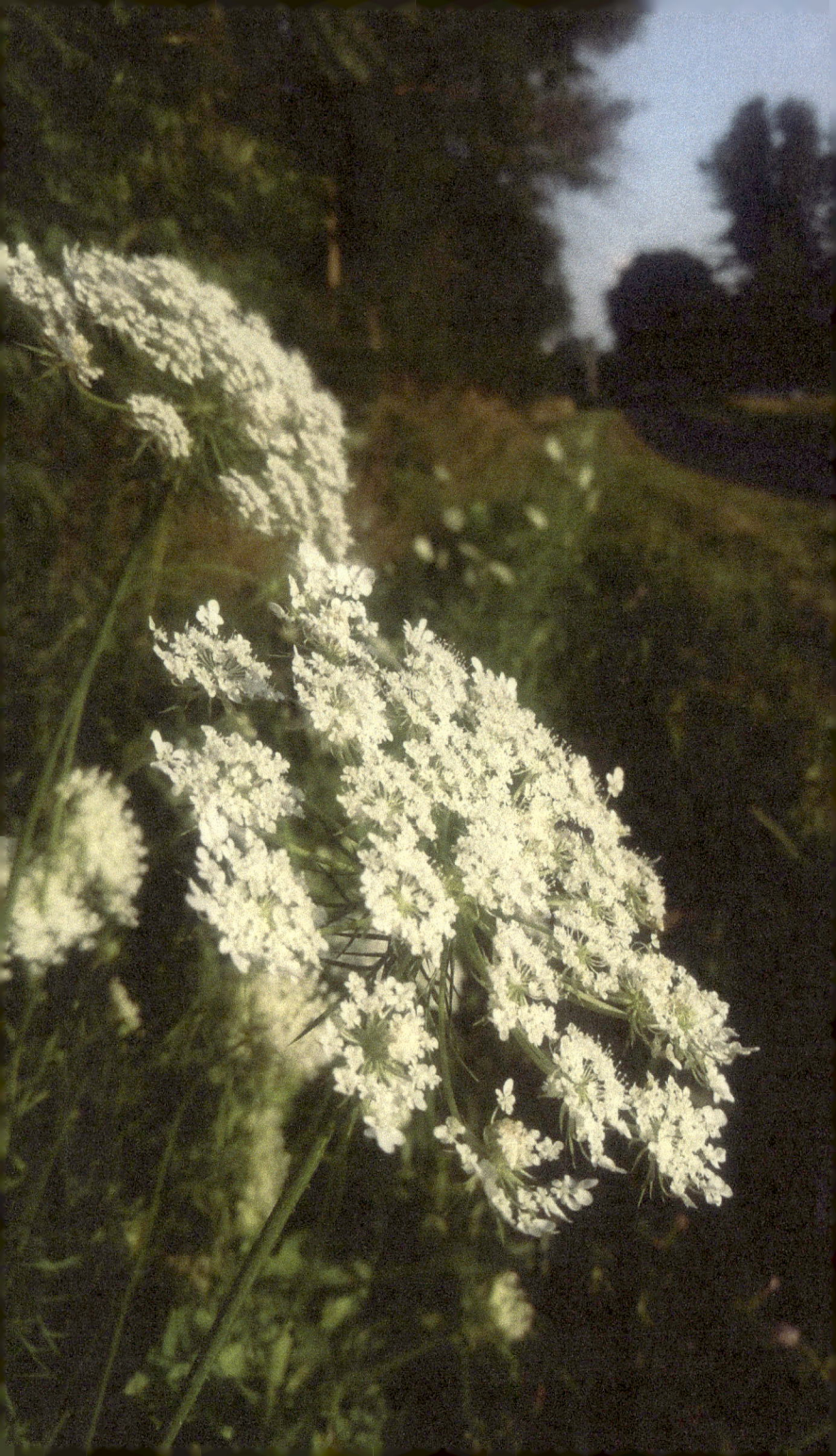

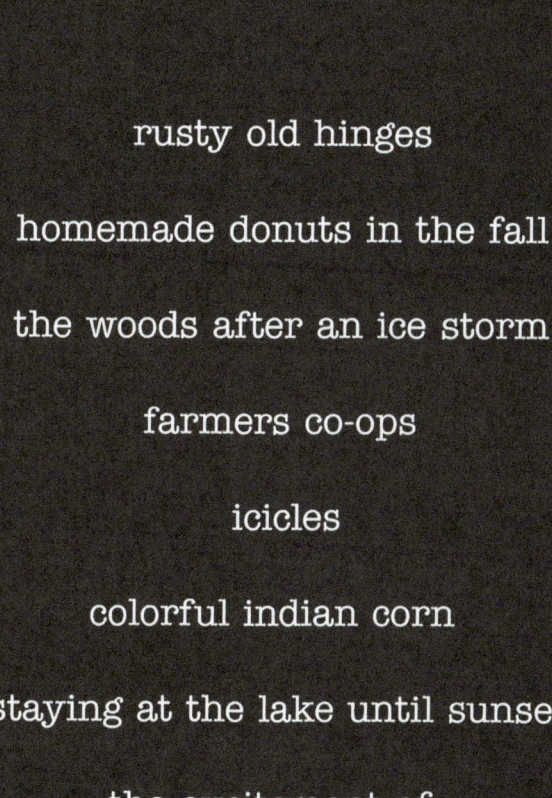

rusty old hinges

homemade donuts in the fall

the woods after an ice storm

farmers co-ops

icicles

colorful indian corn

staying at the lake until sunset

the excitement of Christmas Eve

synchronicities

little danish flags on a string

hand painted wooden tree ornaments

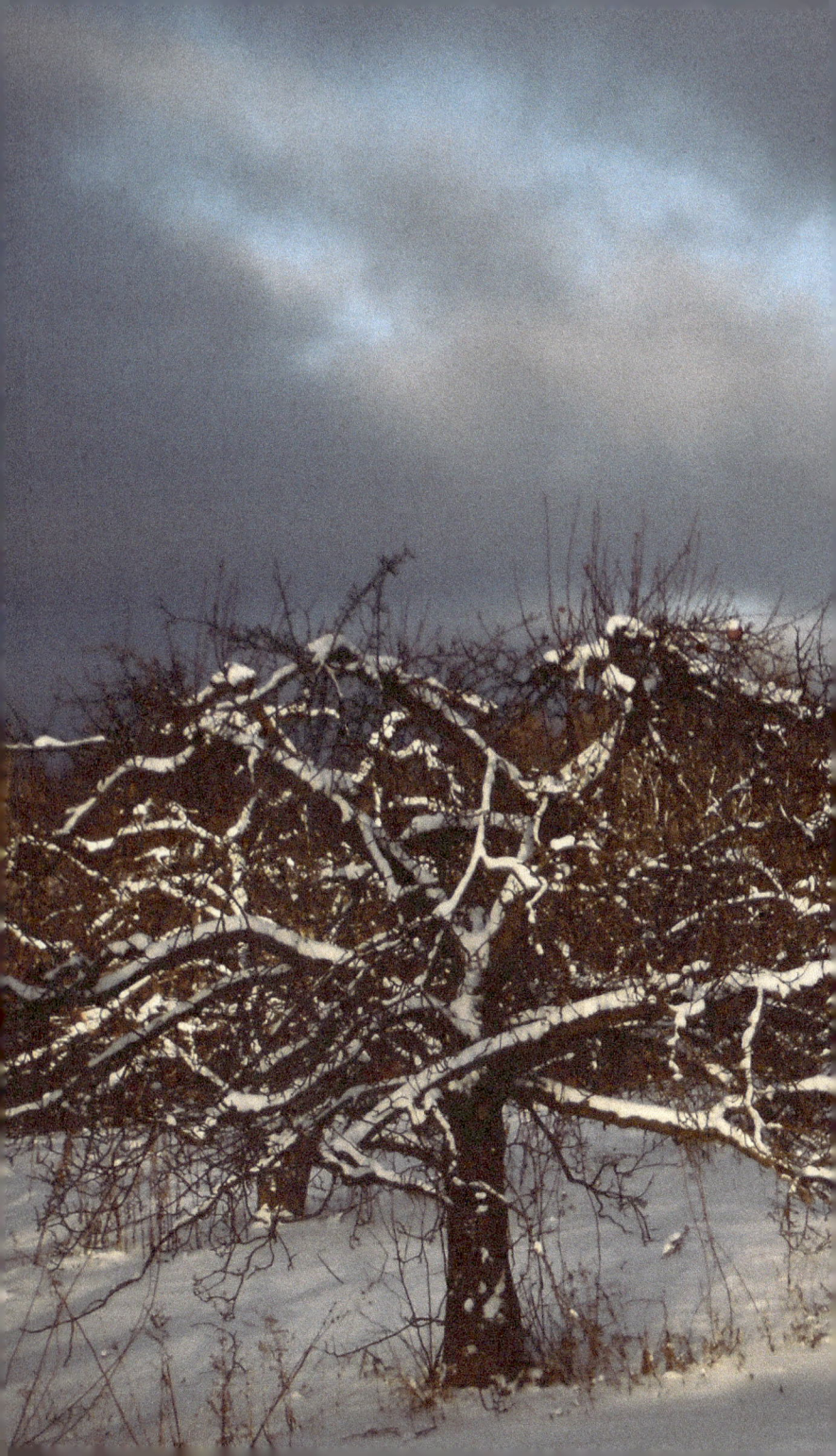

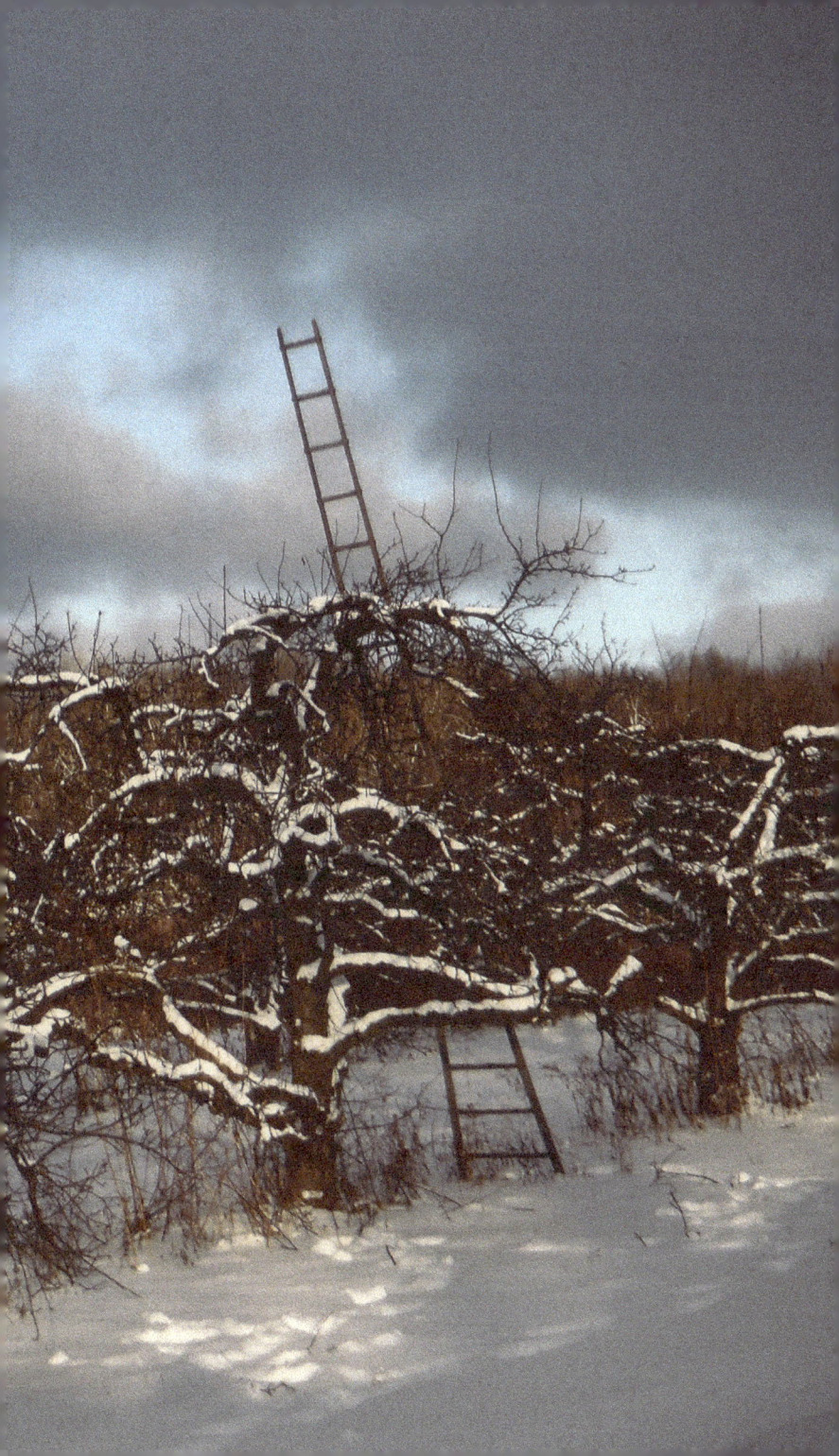

jack frost

oracle cards

positive quotes on colorfully painted rocks

twine for making garden rows

blacksmith

battery operated candles in every window

the state fair

when waitresses know you enough to know your order

pink roses

barn weddings

planting crops by the phases of the moon

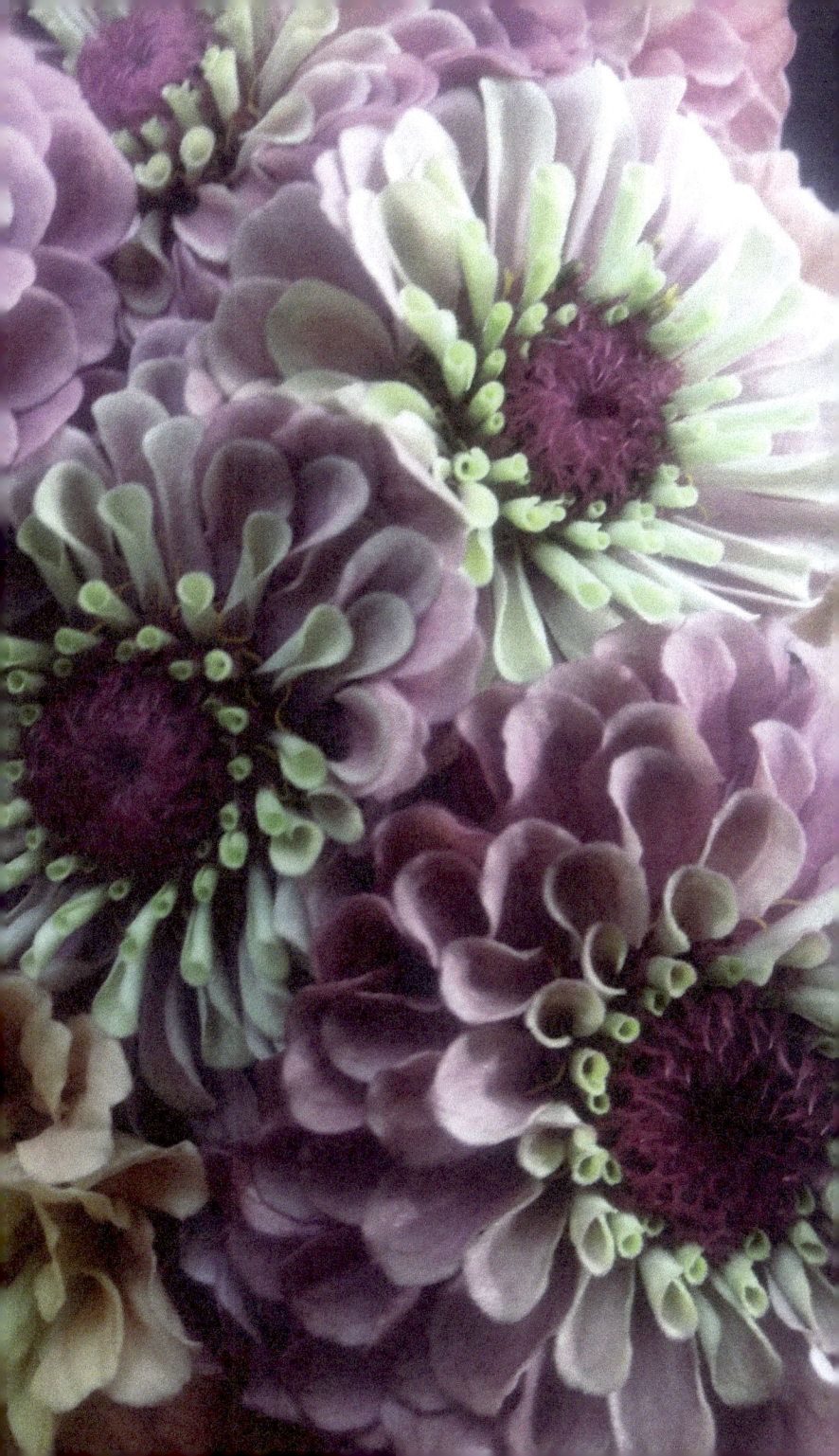

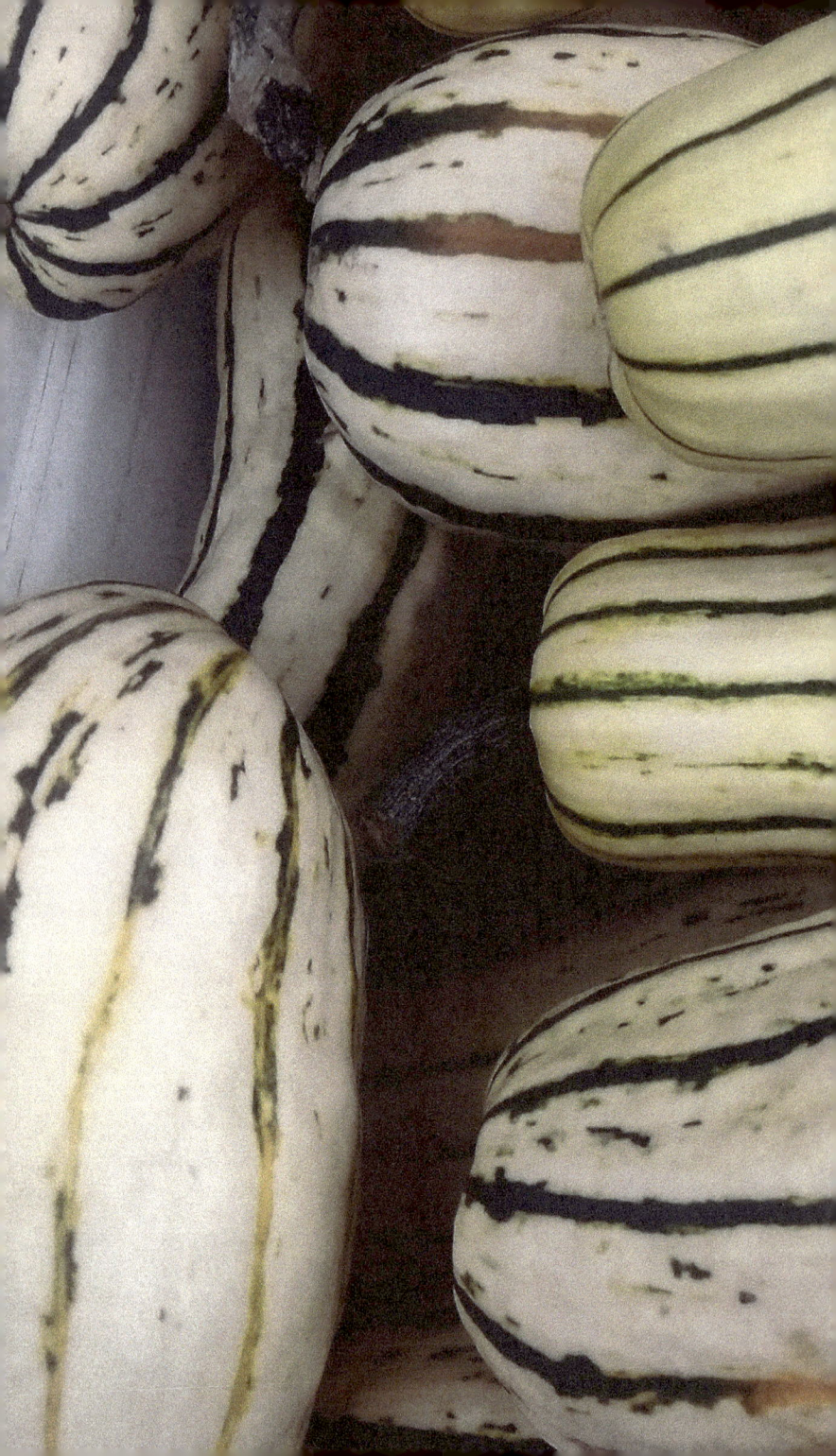

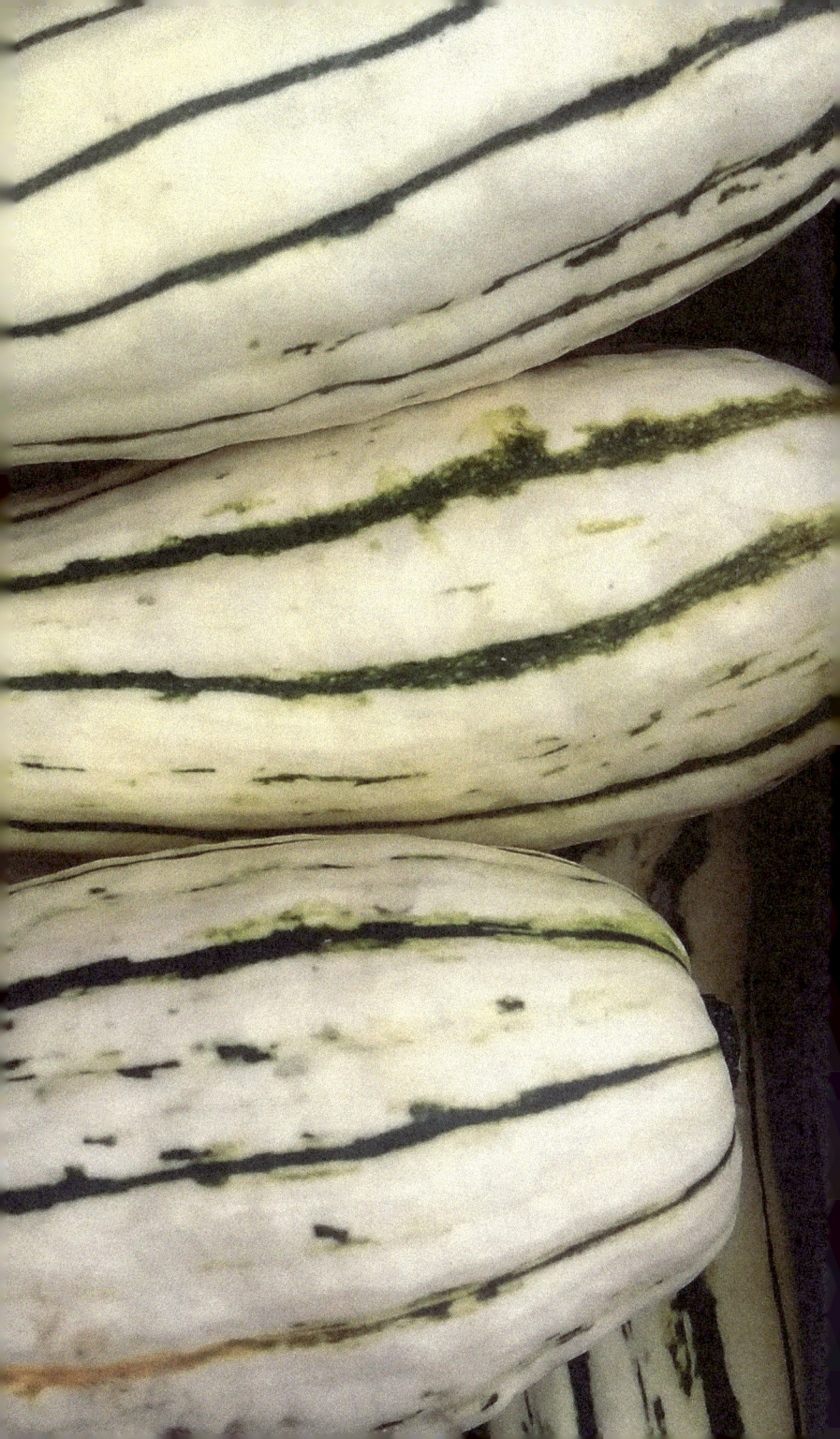

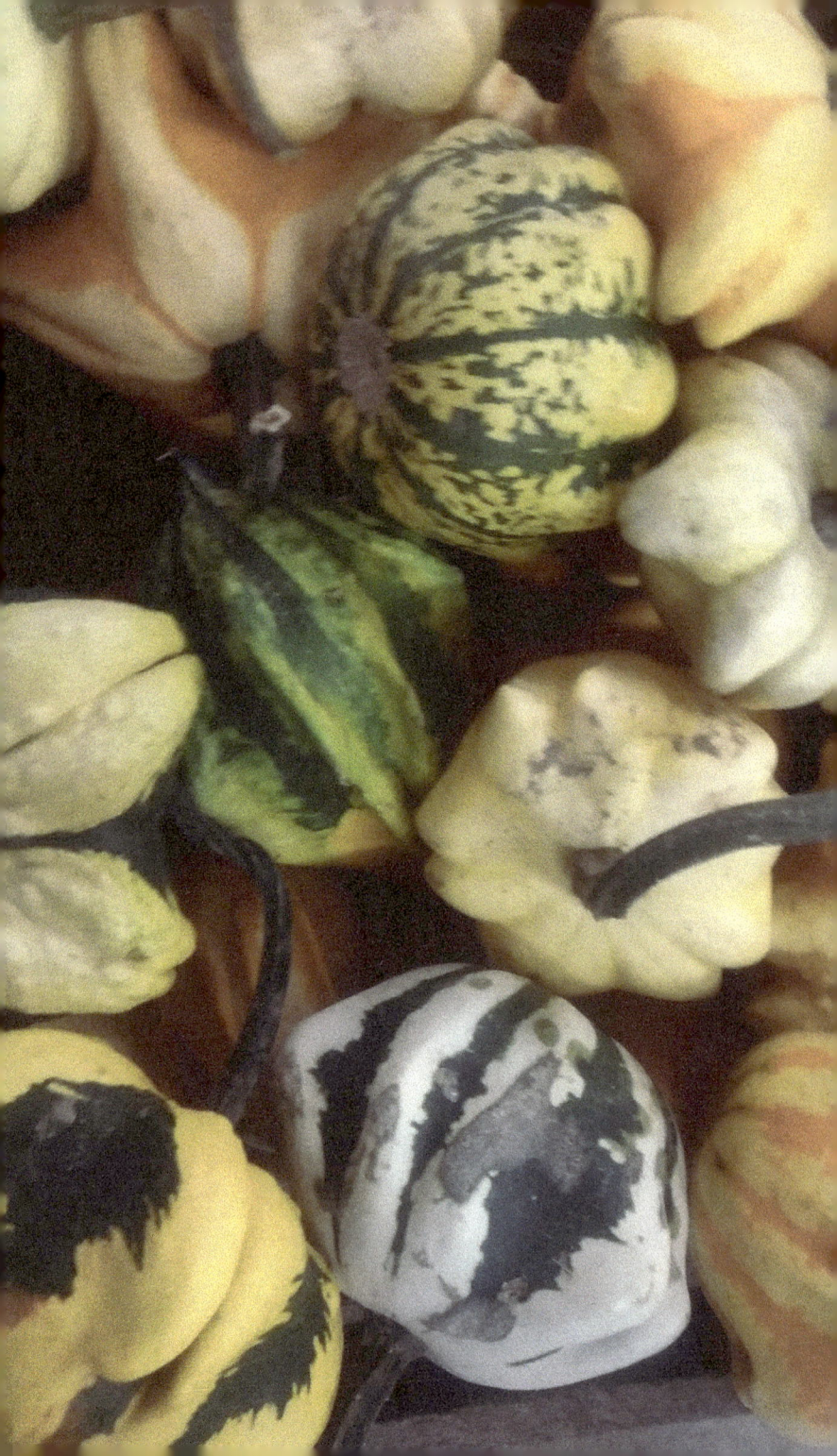

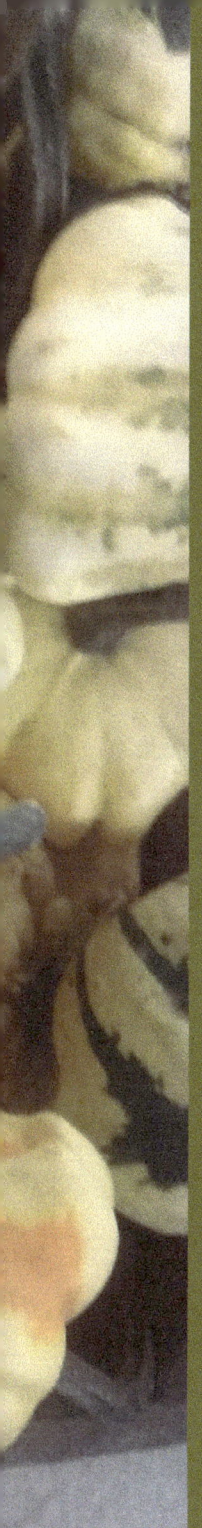

gourds

scratch art paper

teddy bears that wind up and play a comforting song

being read to

wooden rocking horses with folk art designs

floral wallpaper

spirit animals

agate slices

geodes

lanterns glowing with candlelight

cotton candy

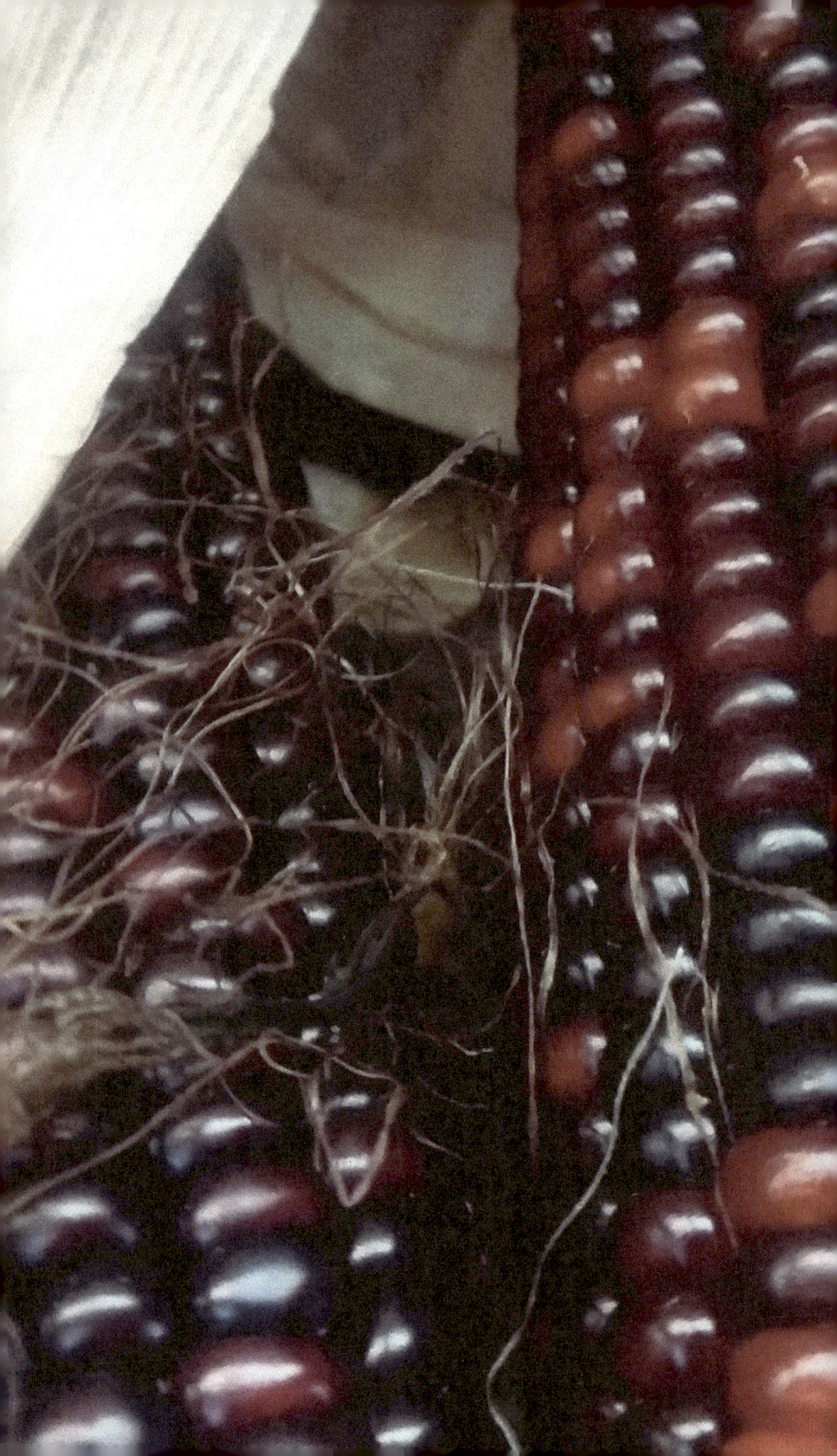

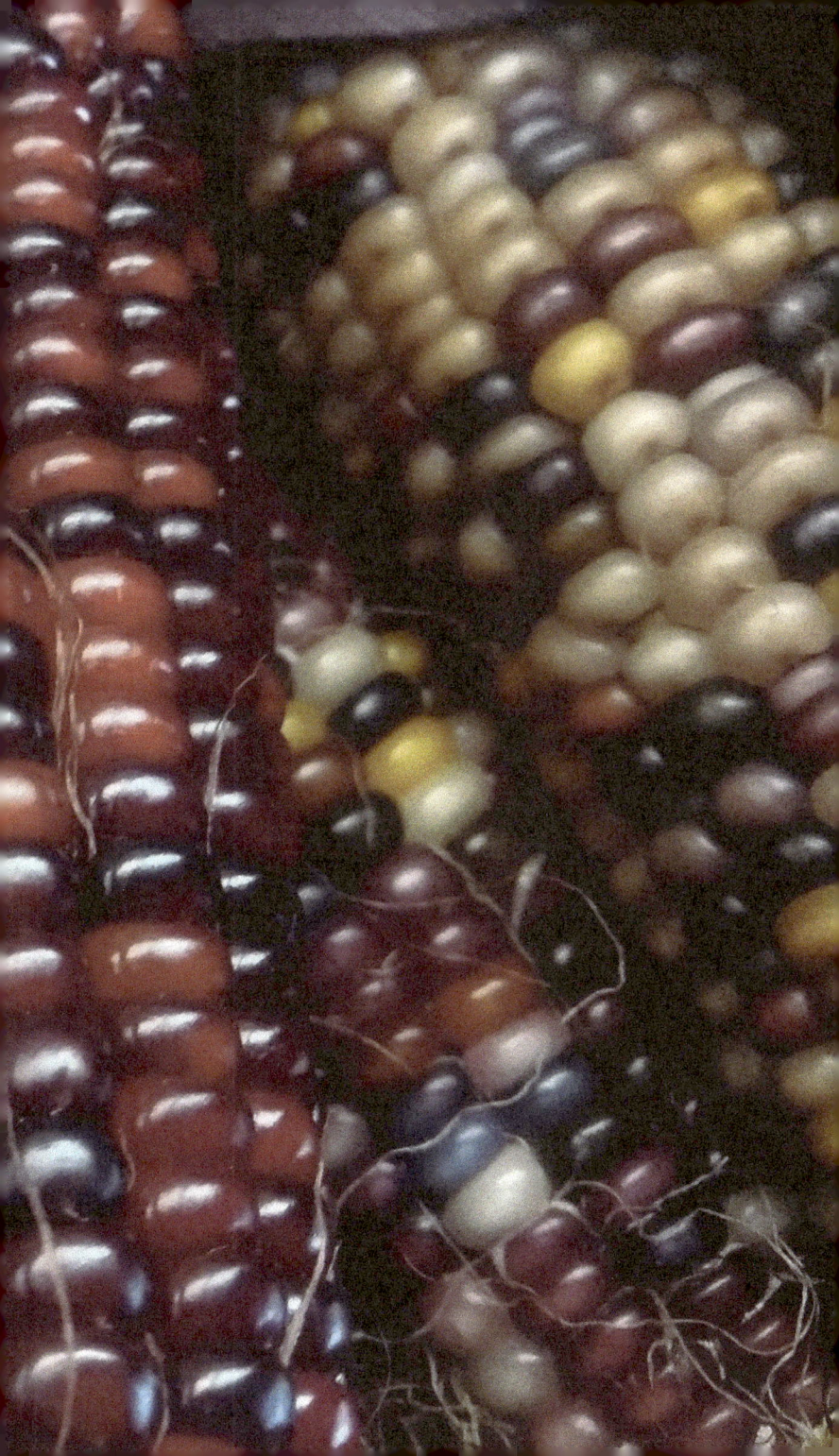

corn mazes

being able to feel the water in
the air before you get to
the lake

writing in the margins of
books

moss on tree trunks

circular rainbows around the
sun on clear days

cobblestone houses

the smell of coconut

crescent moons

old one room school houses

duct tape

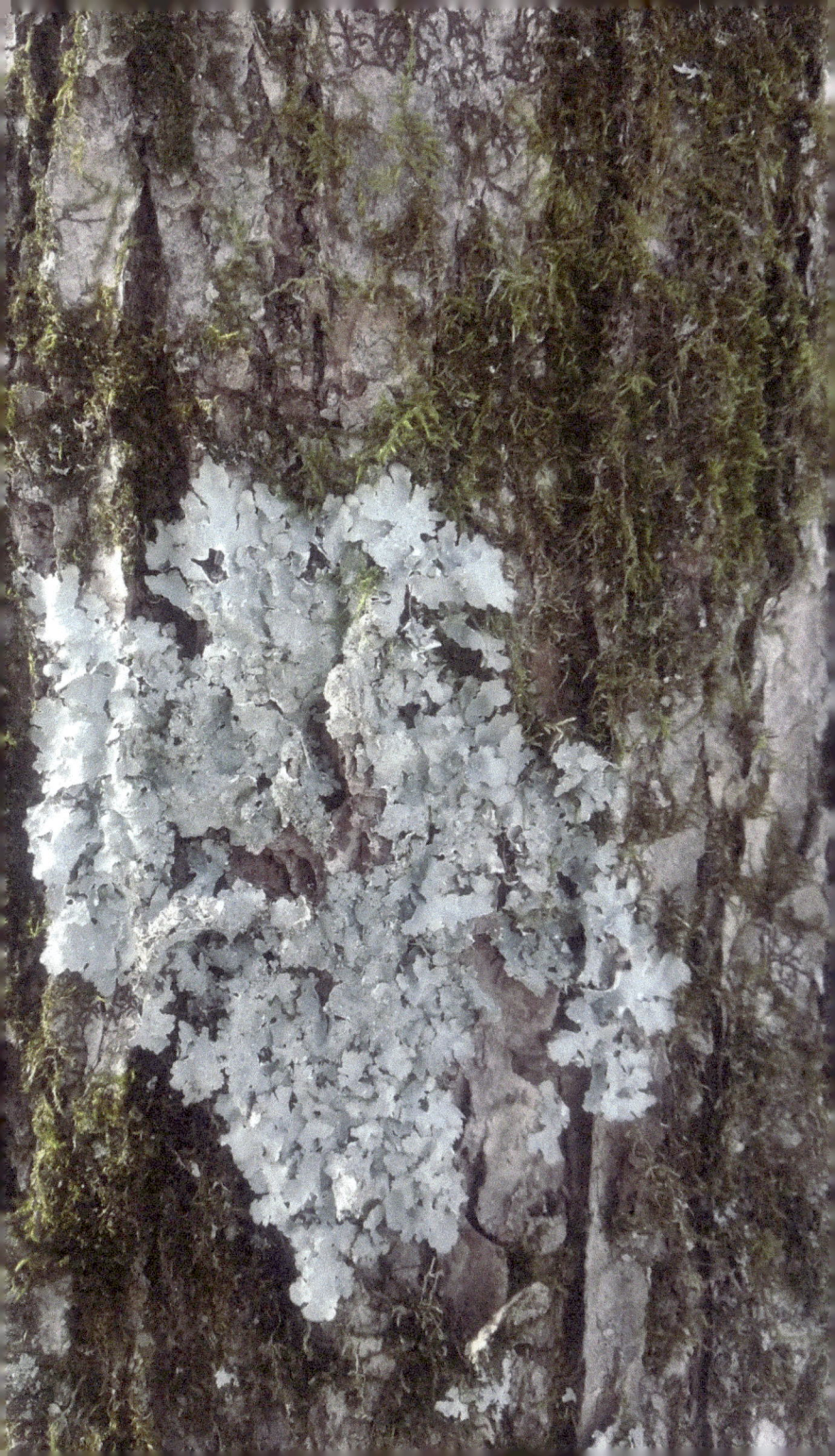

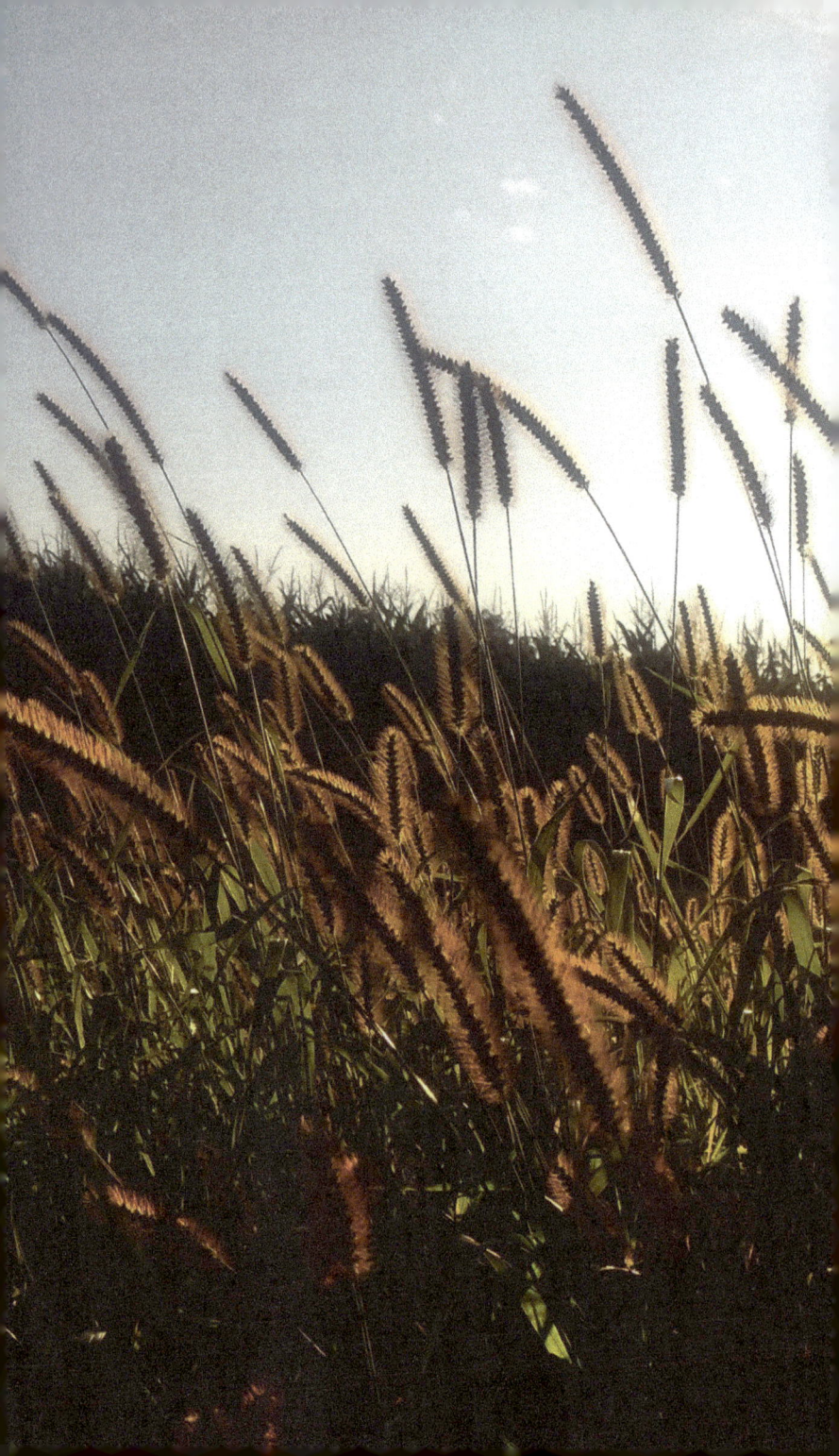

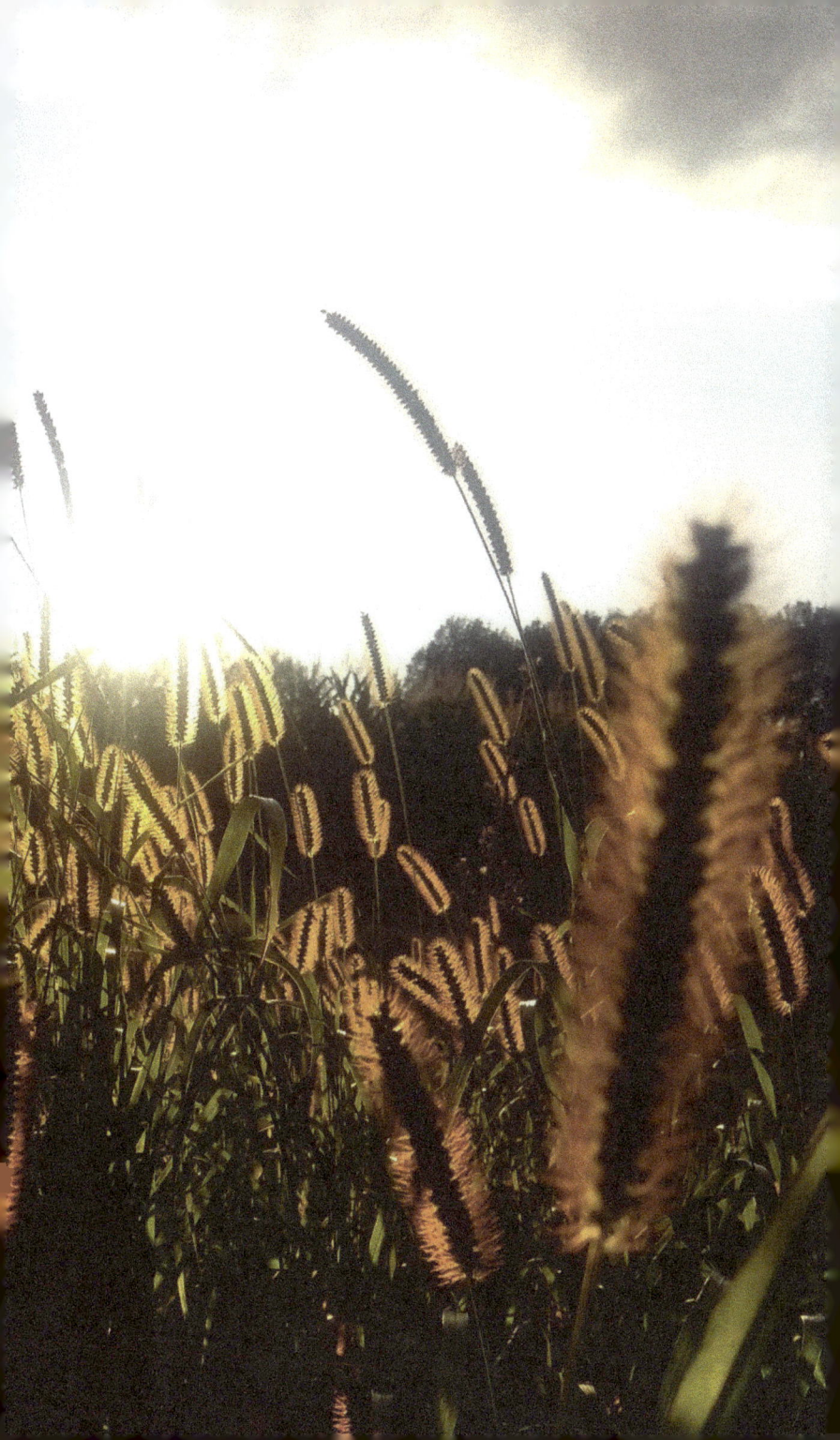

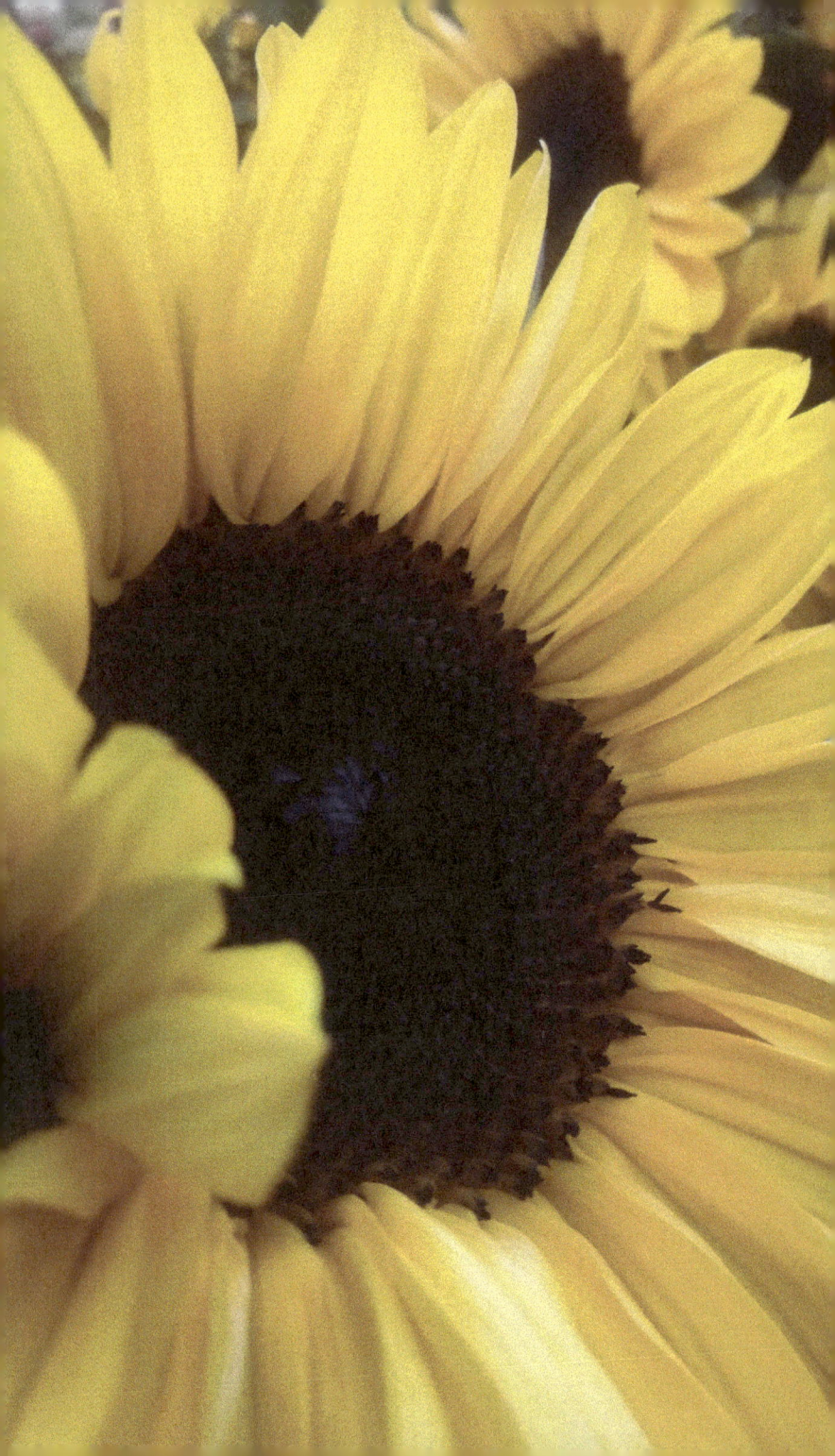

Halloween parties at small town bars

windowsills lined with nature collections

Christmas cards lining the archway of the living room

the first wood fire of the year

sunflower skeletons in the winter garden

kittens

mums on porch steps

cowboy boots with colorful stitching designs

mud bogs

sun dried tomatoes

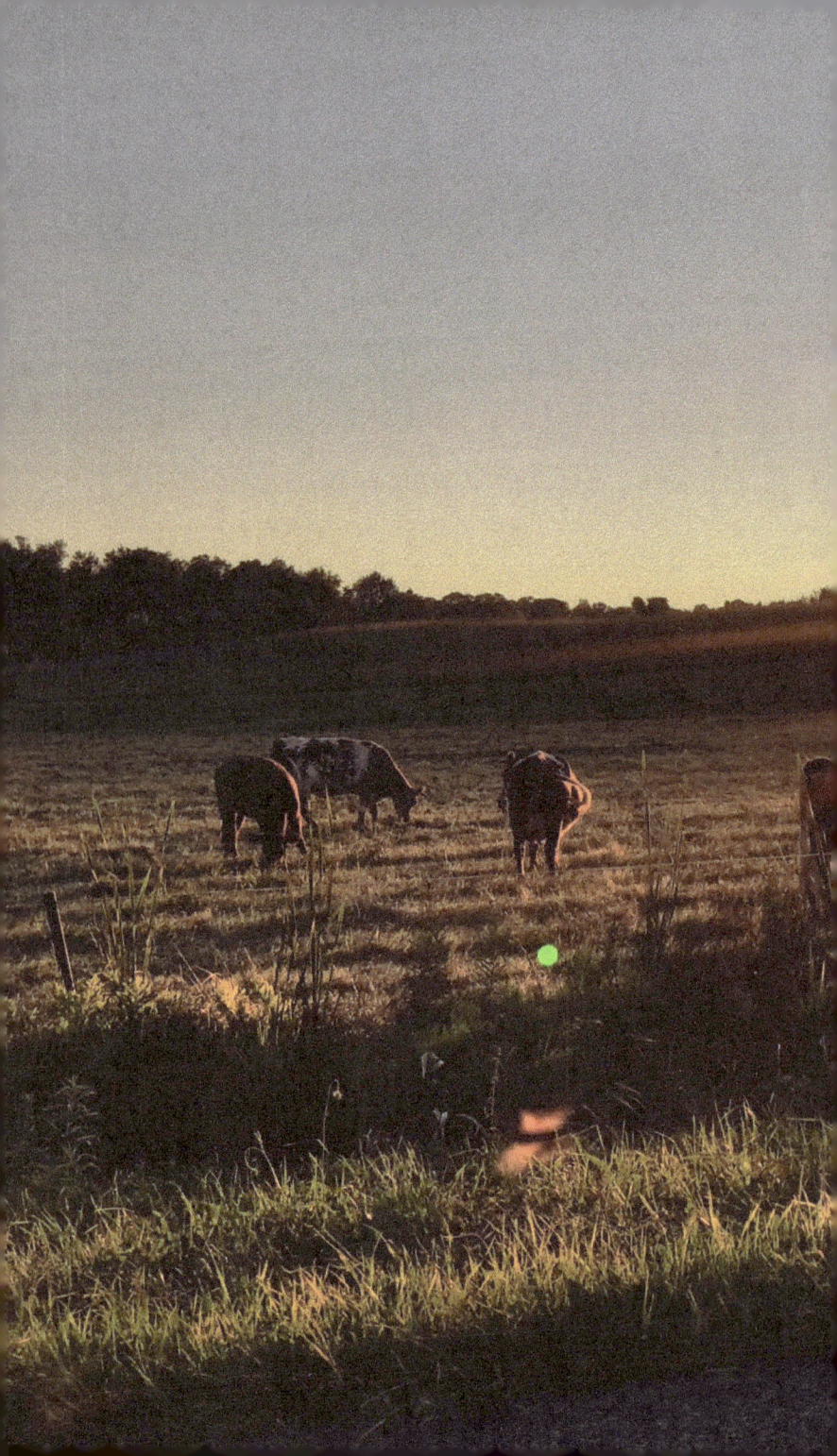

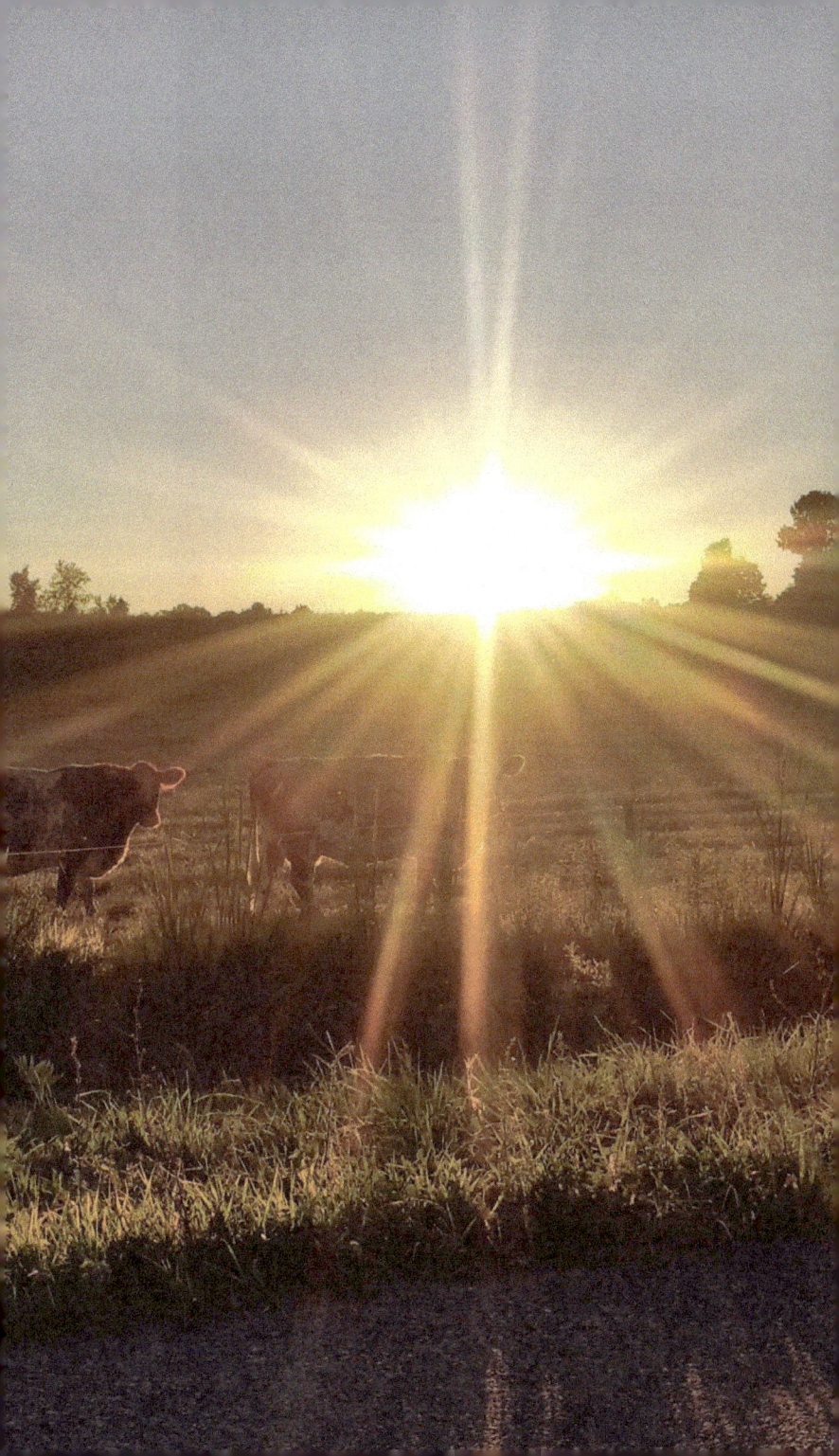

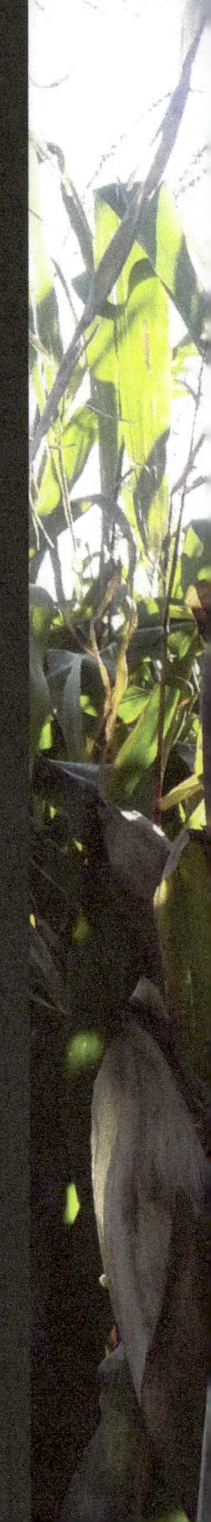

Samhain

pit bull puppies

creeks that flow to the lake

sacred spaces

glass tree ornaments of vegetables and pine cones

natural dyes

moonshine

cranberries and pine to decorate at thanksgiving

the refreshing feeling of new years day

u-pick apples

bringing seashells home from the beach

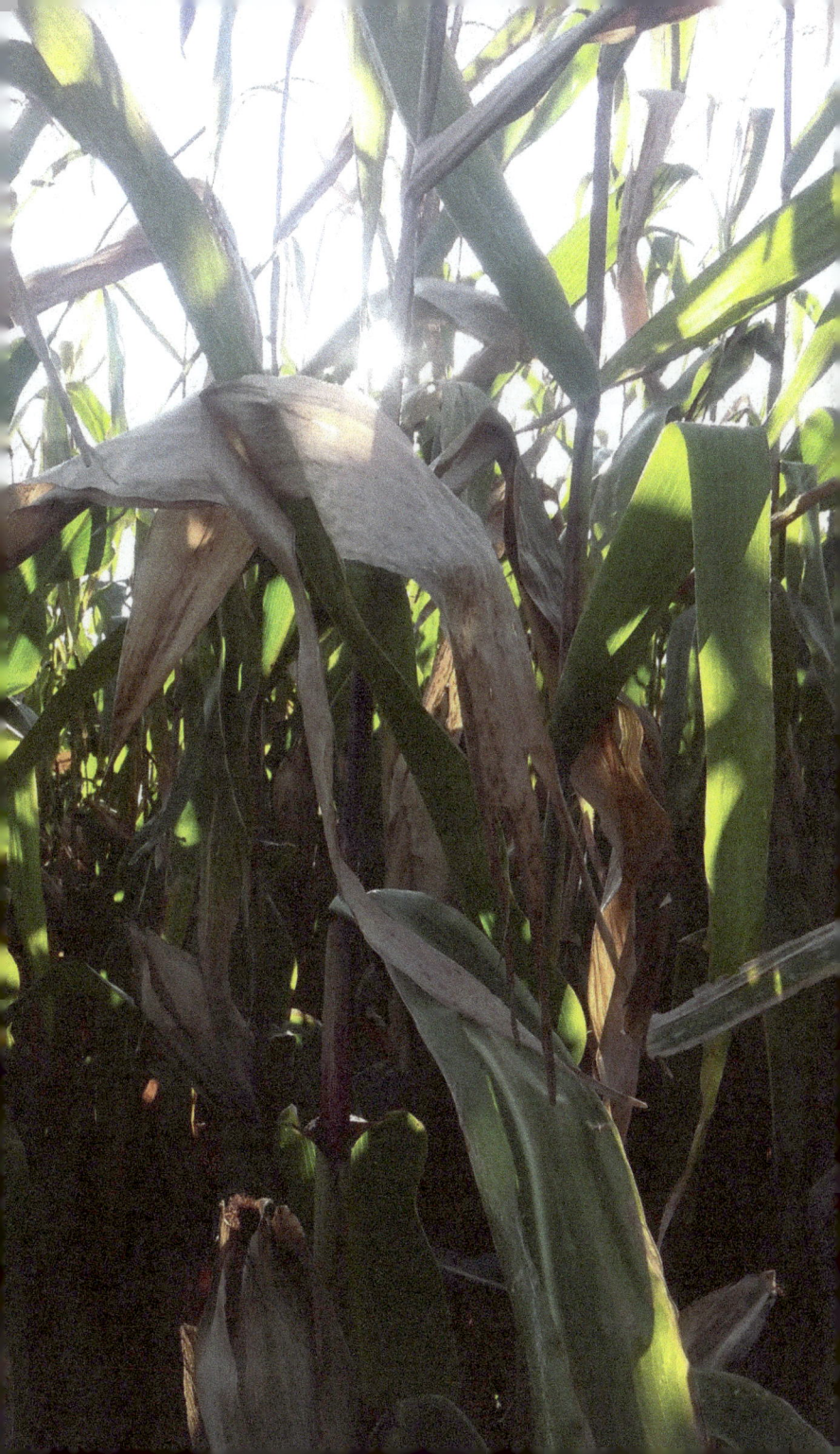

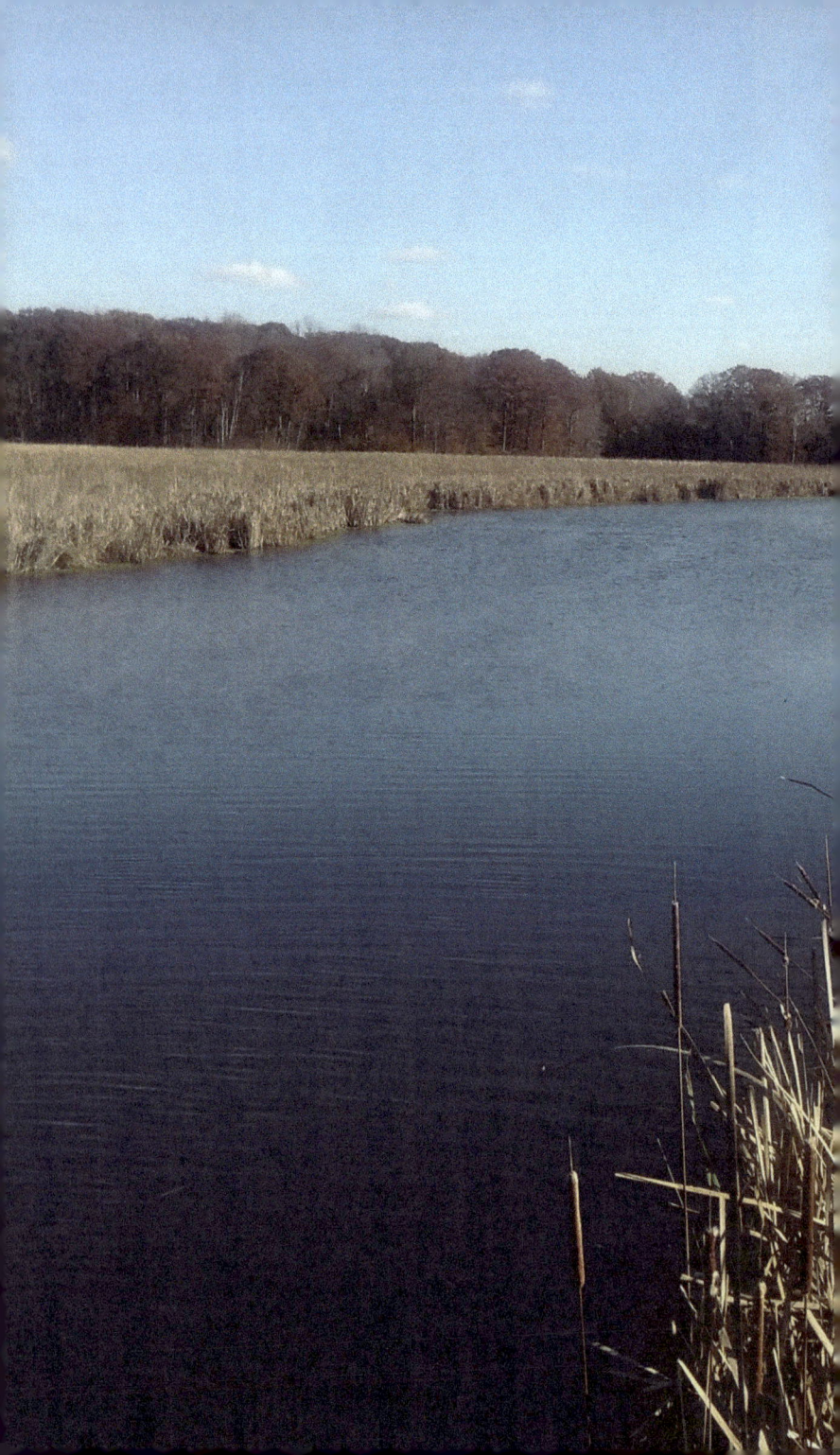

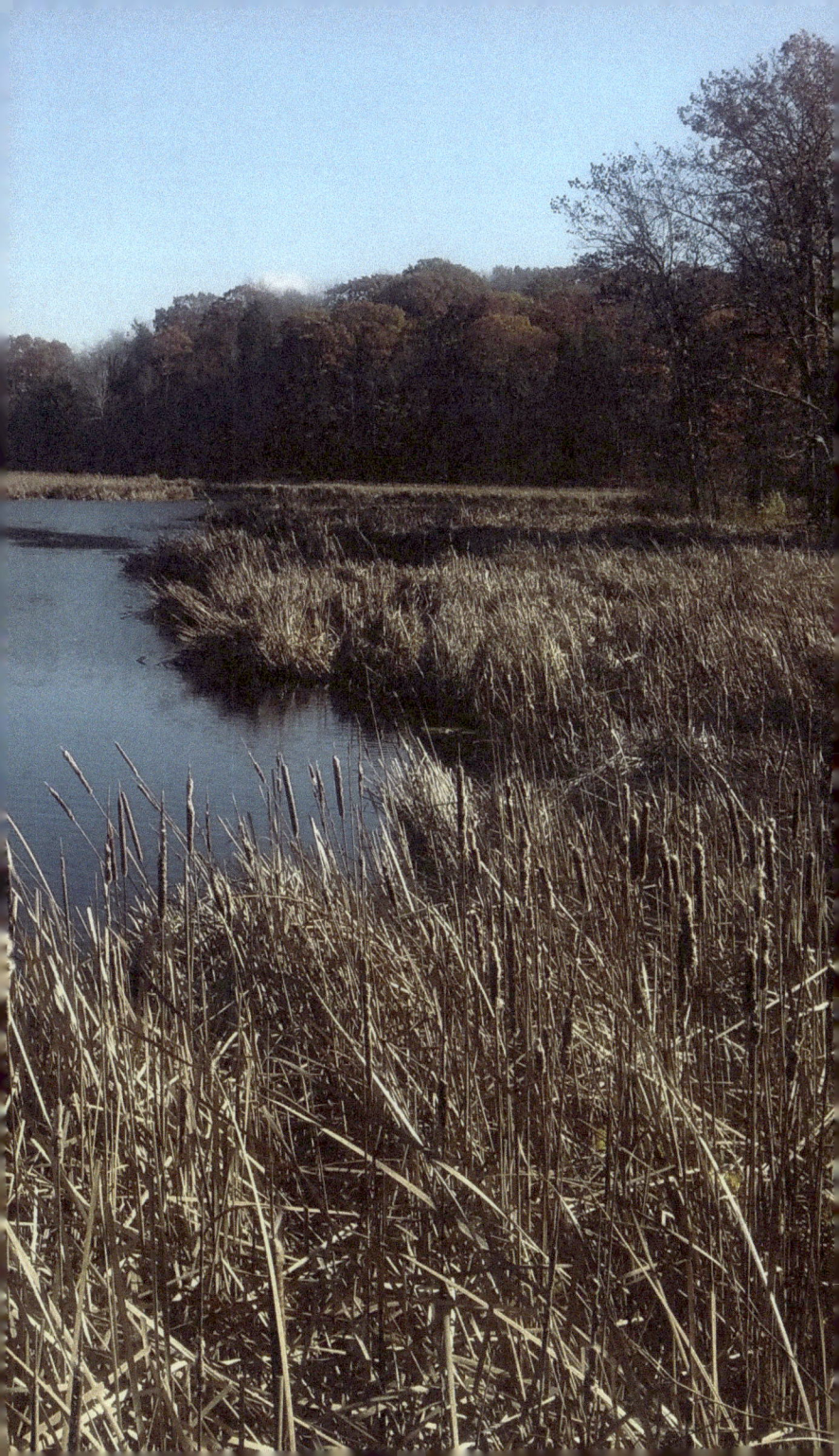

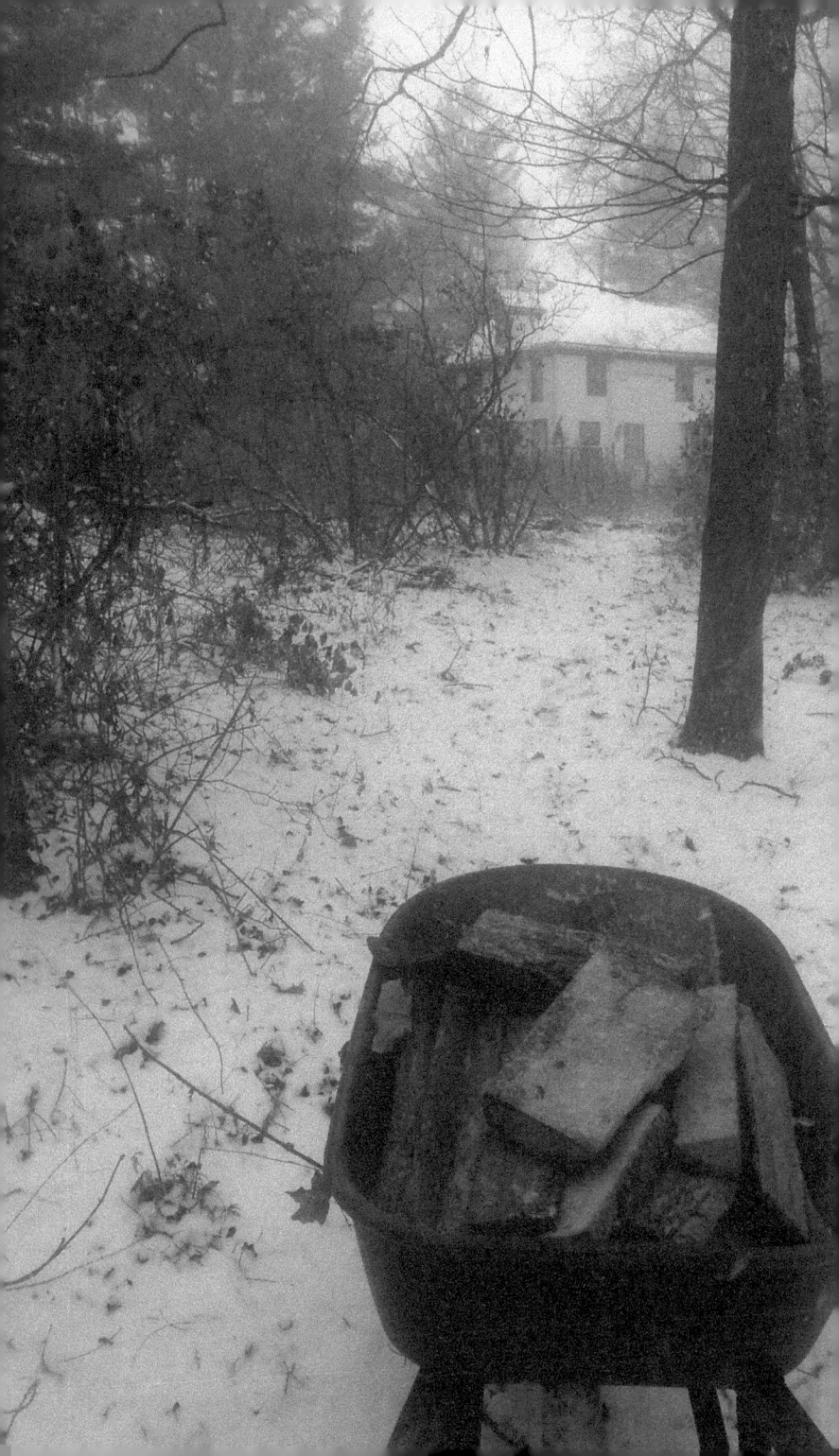

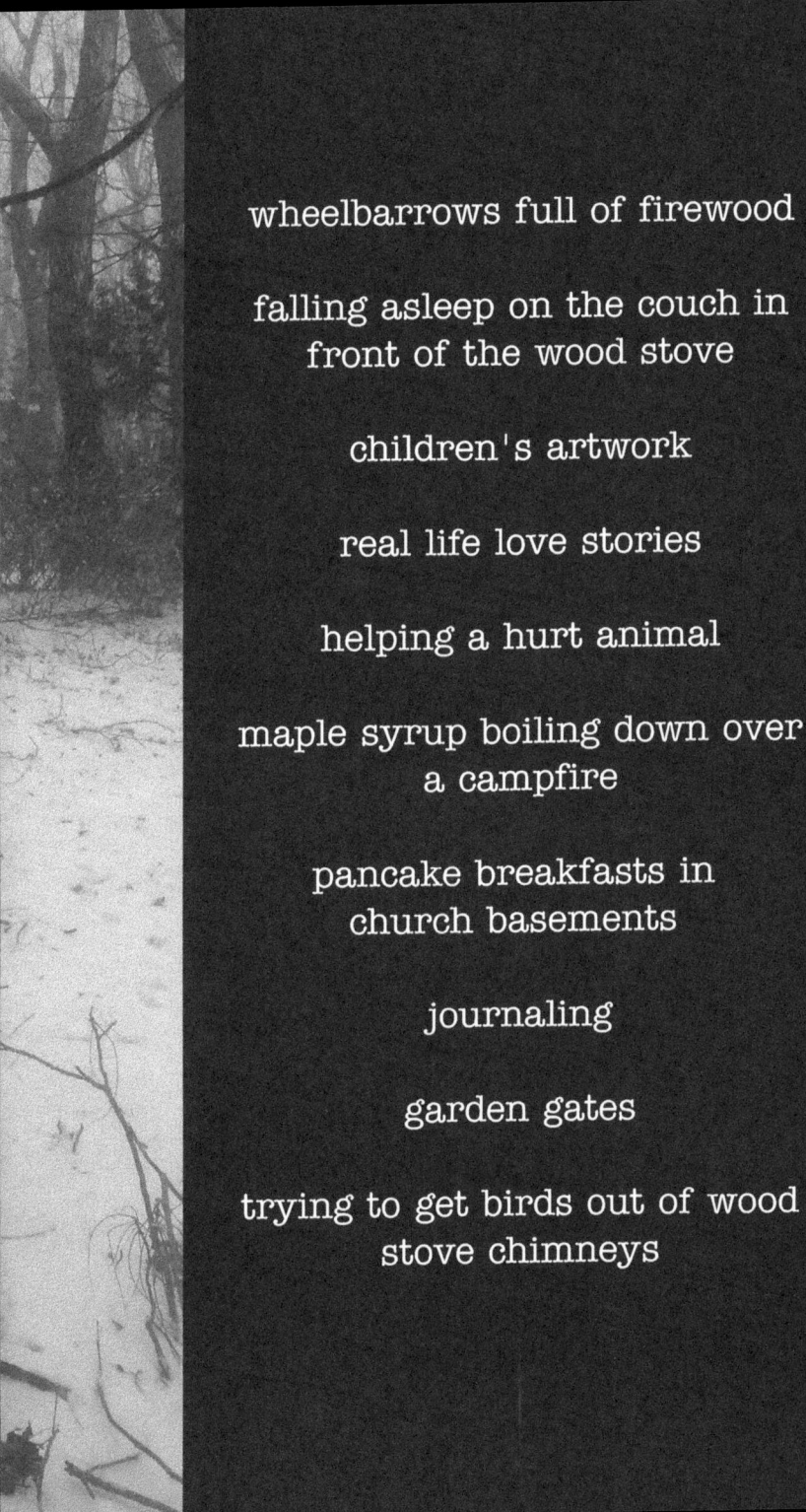

wheelbarrows full of firewood

falling asleep on the couch in front of the wood stove

children's artwork

real life love stories

helping a hurt animal

maple syrup boiling down over a campfire

pancake breakfasts in church basements

journaling

garden gates

trying to get birds out of wood stove chimneys

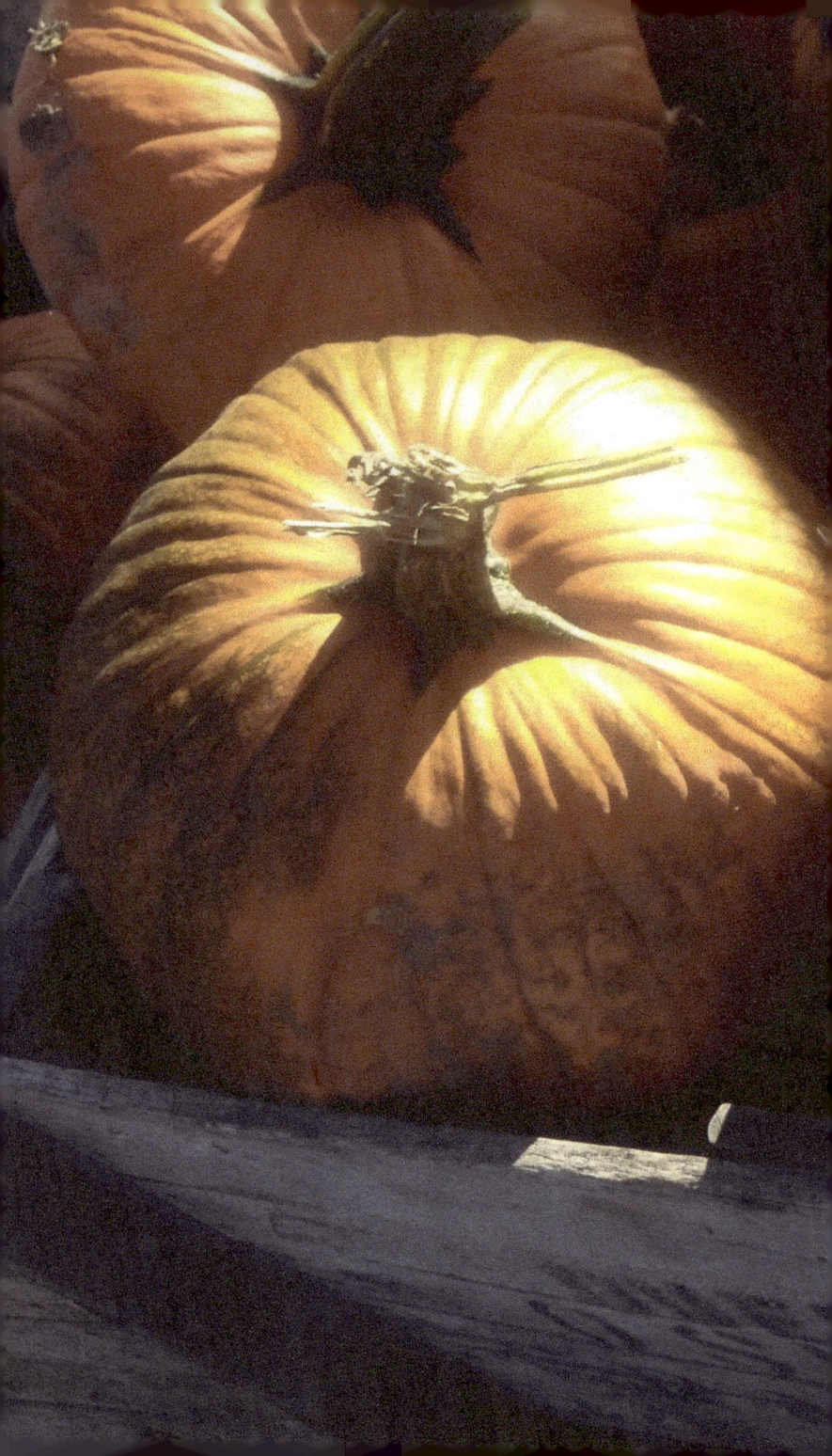

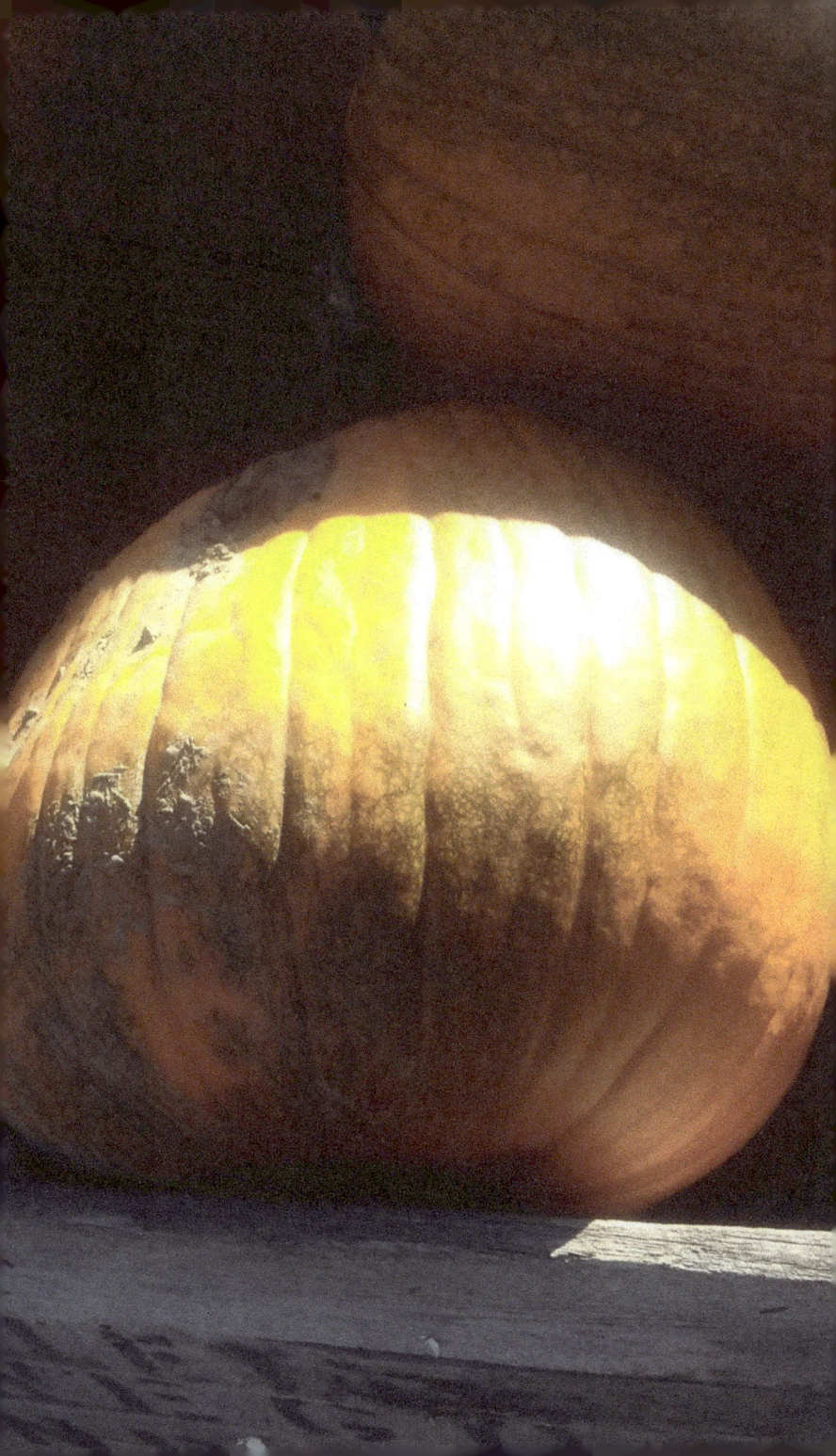

seed paper

favorite baseball hats

lavender honey

coffee flavored ice cream

carnivals

red and white striped
barber poles

middle school plays

typewriters

love letters from the 1940's

candy cane Christmas
countdown calendars

handmade valentines
with glitter

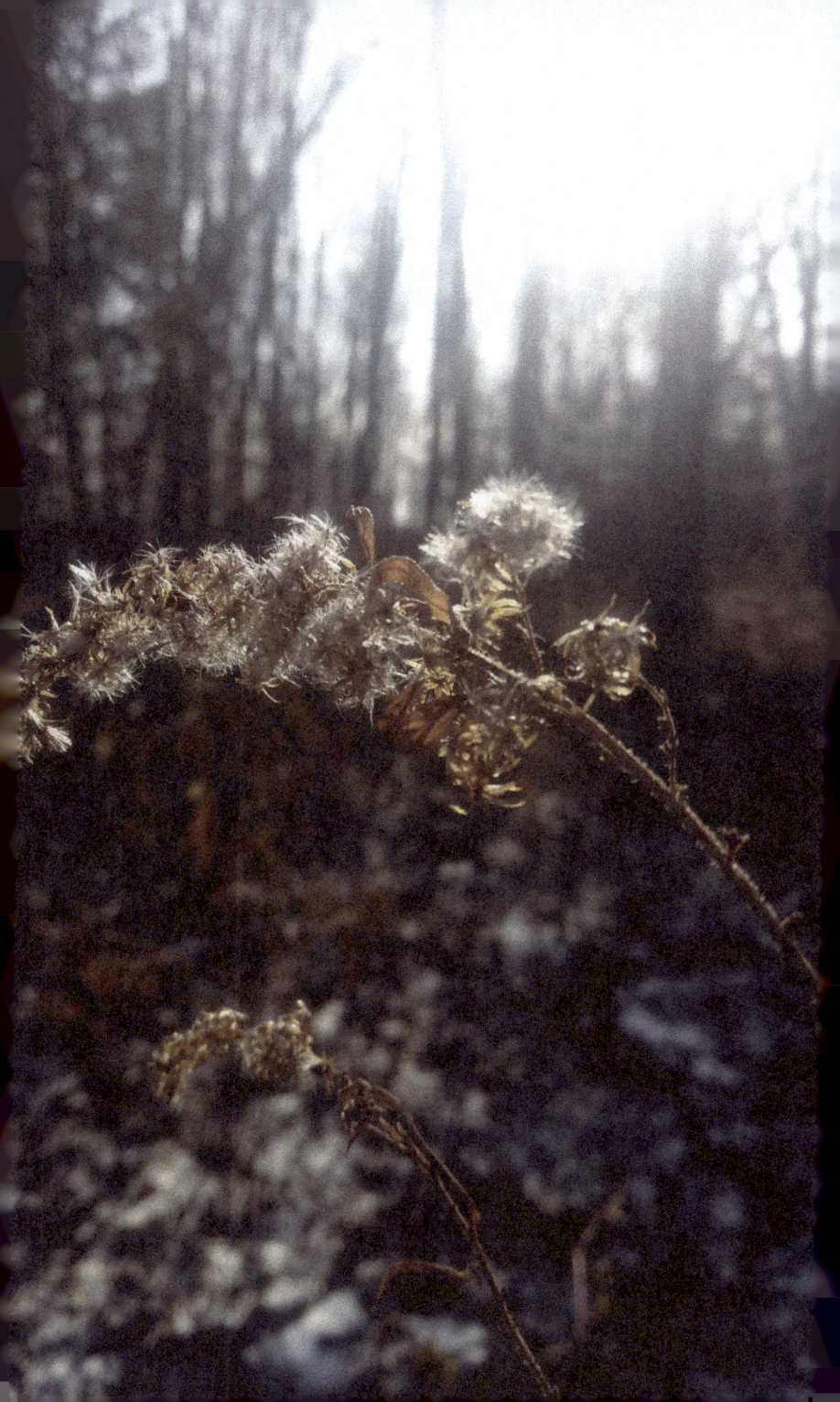

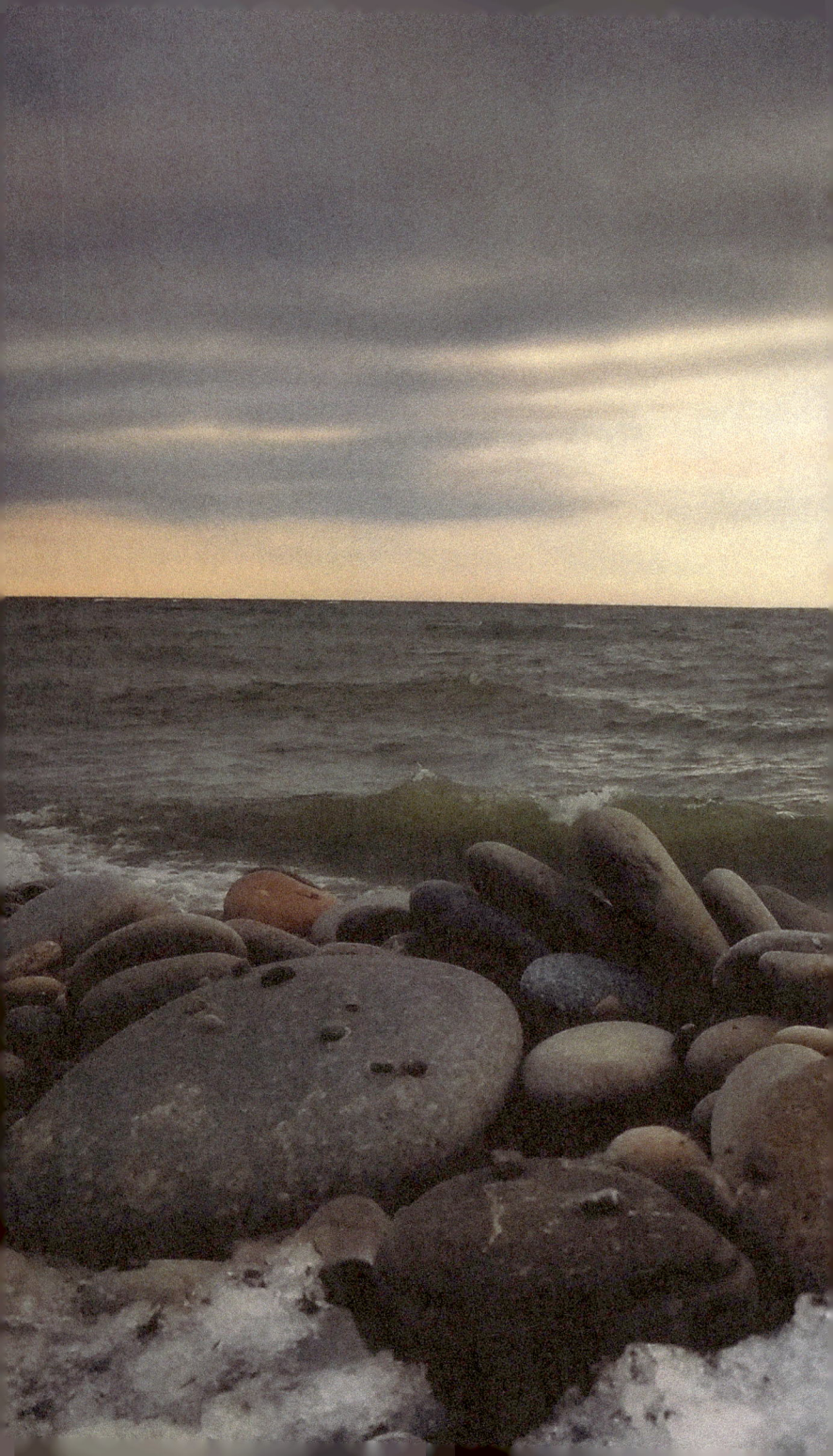

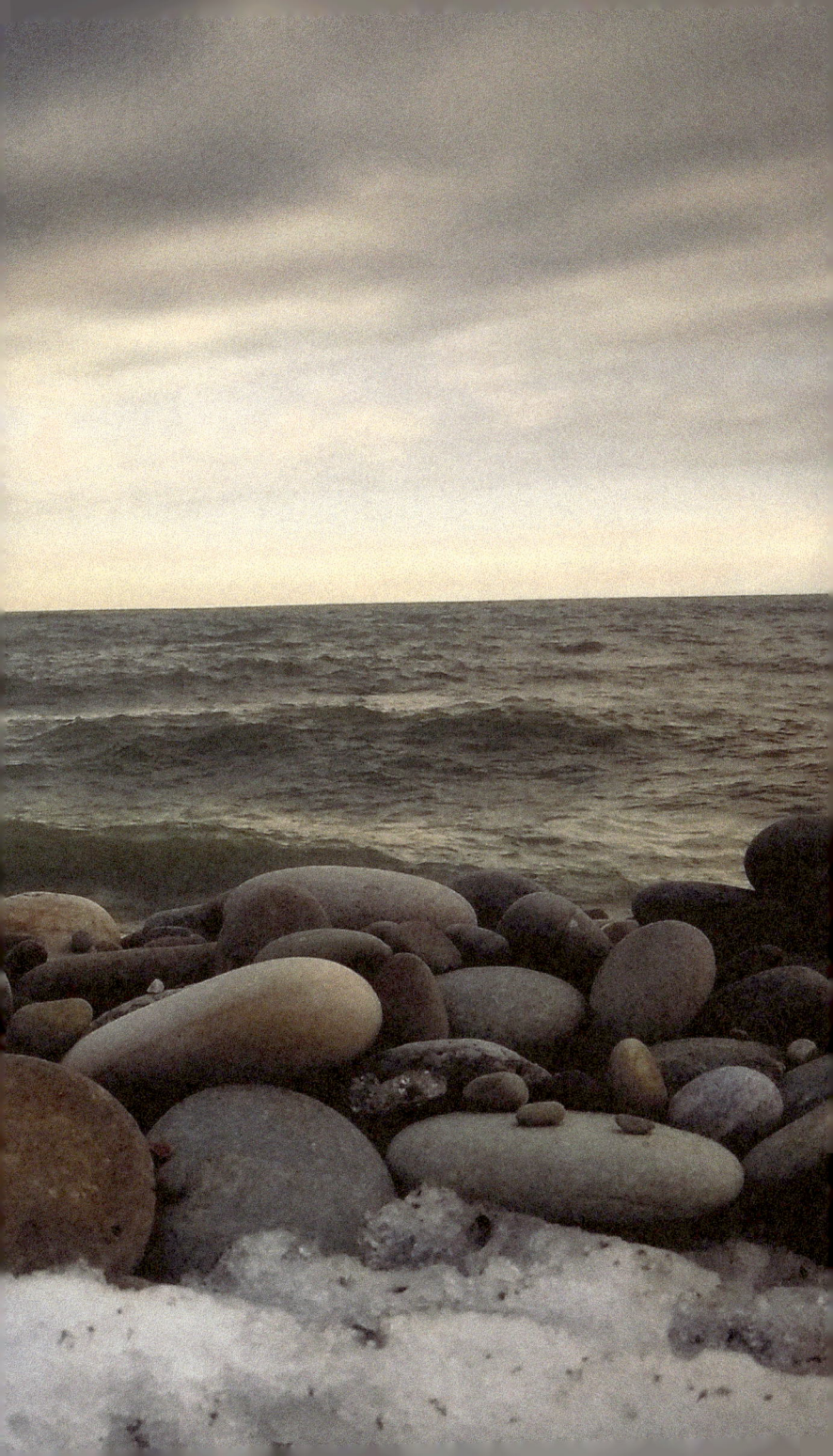

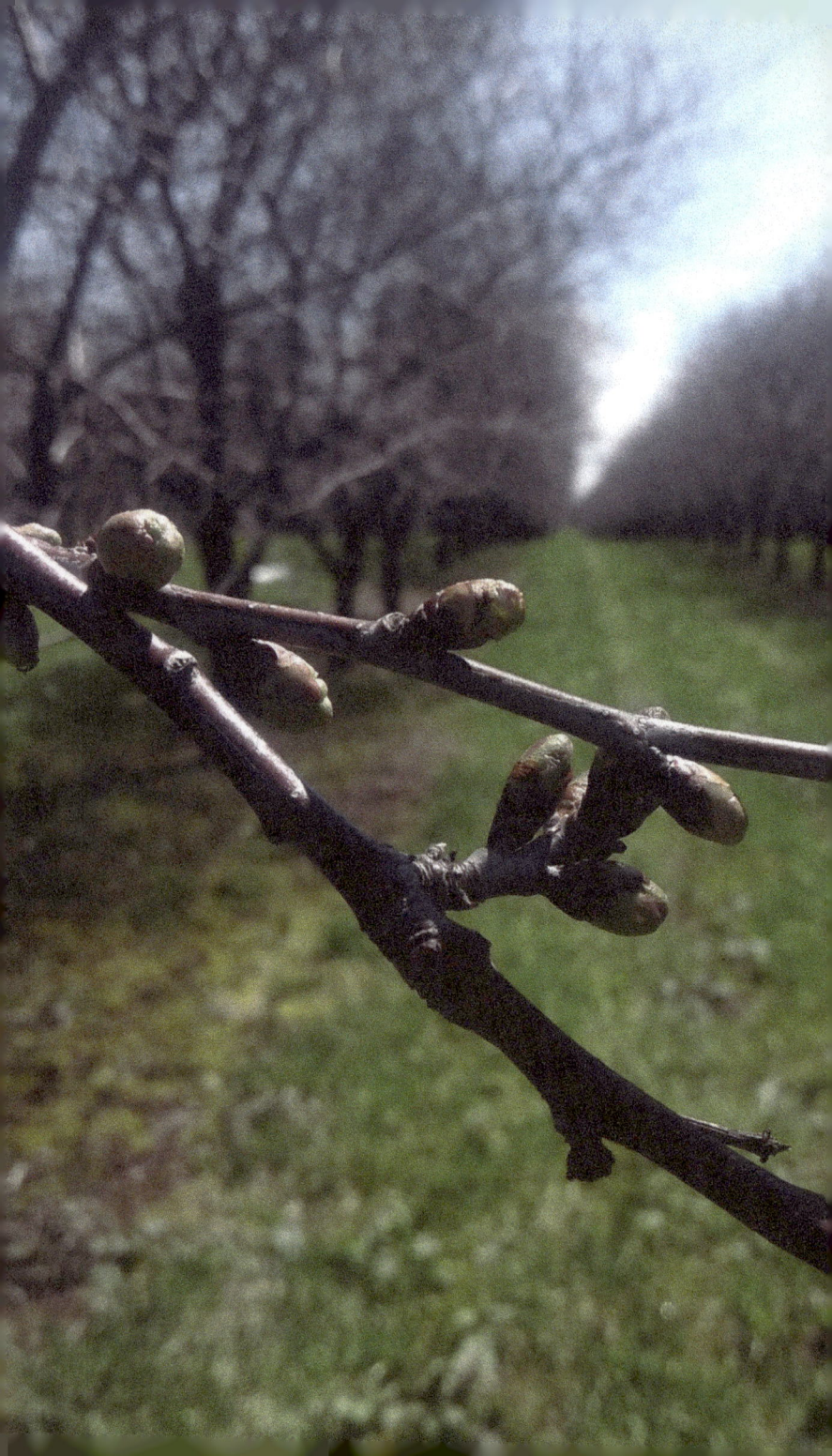

blue jay feathers

wild turkey gobbles from the woods

the color superstition purple

dogs stretching when they get out of bed

postage stamps

jeans with hand sewn patches

artist aprons covered in paint

wooden barns full of old time treasures

stories passed down from generation to generation

wood cut printmaking

rock candy

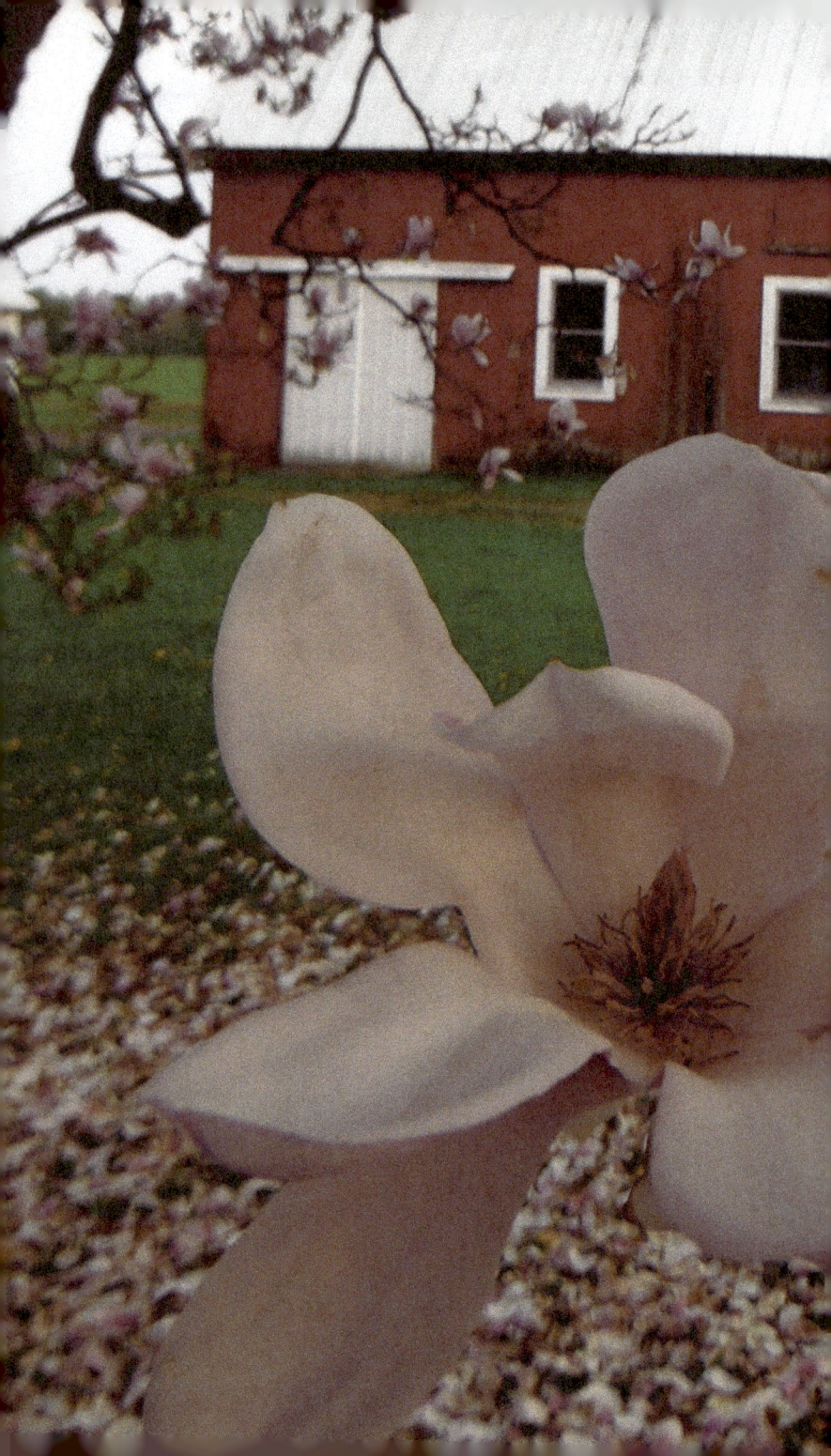

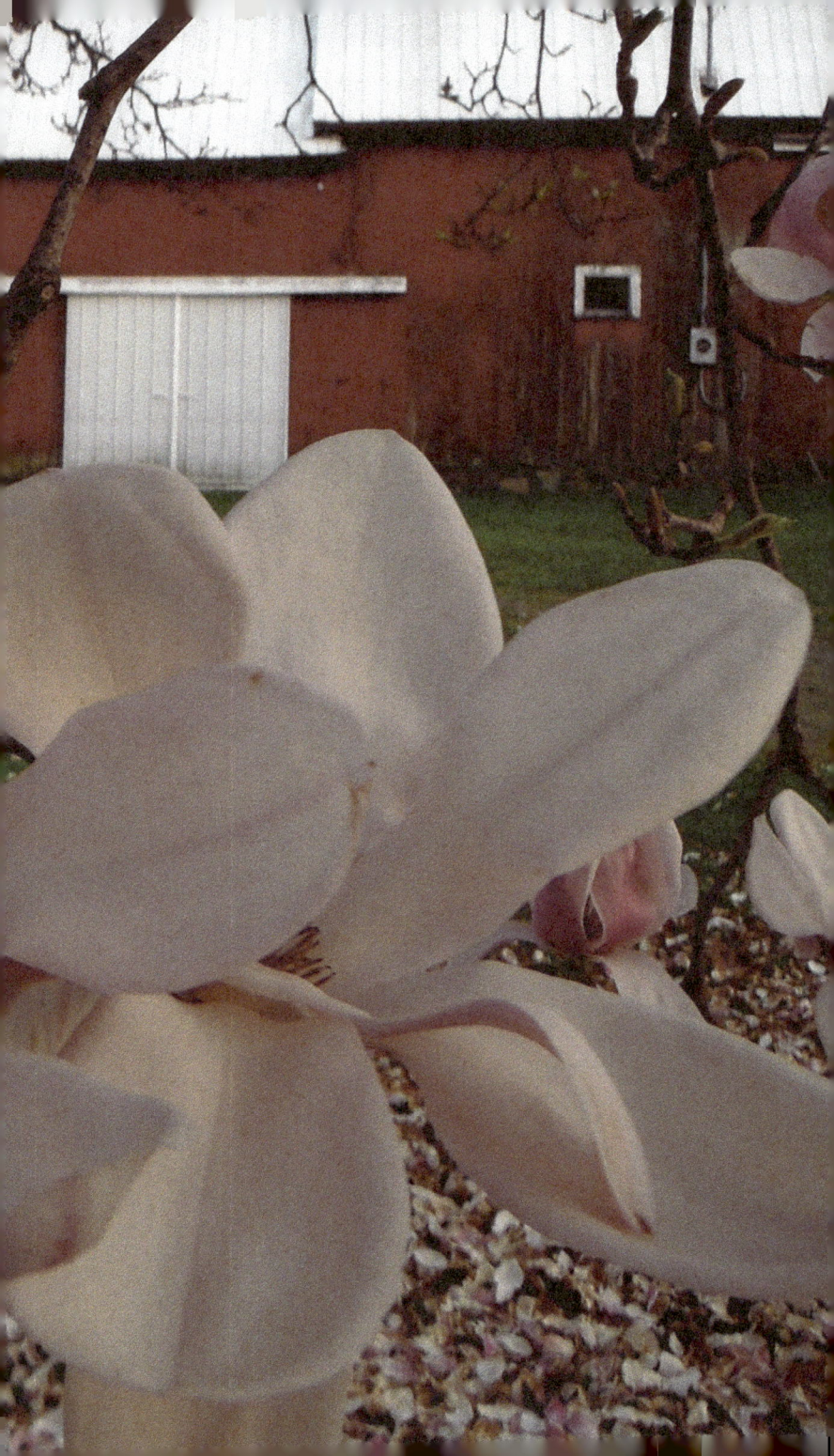

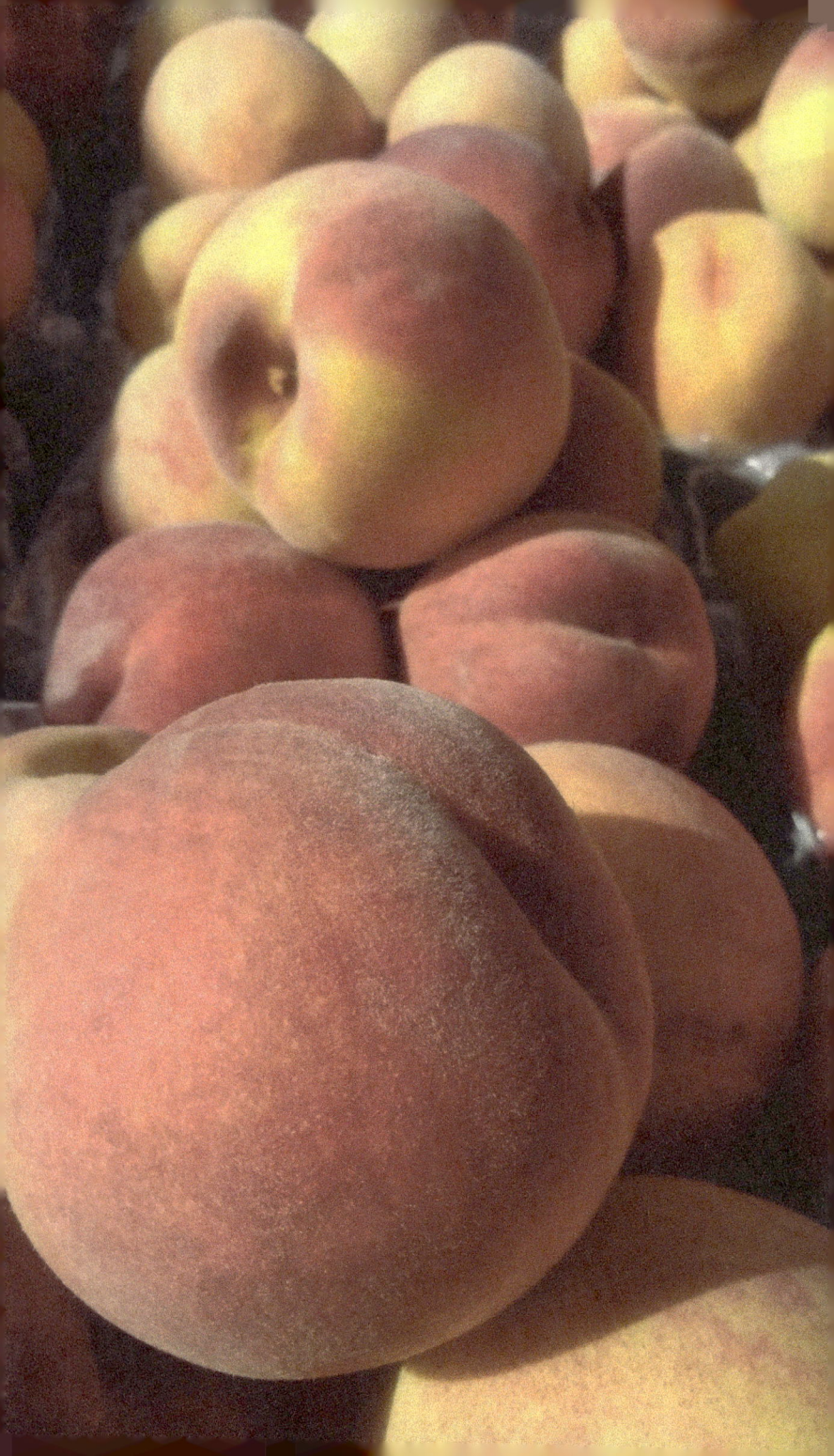

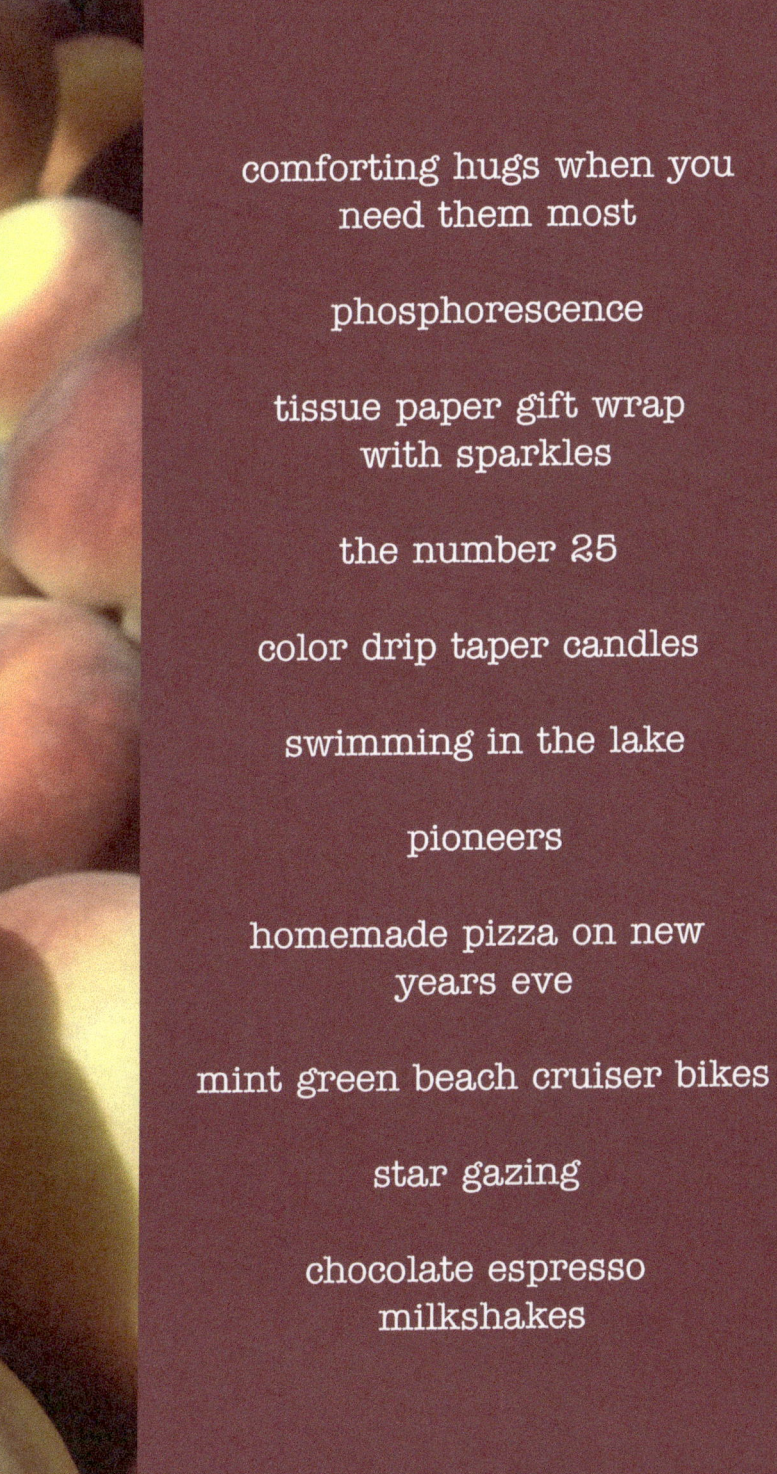

comforting hugs when you
need them most

phosphorescence

tissue paper gift wrap
with sparkles

the number 25

color drip taper candles

swimming in the lake

pioneers

homemade pizza on new
years eve

mint green beach cruiser bikes

star gazing

chocolate espresso
milkshakes

horseshoes for luck in
cement sidewalks or hung
above front doors

homemade tie die t-shirts

the smell of vanilla milk
replacer at a dairy farm

UV changing plastic
pony beads

silver glitter glue

magazine collections

fringe

leather purses with
tooled western designs

making new traditions

framed collages for
inspiration

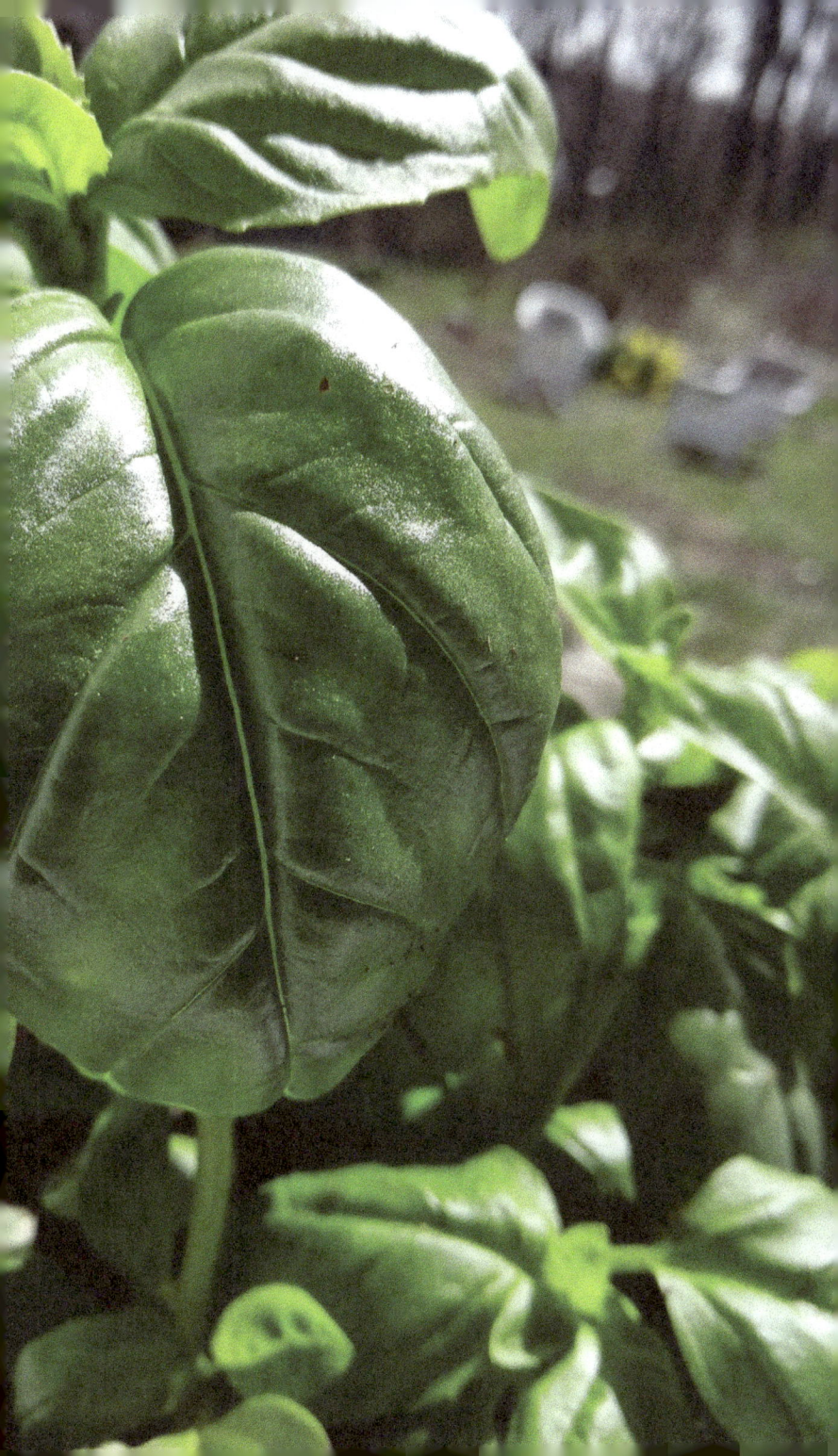

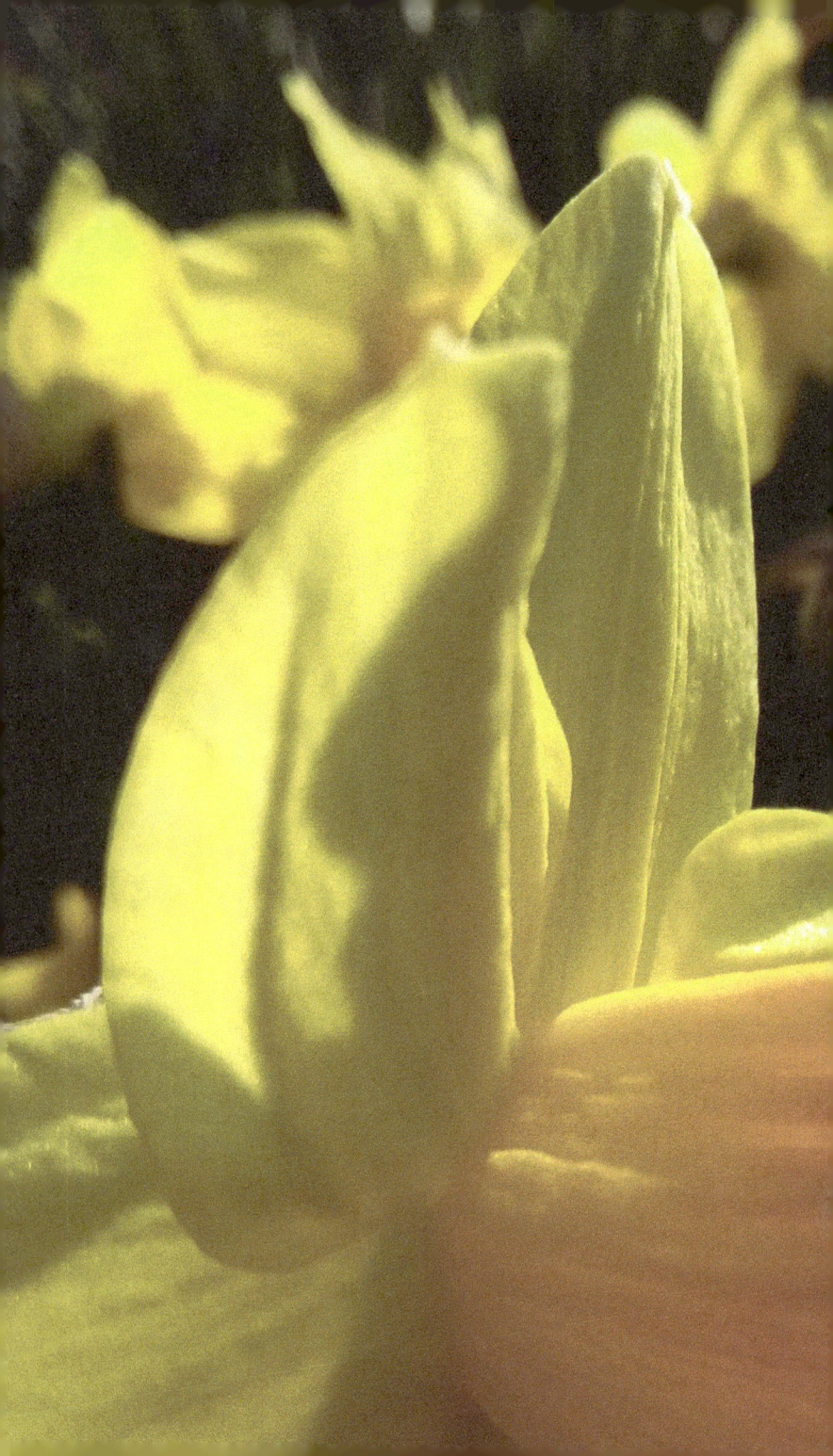

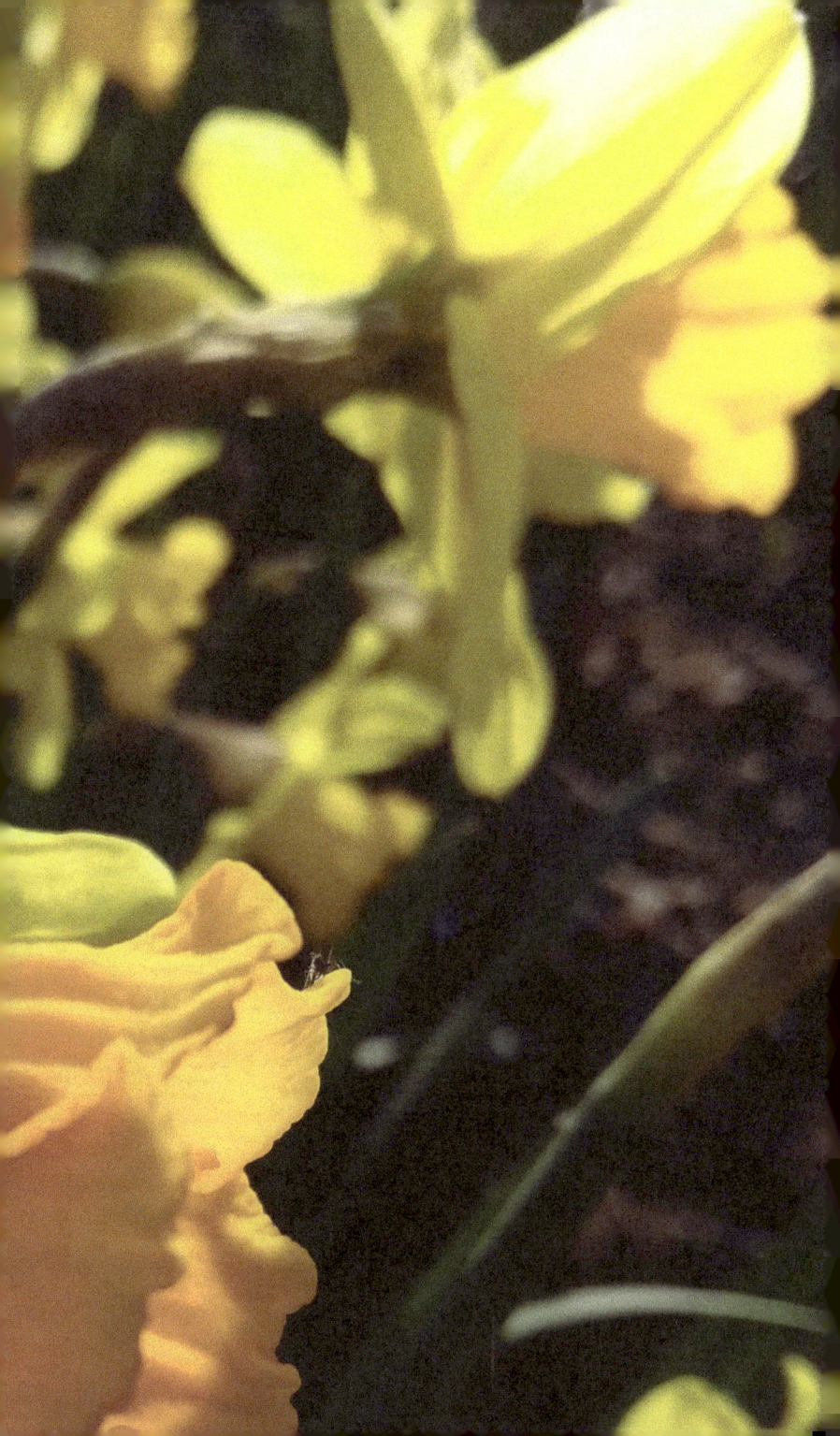

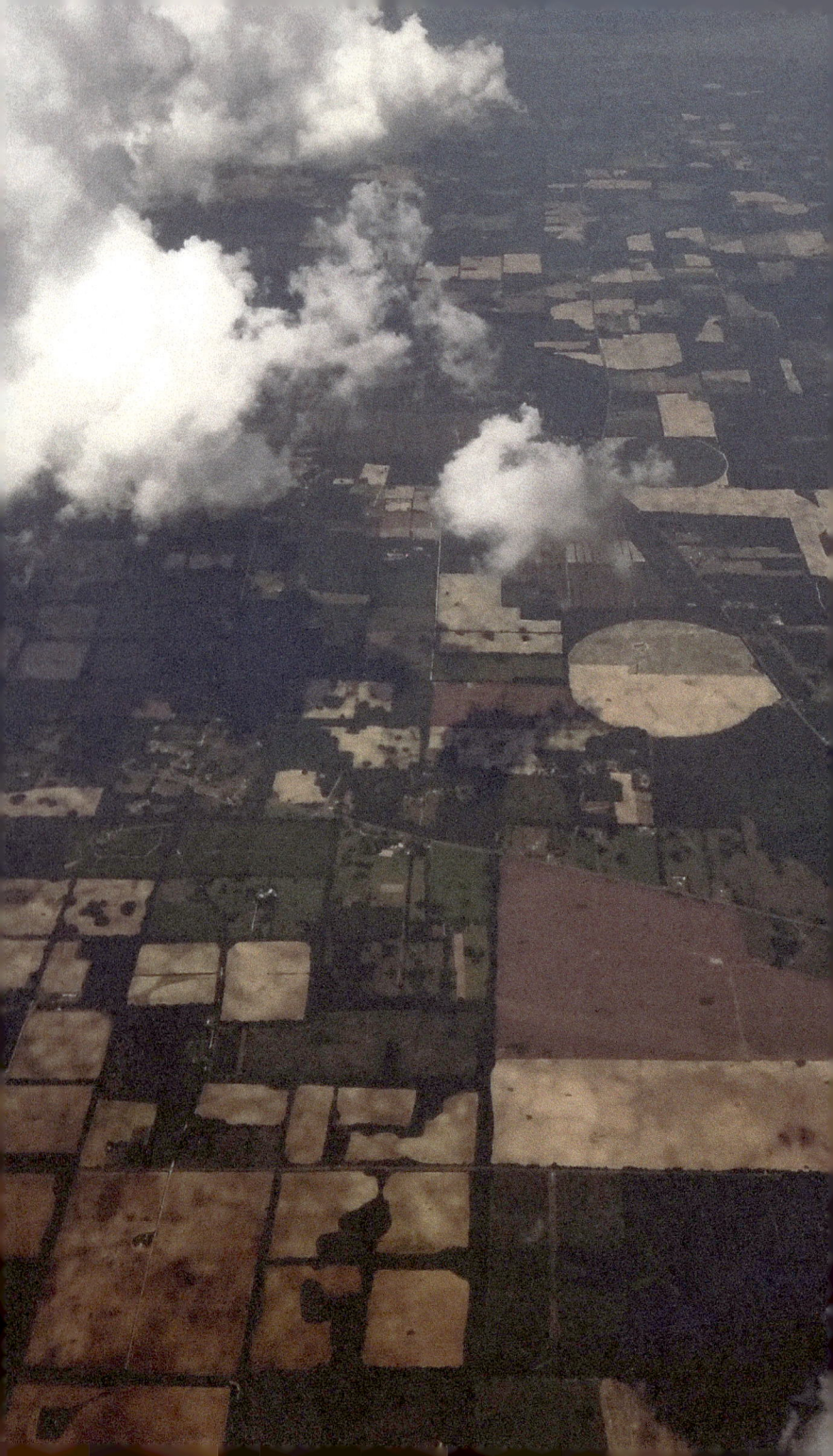

driving mountain roads
in the fall

heat lightning

sledding down hill

rock cairns

meteor showers

mountain ski lift rides to see
the changing leaves

small town granges

college roommates turning
into best friends

family farms

chocolate chip cookie
sandwiches with espresso
frosting in the middle

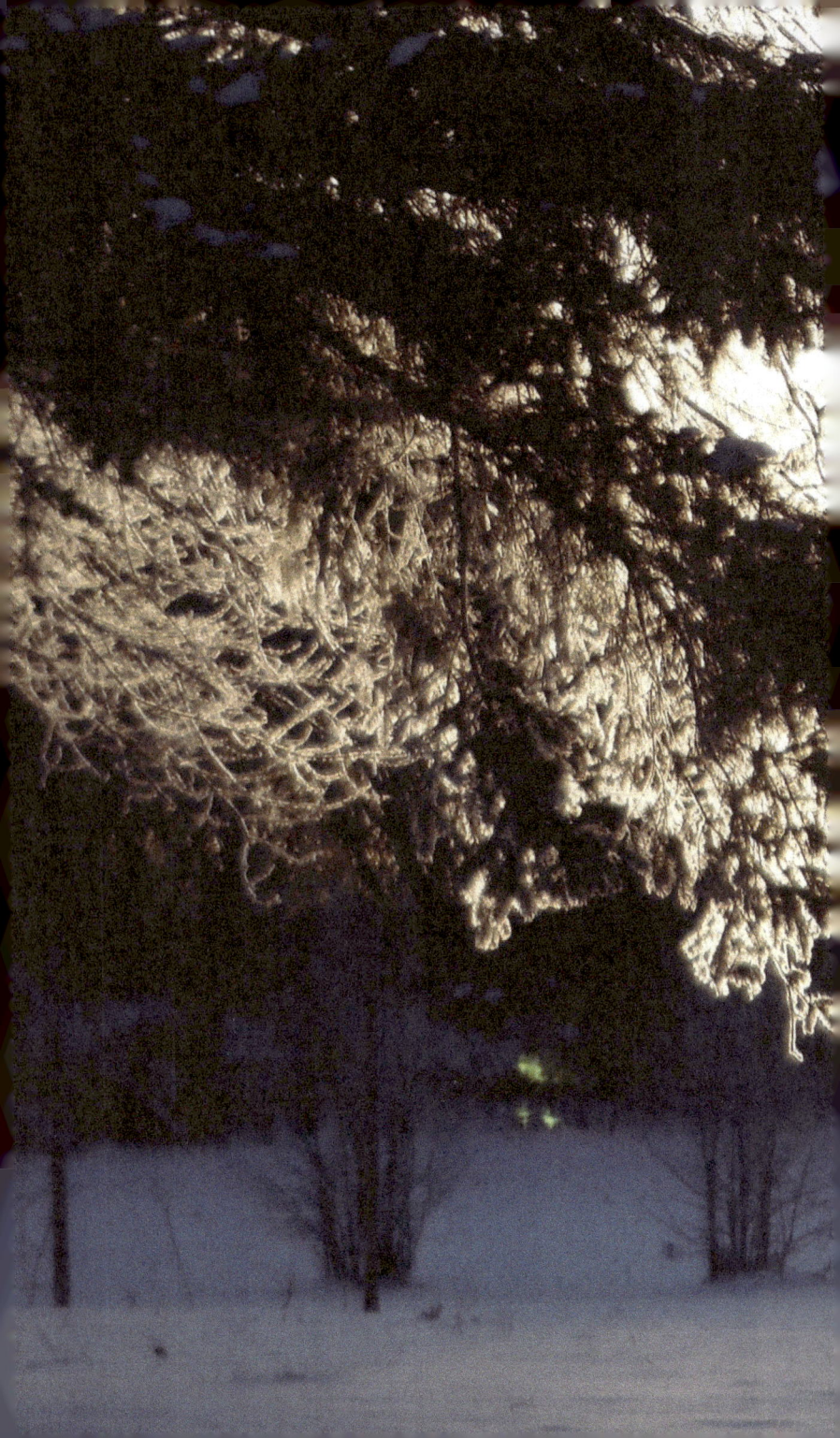

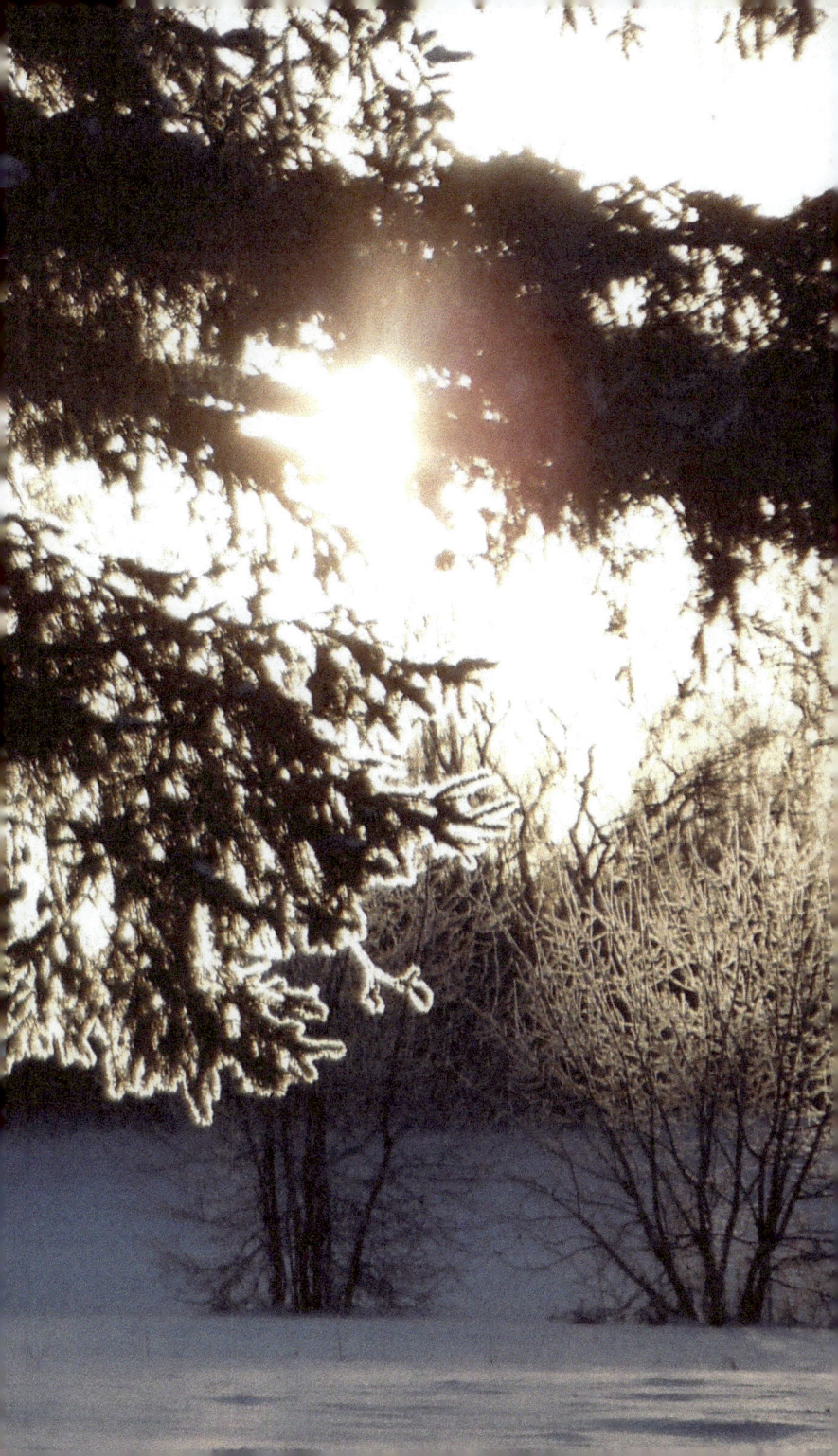

blackberries with milk
and sugar

yule

jersey cows

black and white photo
booth strips

cold iced tea with lemon

garden scarecrows in
old faded overalls

carving pumpkins

peppermint oil

love notes left on post its

sweatpants tucked into wool
socks, ready for winter boots

chimneys with thick wooden
hearths

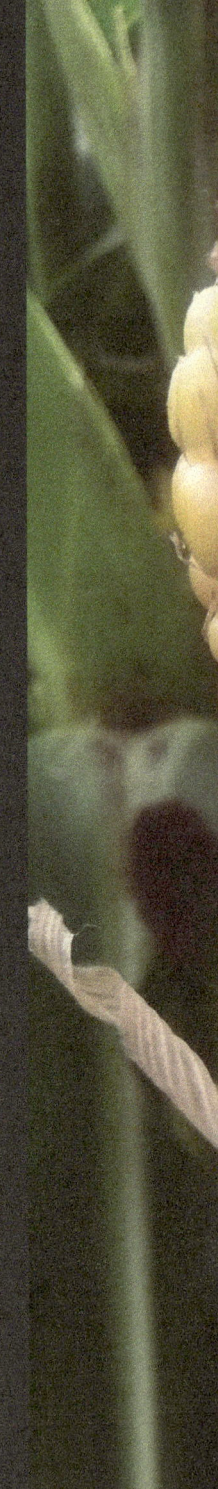

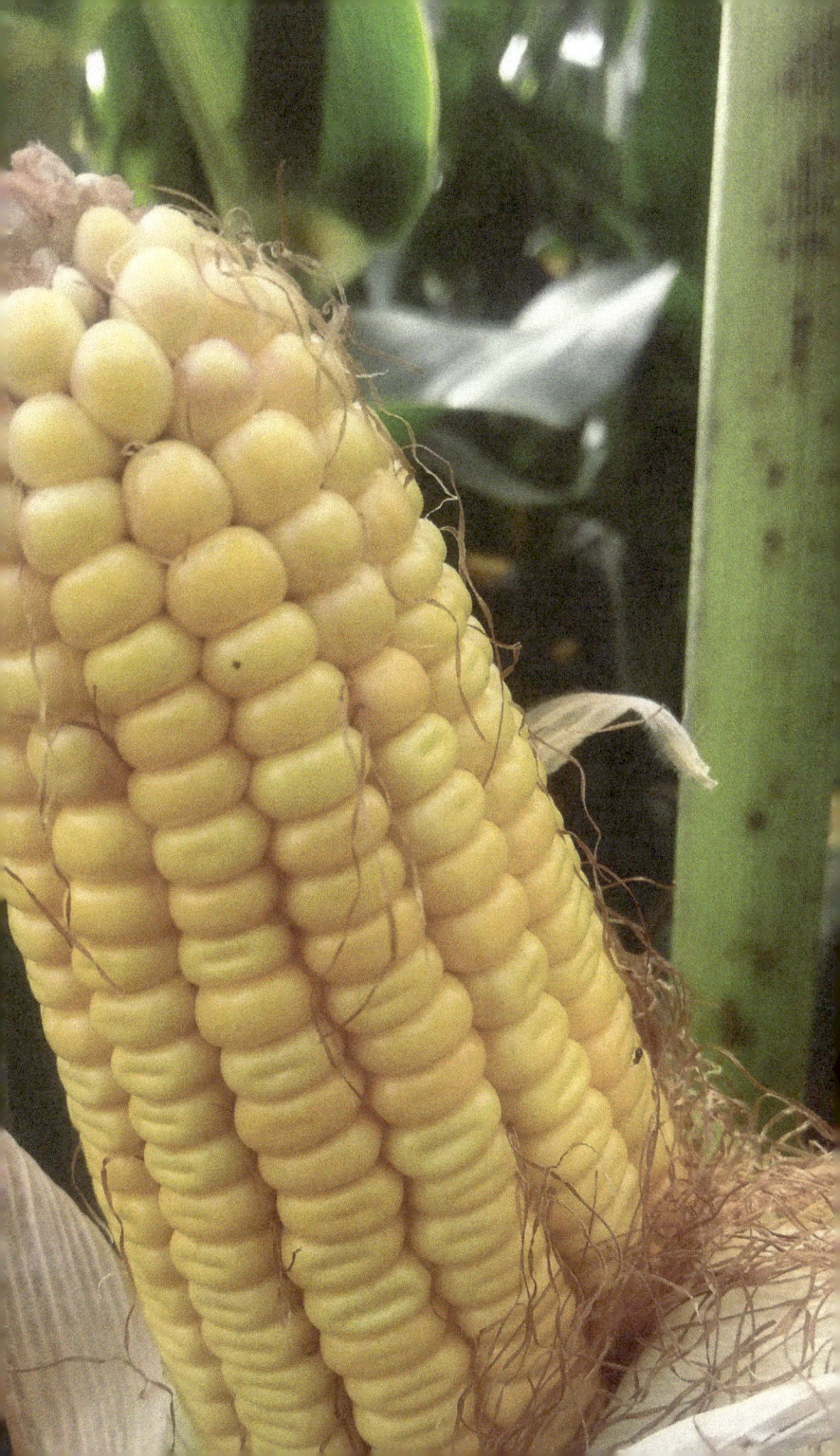

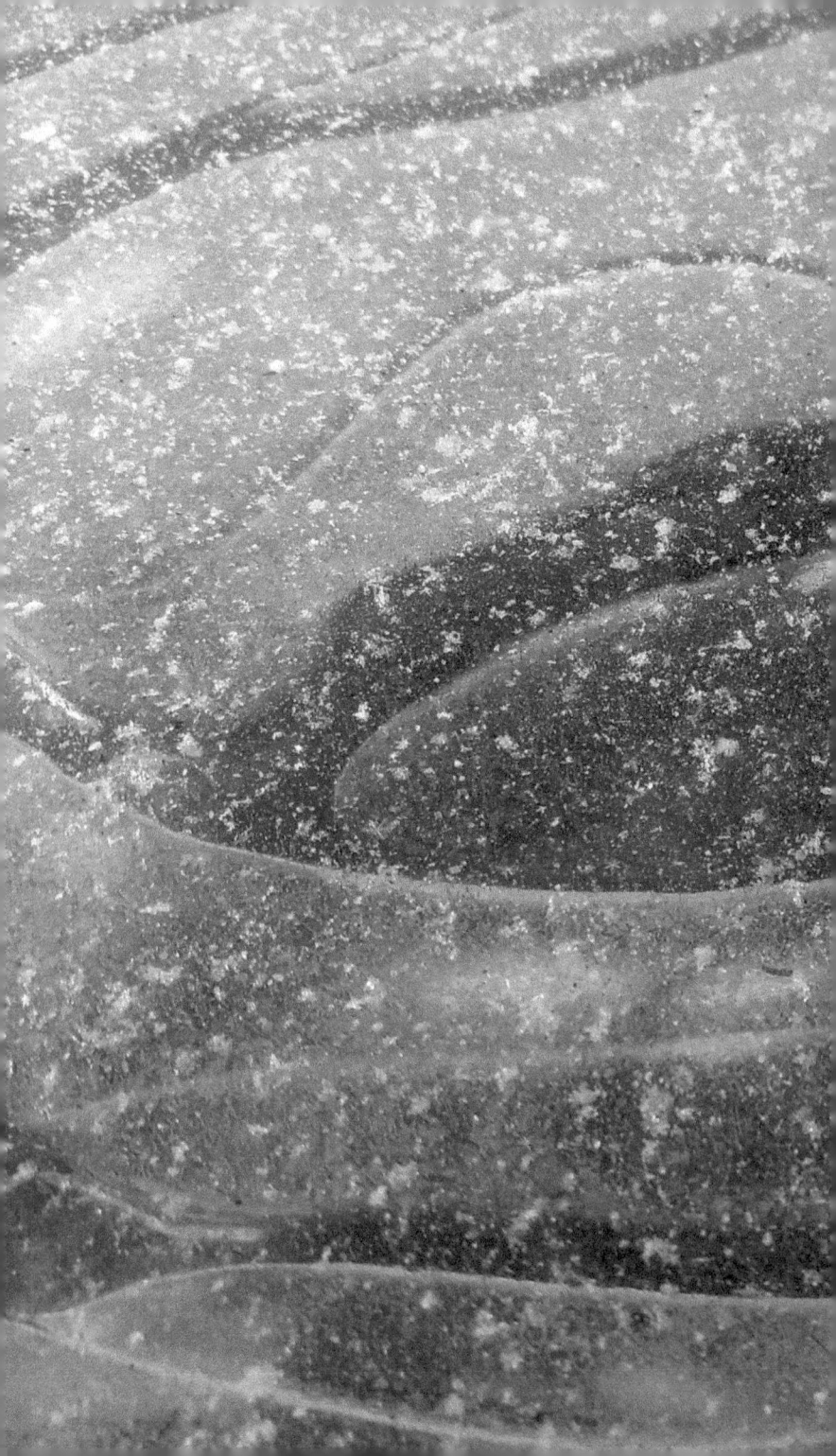

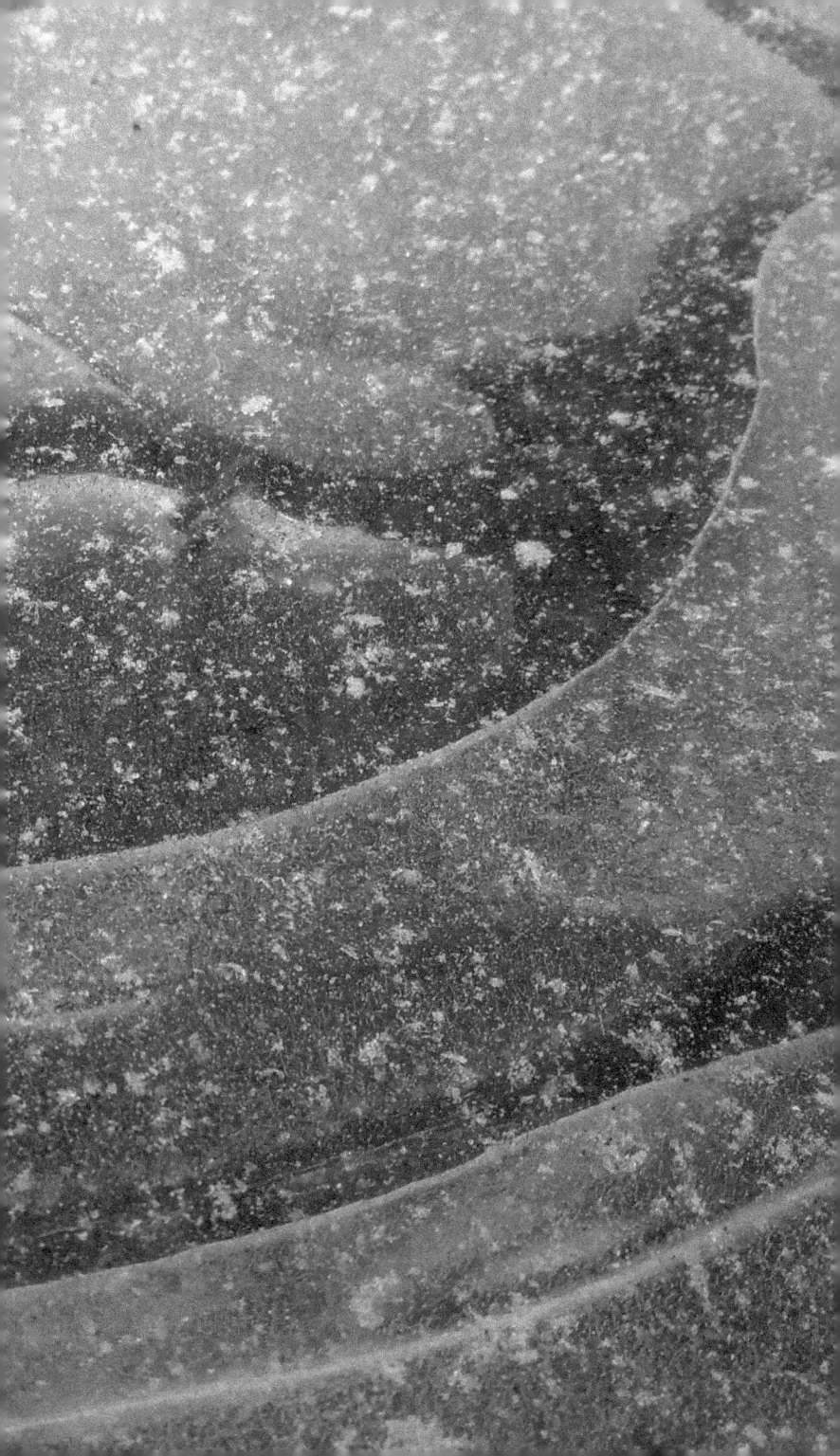

vintage sewing machines

crows feet wrinkles
from the sun

boxes of free books at the
library

dill pickles

old faded recipes in different
languages passed down from
great grandparents

folding the flag

junk drawers full of
odds and ends

farmhouse kitchens

old wood cook stoves

red bandannas worn as
headbands

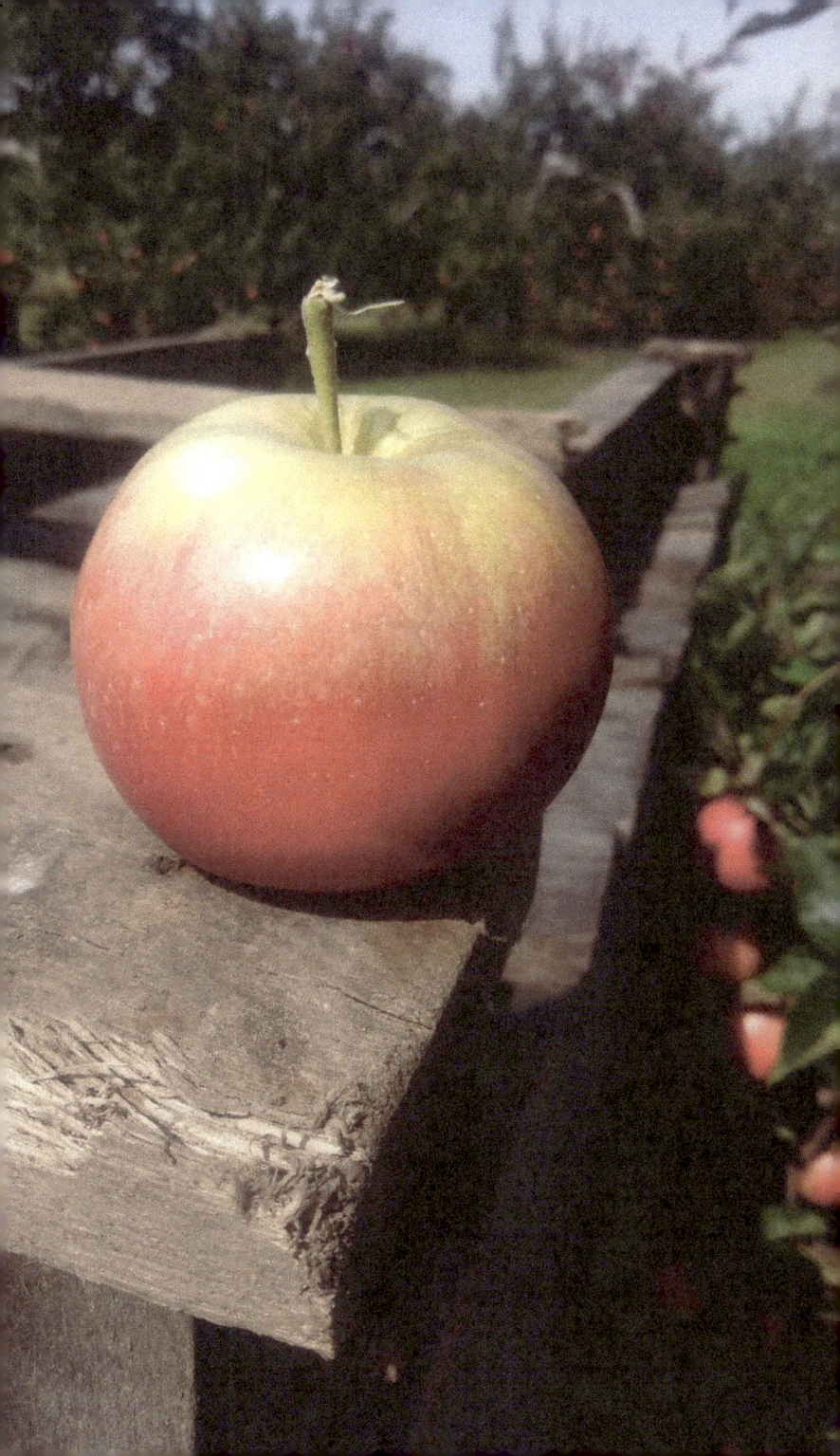

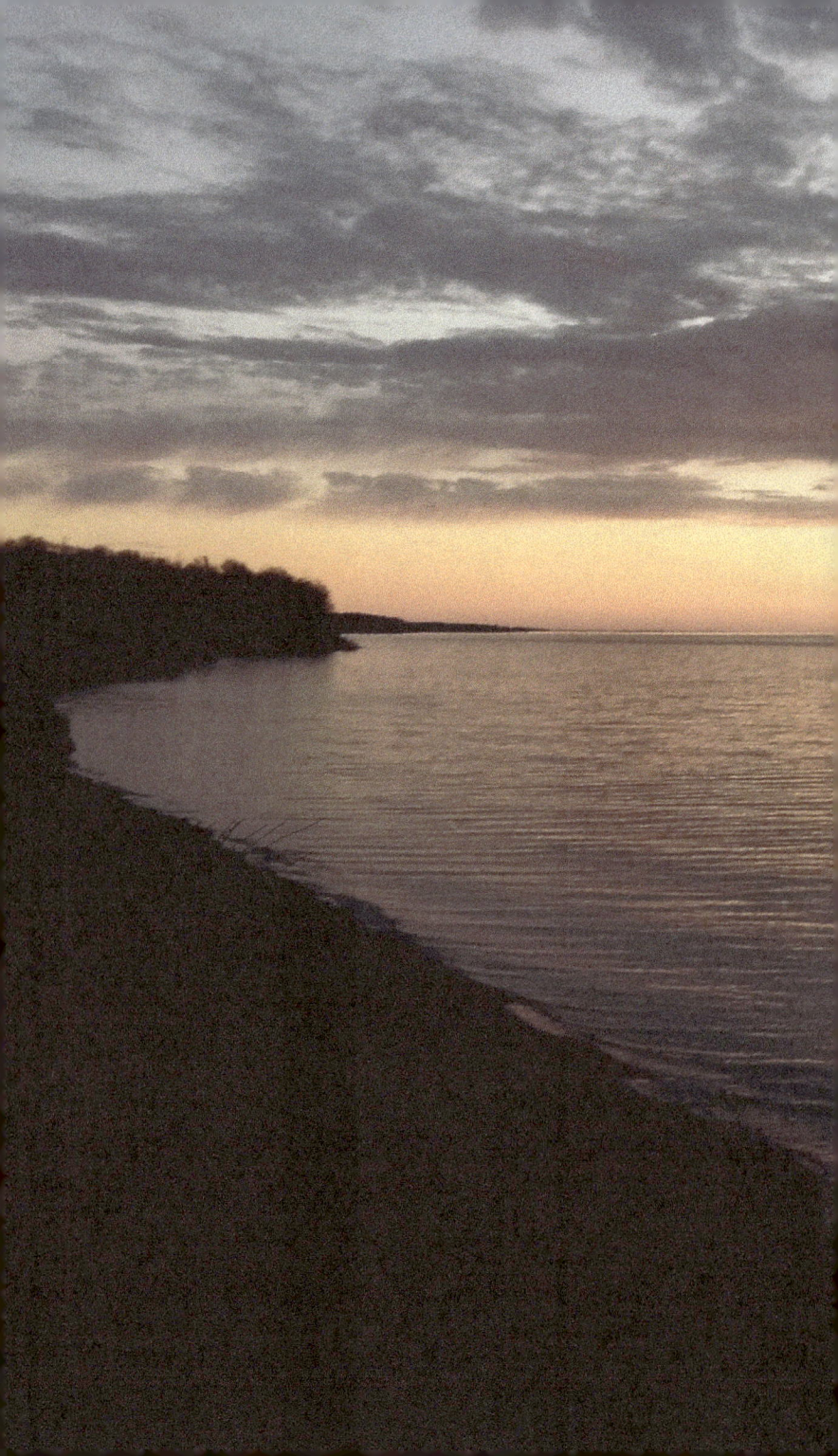

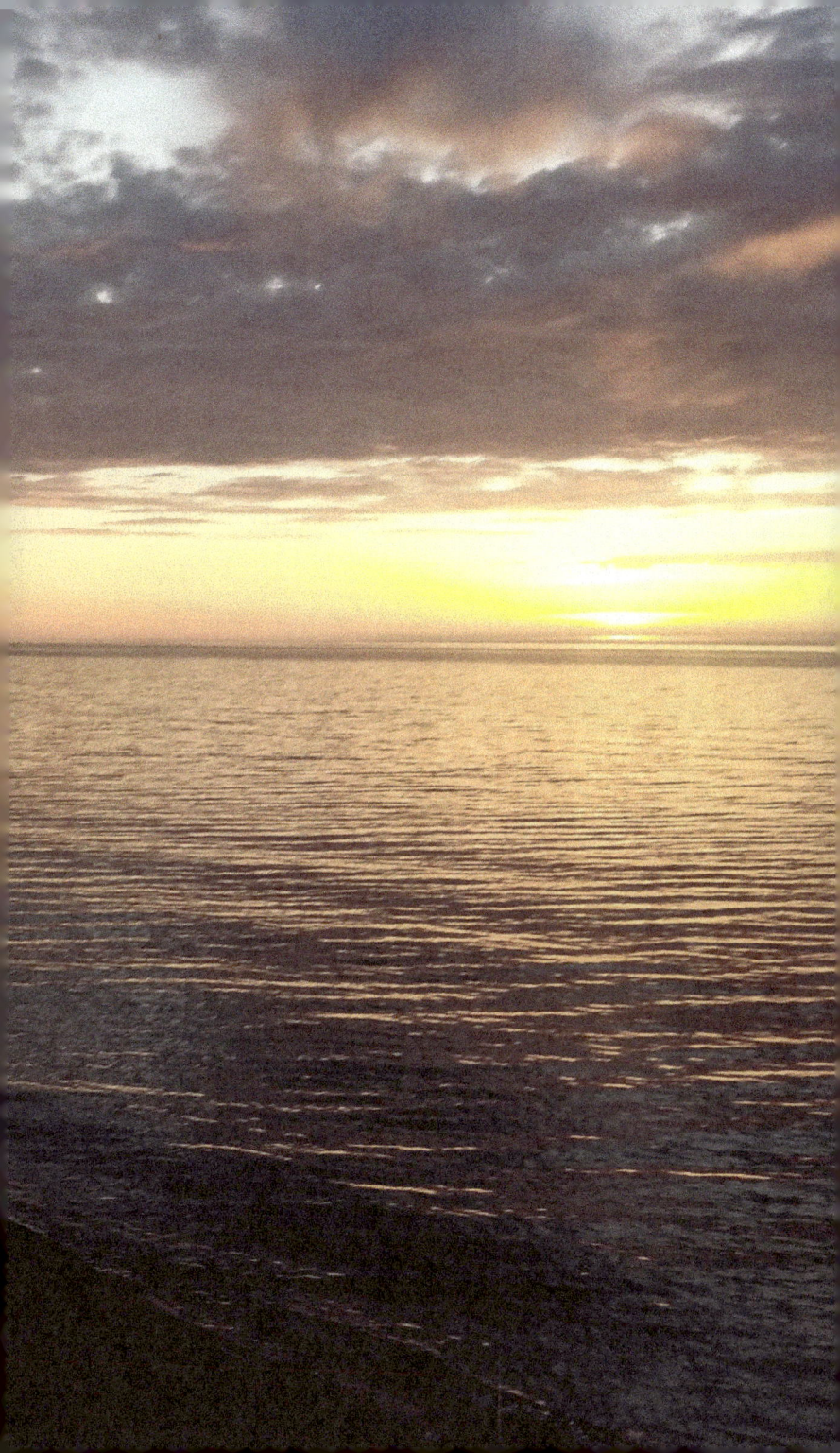

weeping willow trees

the taste of anything cooked
while camping

ladybugs

barn swallows

maple sugar candy

pinion pine incense

water witching

farmers harvesting
by moonlight

the American flag waving in
the breeze

pumping water by hand

folk art

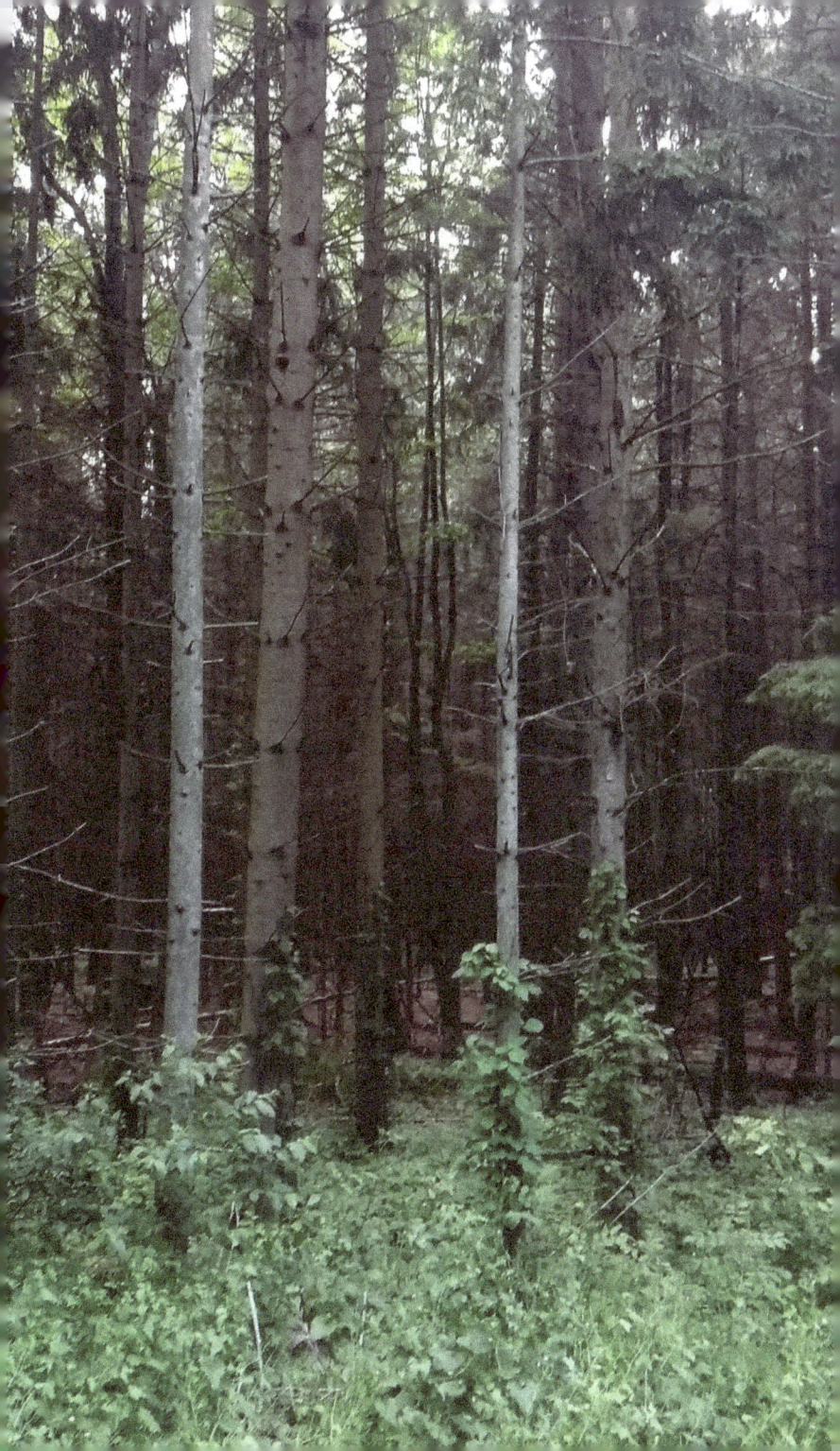

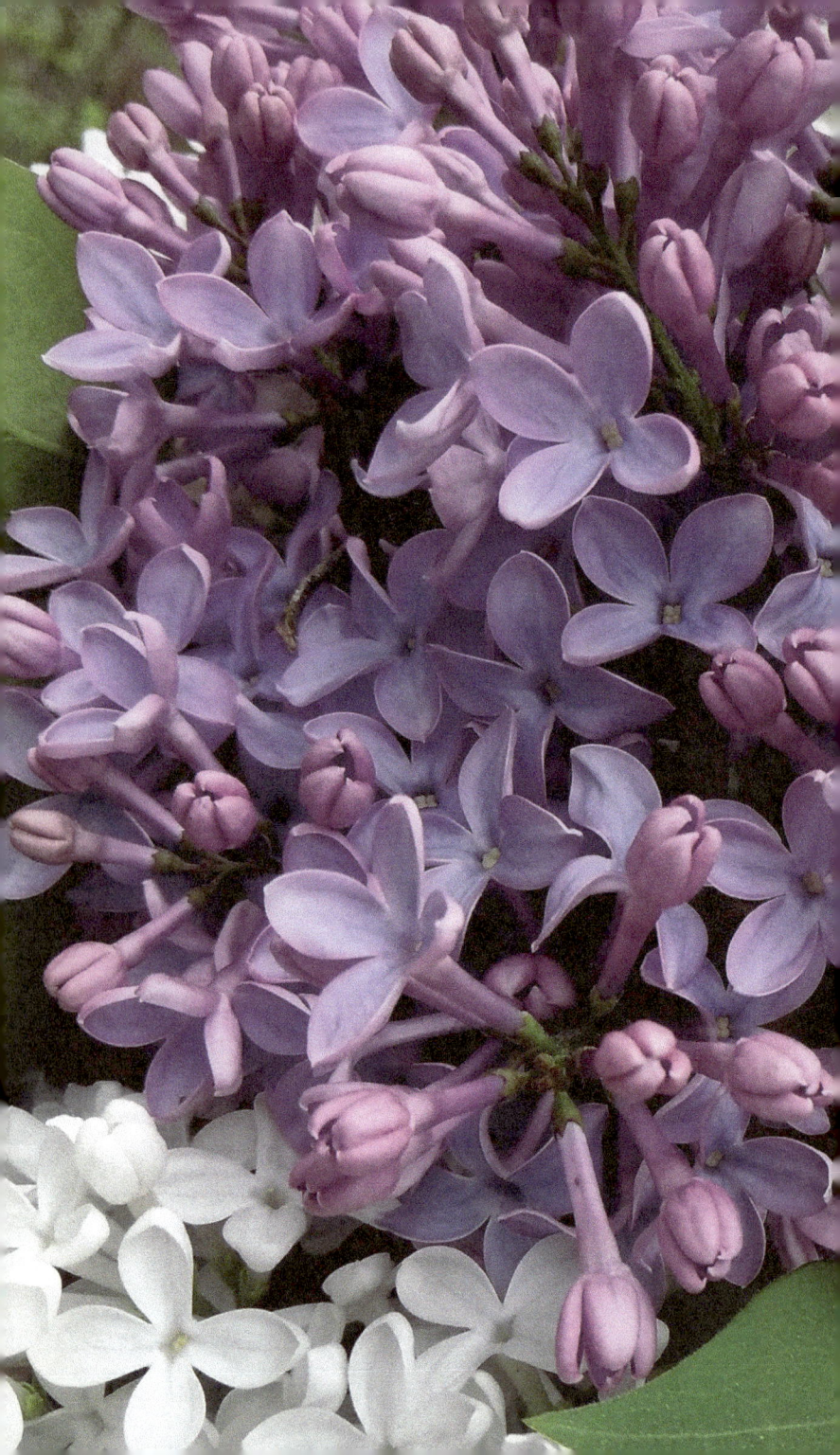

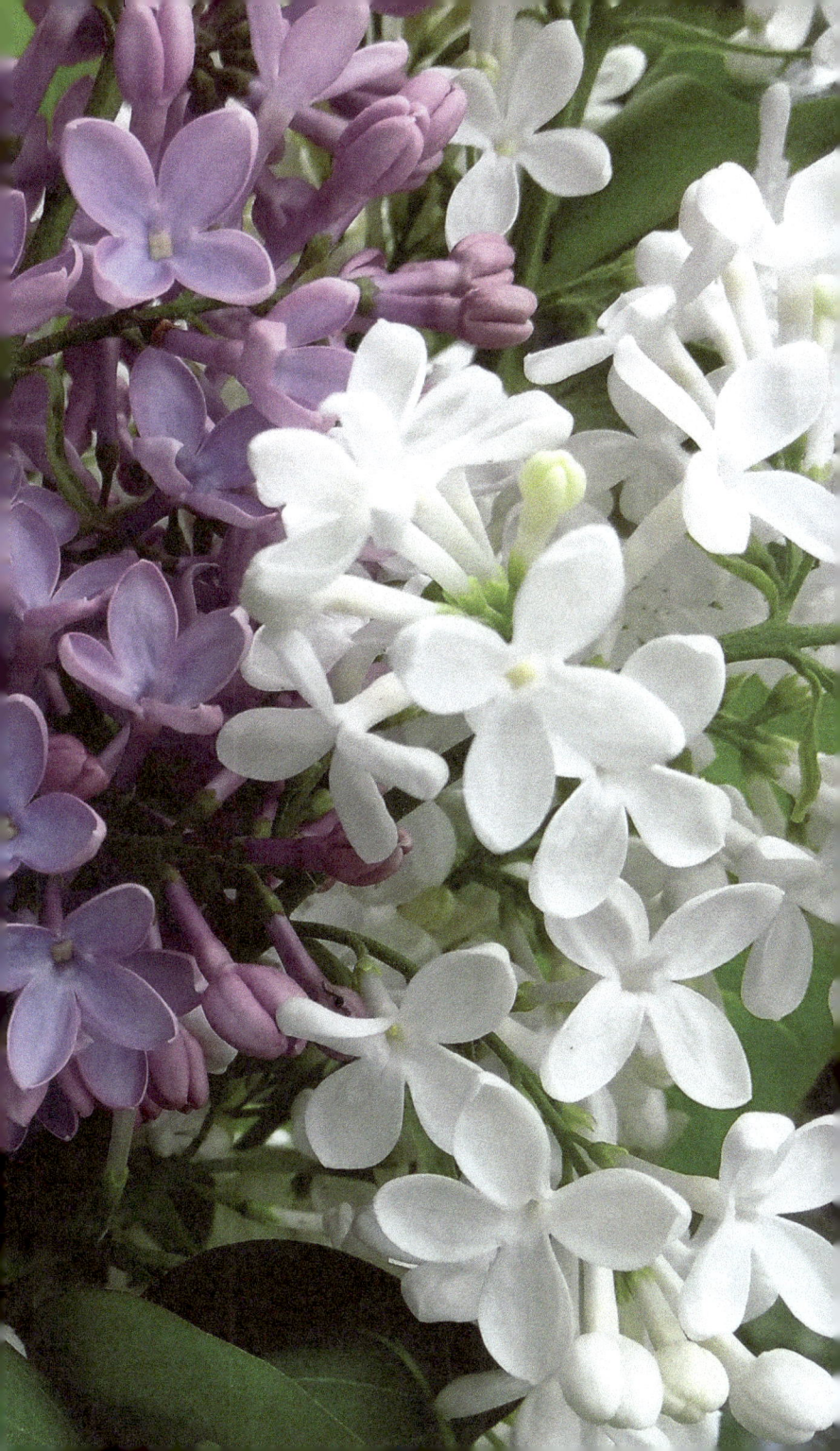

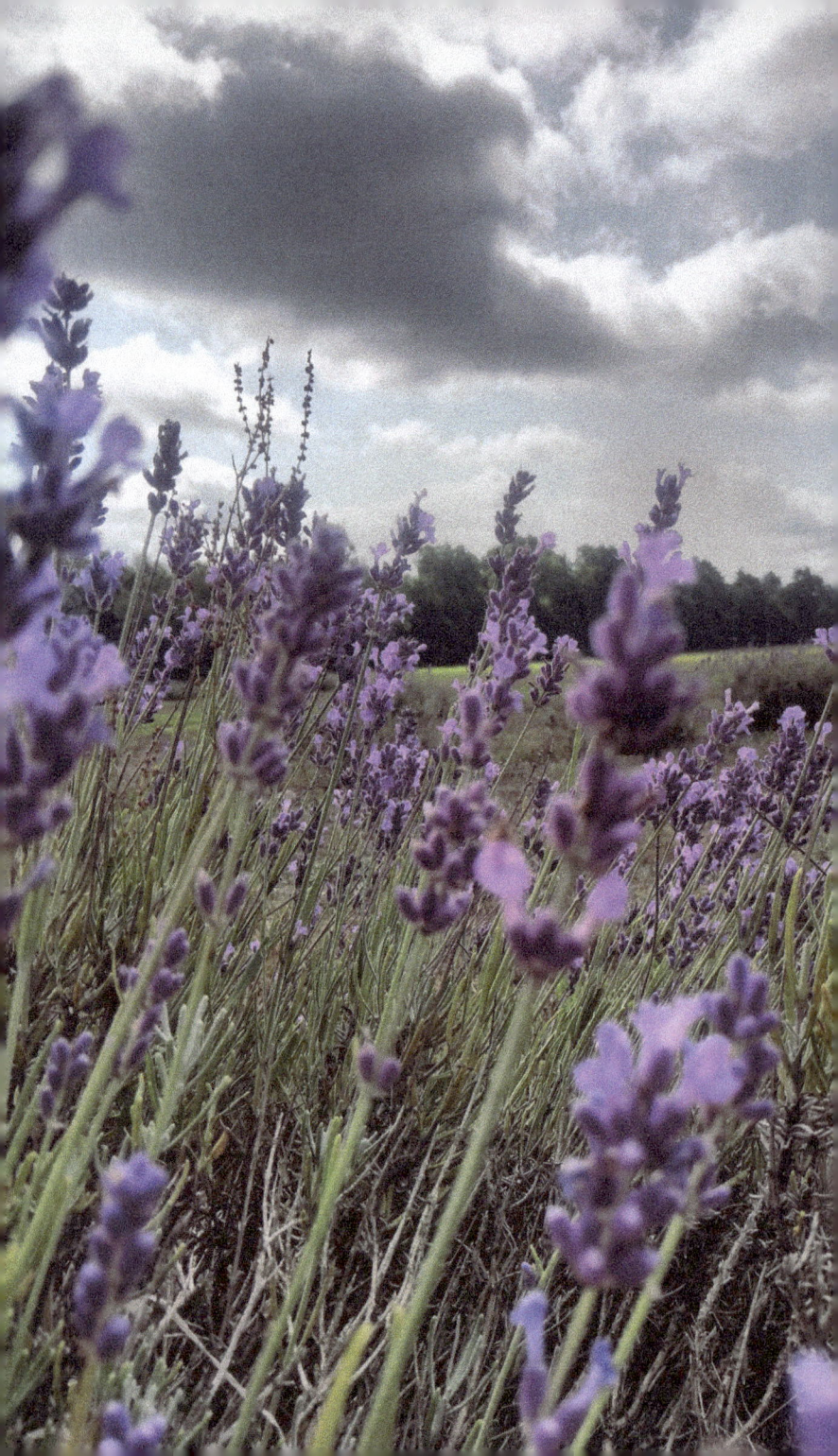

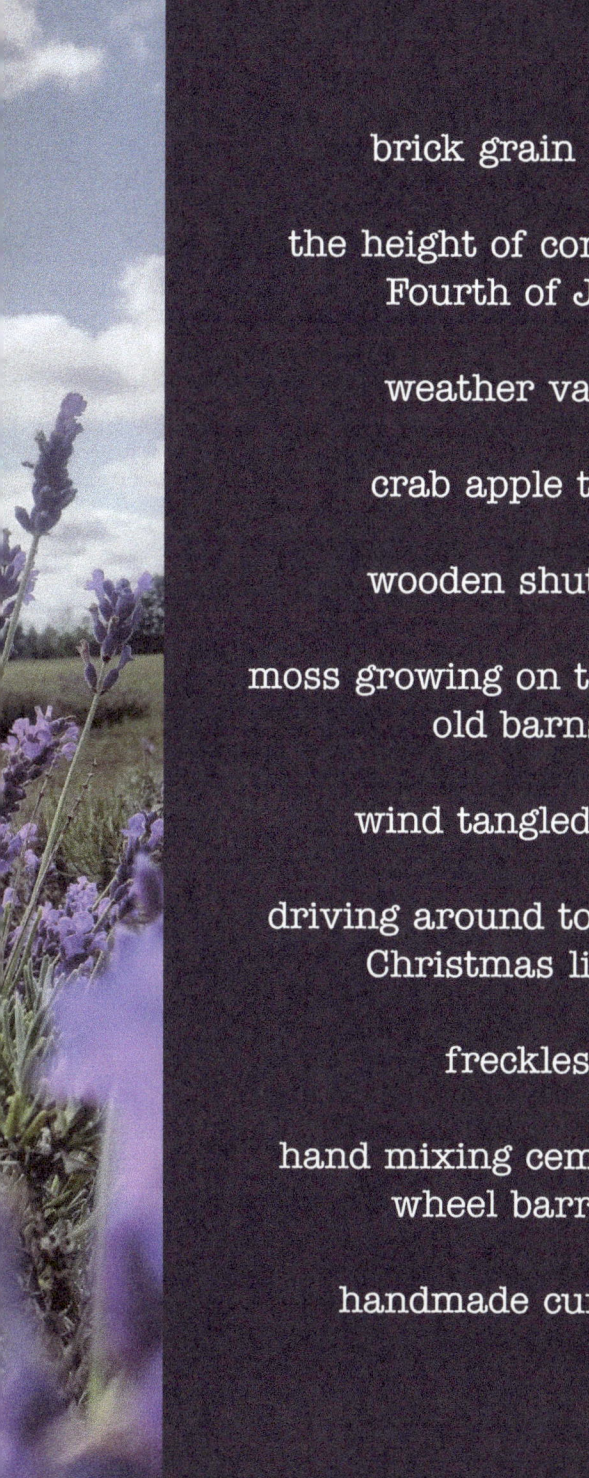

brick grain silos

the height of corn on the Fourth of July

weather vanes

crab apple trees

wooden shutters

moss growing on the roofs of old barns

wind tangled hair

driving around town to see Christmas lights

freckles

hand mixing cement in a wheel barrow

handmade curtains

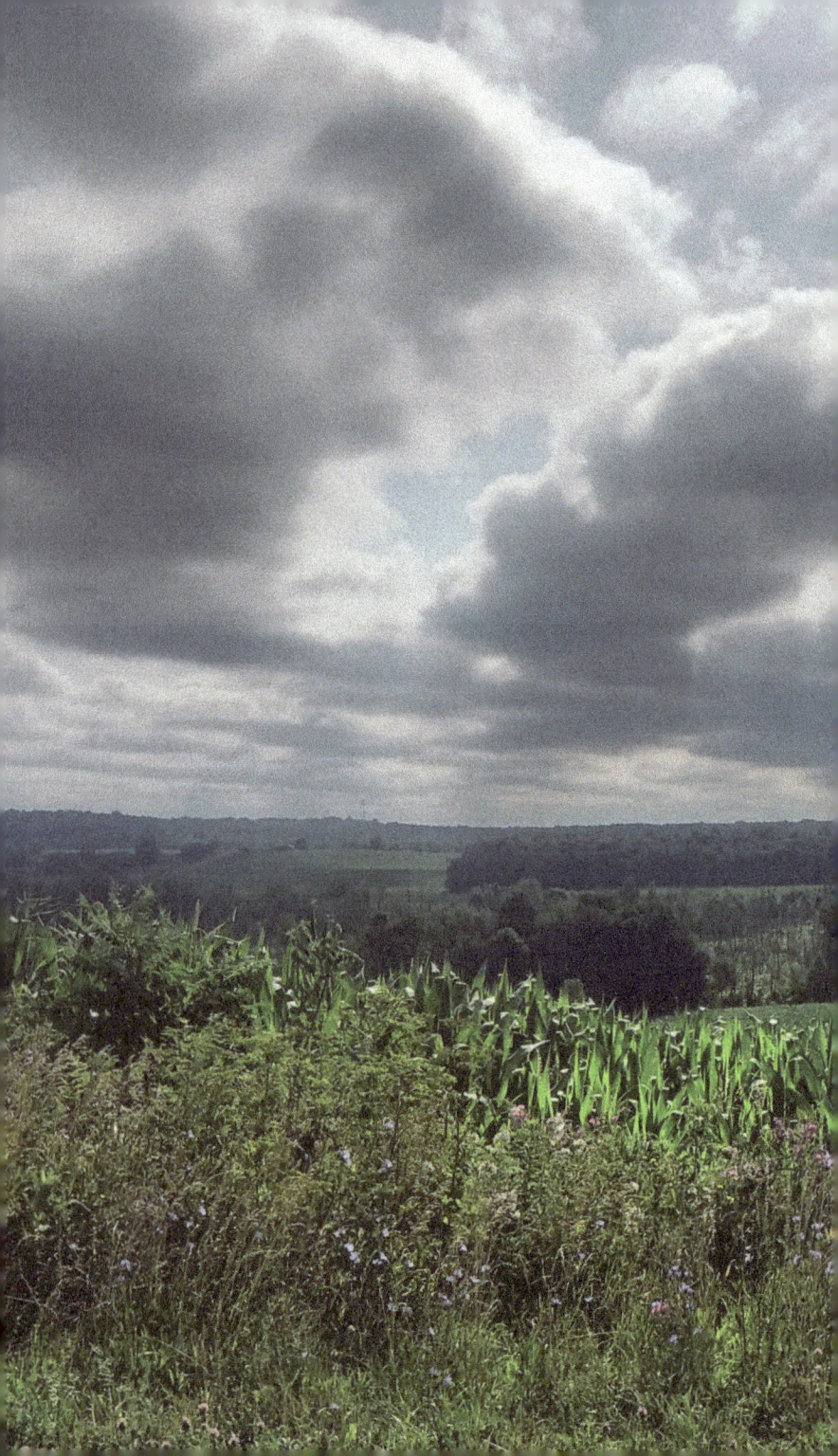

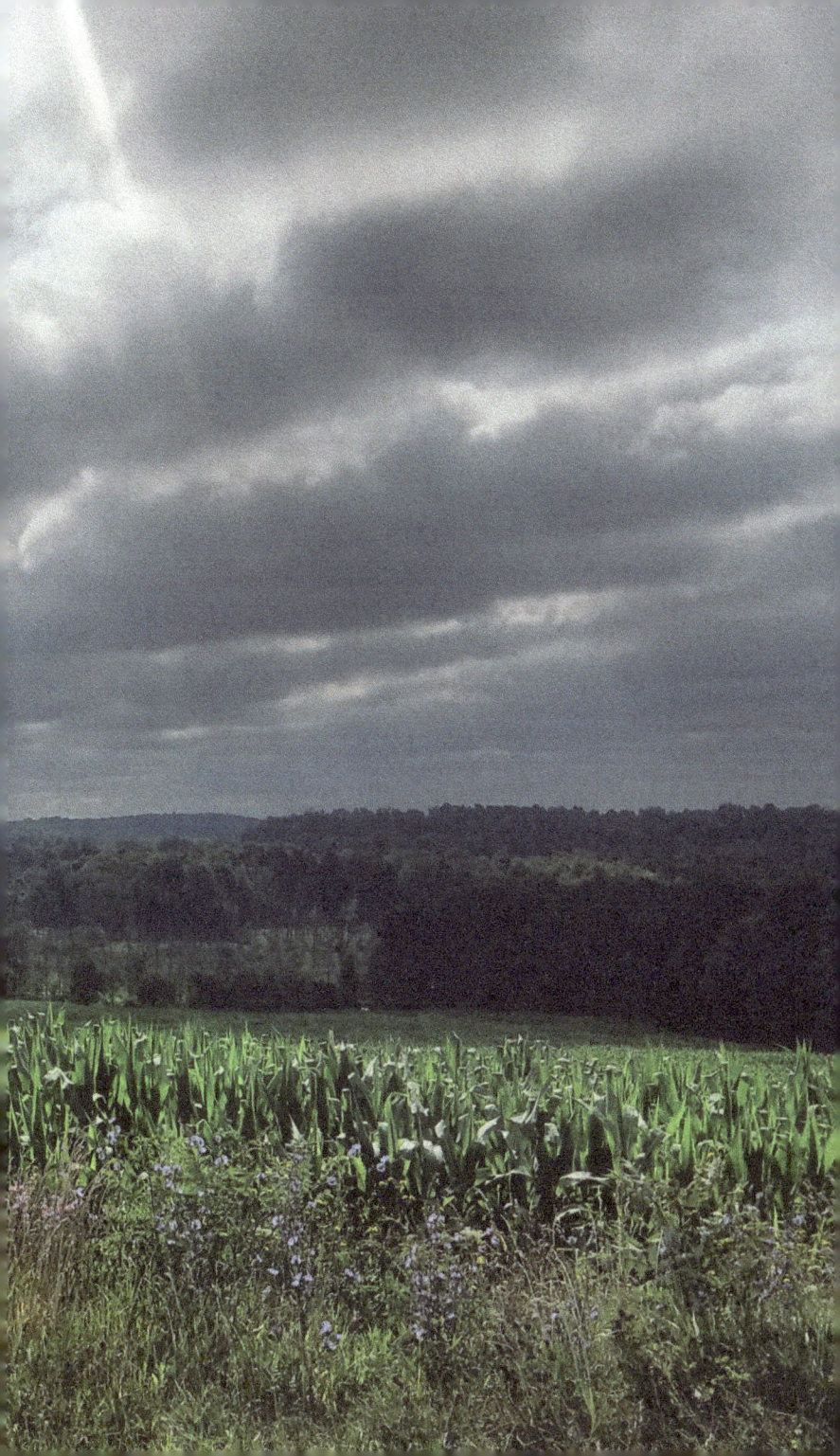

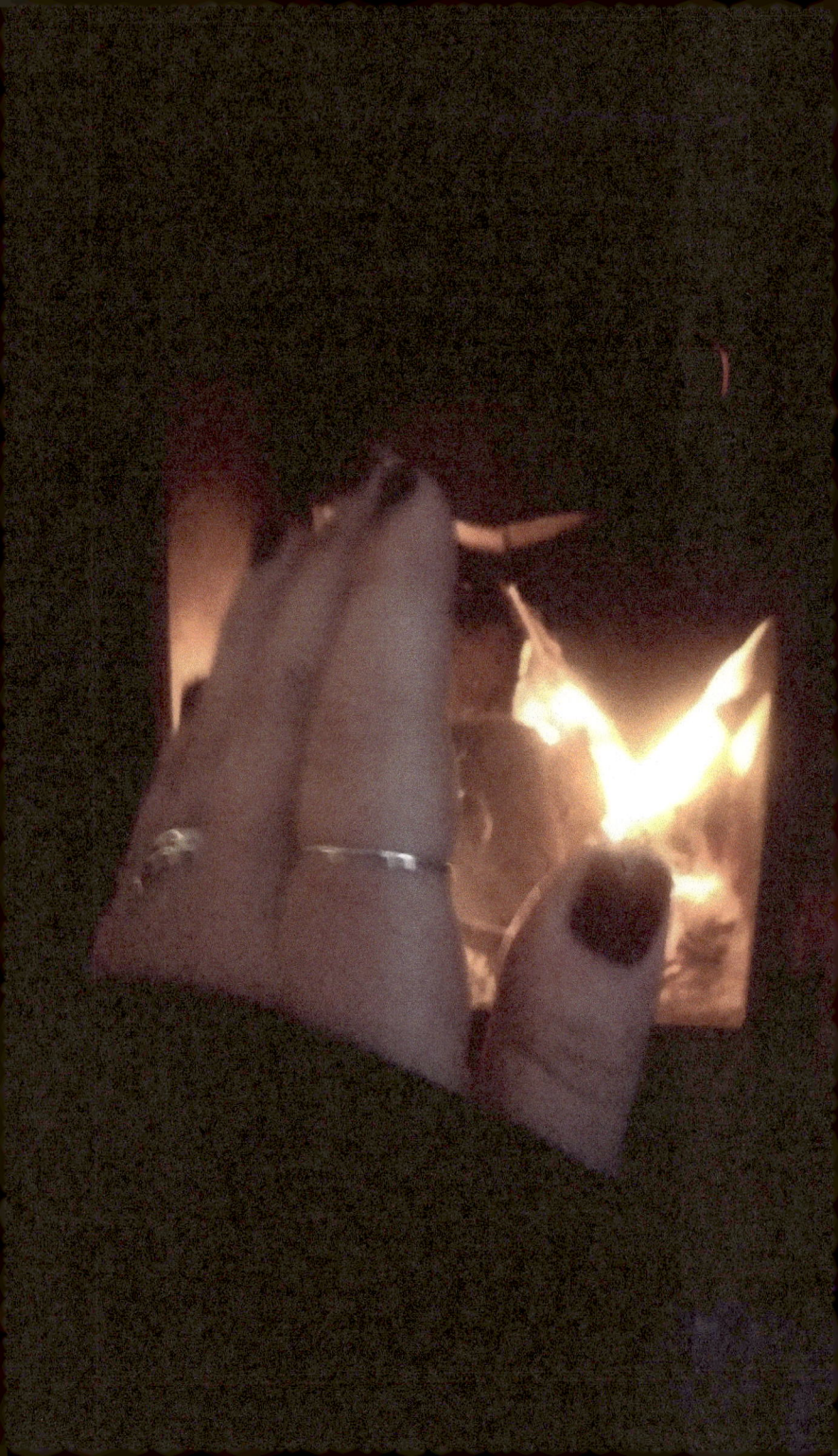

the warmth of a wood fire

fancy trim work on
farmhouse porches

wearing layers when it's cold

solar lights lining
garden paths

drinking water from the
garden hose

taking walks before sunrise

sparklers

lists of ice cream flavors

moon flowers

buying gladiolas from
roadside garden stands

grandpas

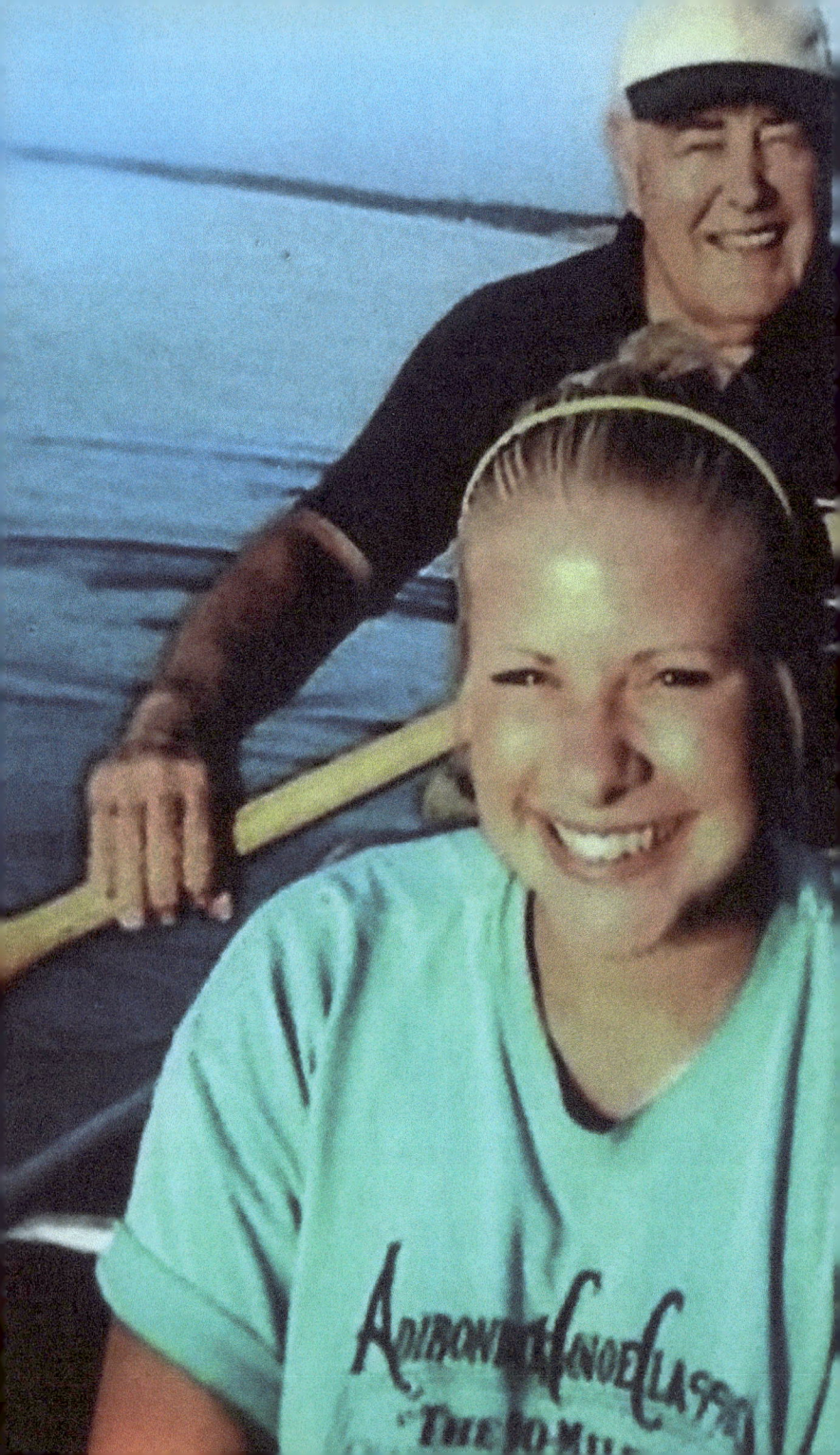

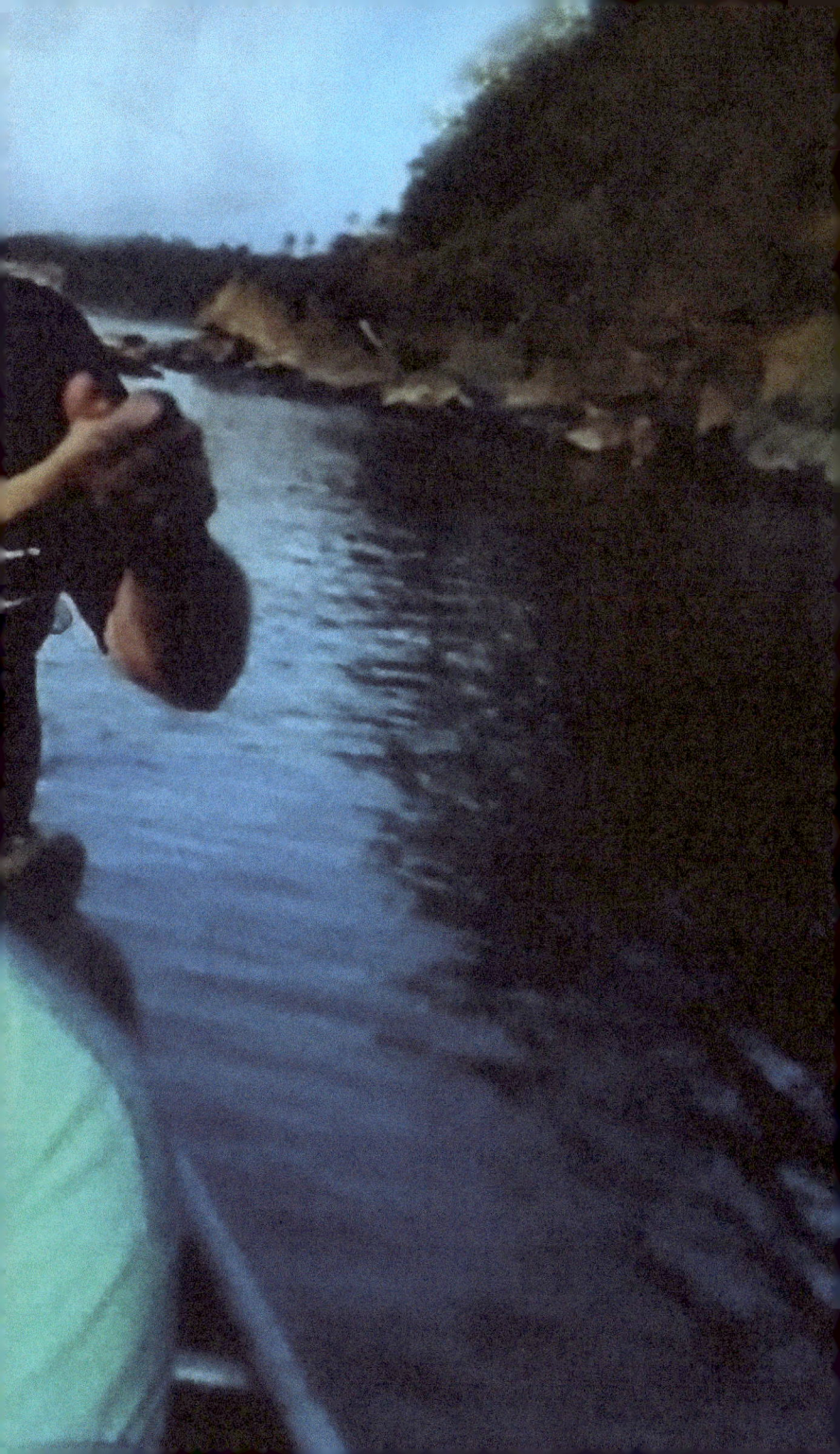

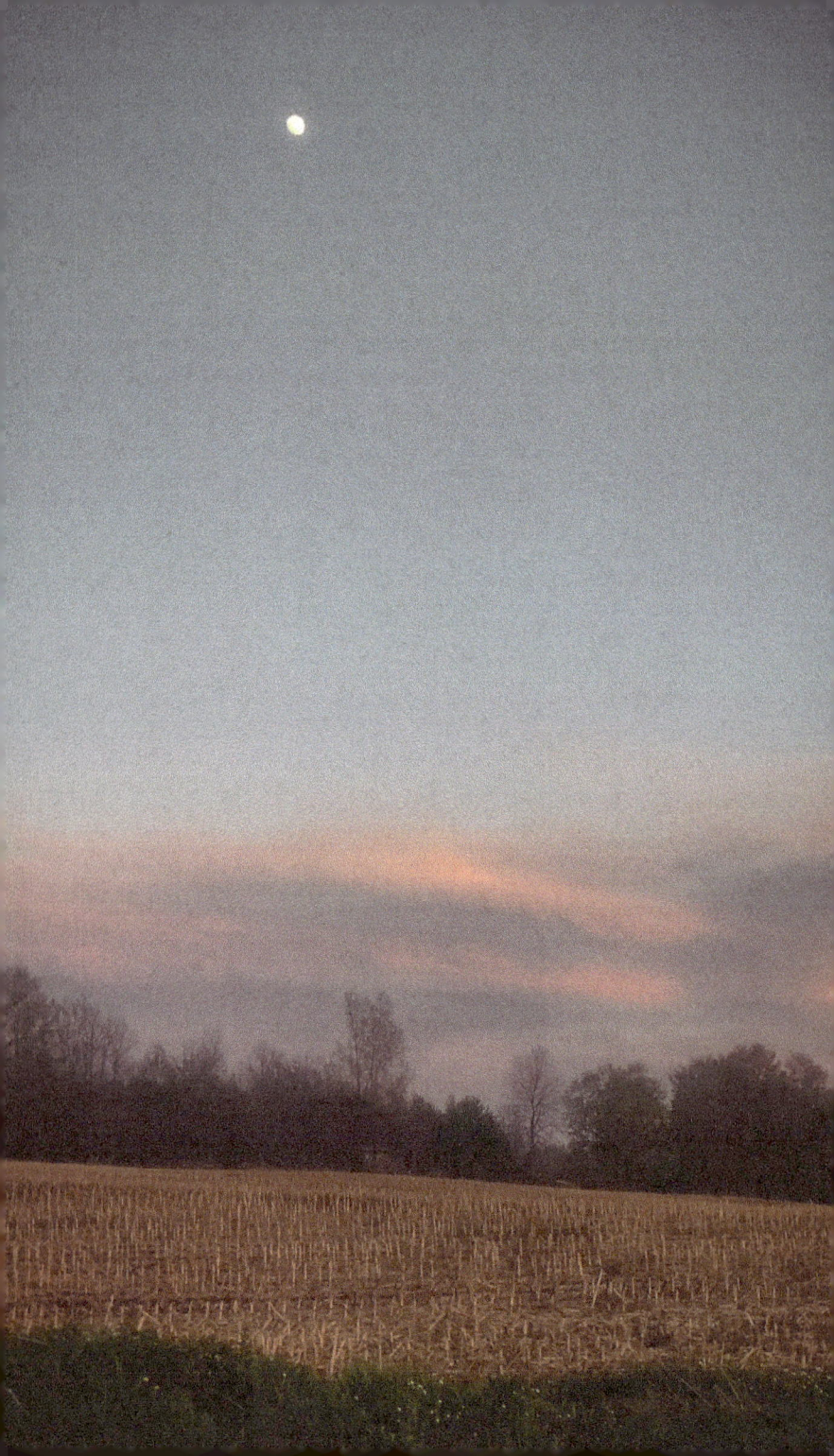

About the Author

Kelly Jackson is an old fashioned country girl who lives in an 1870's farmhouse on the shores of Lake Ontario. Kelly lives in the woods with her husband Steven, dog and cat. She loves to paint, garden, journal, write, quilt, crochet and be outside in nature. Kelly has her Bachelors Degree in Fine Art (BFA) with a concentration in Illustration and Book Arts and her Masters in Art Education from SUNY Oswego. Kelly is an elementary school Art Teacher, the Vice President of the local Arts Center, and a working artist. Kelly is also passionate about local history and agriculture. This is Kelly's second book, a compilation of her favorite photographs and lists of her favorite things.

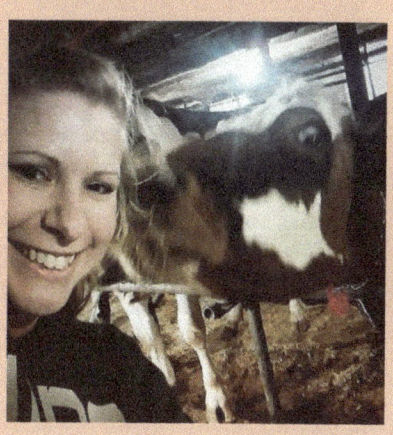

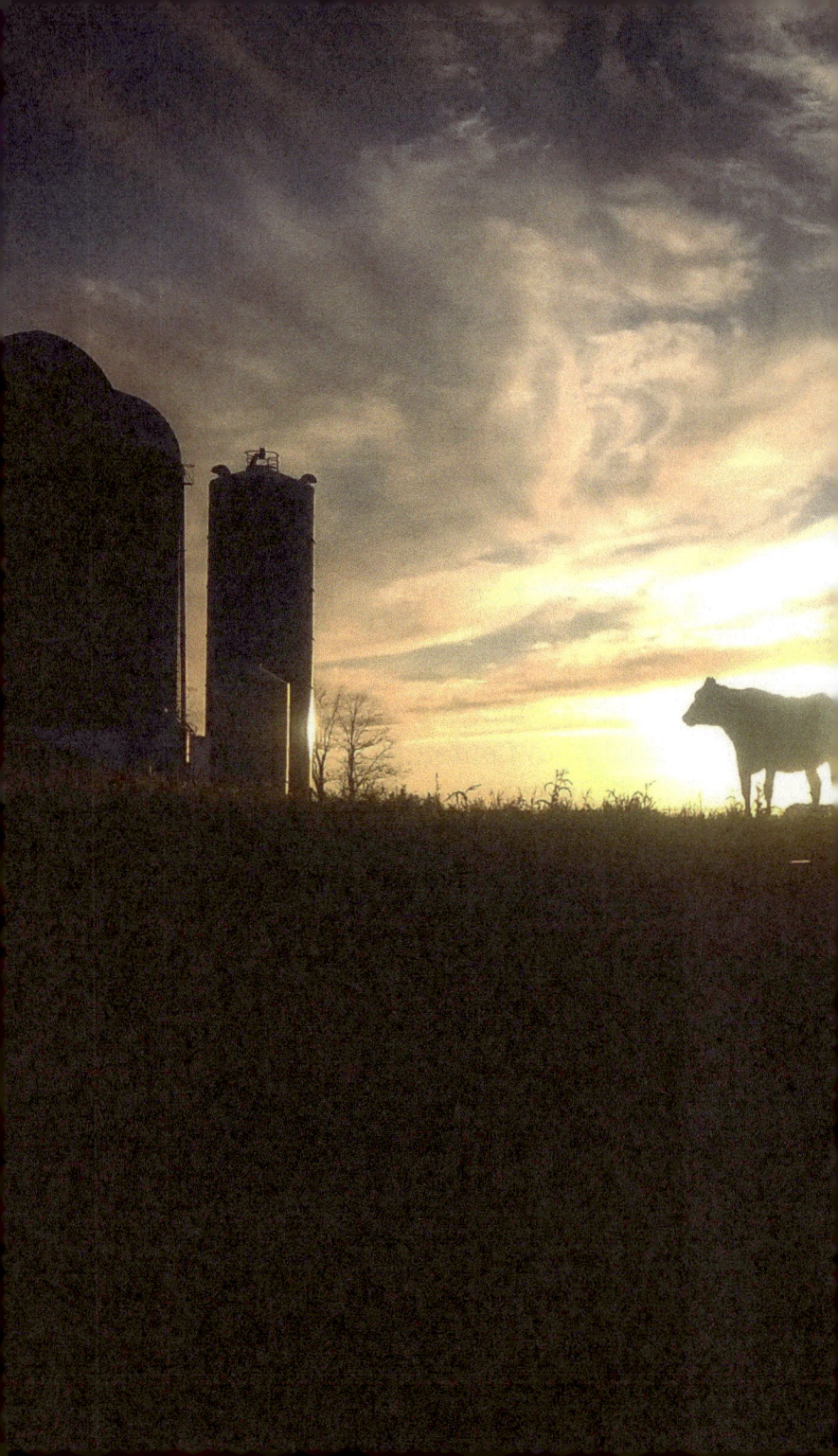

Lightning Source UK Ltd.
Milton Keynes UK
UKHW020216050920
369297UK00003B/26